PRENTICE HALL
LITERATURE

PENGUIN EDITION

Teaching Resources

Unit 2
Short Stories

Grade Seven

PEARSON
Prentice Hall

Upper Saddle River, New Jersey
Boston, Massachusetts

Copyright © by Pearson Education, Inc., publishing as Pearson Prentice Hall, Boston, Massachusetts 02116. All rights reserved. Printed in the United States of America. This publication is protected by copyright, and permission should be obtained from the publisher prior to any prohibited reproduction, storage in a retrieval system, or transmission in any form or by any means, electronic, mechanical, photocopying, recording, or likewise. The publisher hereby grants permission to reproduce these pages, in part or in whole, for classroom use only, the number not to exceed the number of students in each class. Notice of copyright must appear on all copies. For information regarding permission(s), write to: Rights and Permissions Department, One Lake Street, Upper Saddle River, New Jersey 07458.

Pearson Prentice Hall™ is a trademark of Pearson Education, Inc.
Pearson® is a registered trademark of Pearson plc.
Prentice Hall® is a registered trademark of Pearson Education, Inc.

ISBN 0-13-134195-2

4 5 6 7 8 9 10   10 09 08 07

Contents

Part 1 Predicting

Part 2 Making Inferences

"Ribbons" by Laurence Yep

"After Twenty Years" by O. Henry
"He—y, Come on O—ut" by Shinichi Hoshi

Vocabulary Warm-up Word Lists

Study these words from "The Treasure of Lemon Brown." Then, complete the activities.

Word List A

brilliance [BRIL yuhns] *n.* a great brightness
The sun's <u>brilliance</u> filled the room with light.

commence [kuh MENS] *v.* to begin
Swimming lessons <u>commence</u> at 9 A.M. tomorrow.

lifetime [LYF tym] *n.* the length of time that someone lives
In her <u>lifetime</u>, young Allison had already done many things.

memories [MEM uh reez] *n.* the things that one remembers
The family had good <u>memories</u> of their time at the beach.

swirling [SWERL ing] *adj.* going in circles with a whirling motion
The <u>swirling</u> top whirled across the floor.

theaters [THEE uh terz] *n.* buildings in which shows are presented
Which of the <u>theaters</u> on Broadway is showing a musical comedy?

throb [THRAHB] *v.* to beat strongly or fast
When Charles came down with a fever, his head began to <u>throb</u>.

treasure [TRE zher] *n.* something very special or valuable
To Peter, the rocks he collects are a <u>treasure</u>.

Word List B

awaited [uh WAY tid] *v.* was in store for
The assignment, put off all weekend, <u>awaited</u> Michelle.

beckoned [BEK uhnd] *v.* called with a silent motion
Diana <u>beckoned</u> to me with her right hand.

brittle [BRIT uhl] *adj.* having a hard, sharp quality
The old recordings were marked by <u>brittle</u>, scratching sounds.

lecturing [LEK cher ing] *v.* giving a lengthy scolding
When Trevor gets home late, his parents are soon <u>lecturing</u> him.

ominous [AHM uh nuhs] *adj.* threatening; like an evil sign
The scary decorations in the Fun House gave it an <u>ominous</u> look.

revealed [ri VEELD] *v.* made known something that was hidden
Jeremy <u>revealed</u> his sister's gift, which was hidden in the closet.

suspense [suh SPENS] *n.* a state of nervous uncertainty
The <u>suspense</u> of not knowing who would win the contest was almost too great to bear.

youngster [YUHNG ster] *n.* a child or young person
The <u>youngster</u> spent his mornings at a day-care center.

Name _____ Date _____

"The Treasure of Lemon Brown" by Walter Dean Myers
Vocabulary Warm-up Exercises

Exercise A *Fill in each blank in the paragraph below with an appropriate word from Word List A. Use each word only once.*

Marissa loved going to [1] _____ to see live shows. To her those outings were a [2] _____, a most valuable experience. She felt a thrill as the curtain rose and the play would [3] _____. If there was music, the beat of the drums might [4] _____. Dancers would whirl around, the women's [5] _____ skirts creating a flash of [6] _____ under the spotlights. For Marissa, nothing compared with live performances. Although she was only fifteen, she felt she had lived a [7] _____. She would cherish her [8] _____ for years to come.

Exercise B *Answer each question in a complete sentence. Use a word from Word List B to replace each underlined word or group of words without changing the meaning.*

Example: What kind of situation might require you to act <u>gently and sensitively</u>? (delicately) *I would act <u>delicately</u> if I had to give someone bad news.*

1. What <u>threatening</u> thing might <u>have been in store for</u> someone at one time?

   _____

   _____

2. Has anyone ever <u>summoned you with a look</u>?

   _____

3. Have you ever read a story that kept you feeling <u>anxious excitement</u> until the identity of the villain was <u>disclosed</u>?

   _____

   _____

4. Does the <u>hard, sharp noise</u> of chalk scratching the blackboard ever bother you?

   _____

5. When might someone be <u>giving</u> a child <u>a lengthy scolding</u>?

   _____

6. How does a <u>child</u> spend his or her time?

   _____

Name _____ Date _____

Read the following passage. Pay special attention to the underlined words. Then, read it again, and complete the activities. Use a separate sheet of paper for your written answers.

The Harlem Renaissance took place in New York City in the 1920s and early 1930s. It was a time when African Americans produced a <u>treasure</u>, a collection of great literature, music, and art. For the first time in the history of the United States, white society would <u>commence</u> to notice African American writers, musicians, and artists.

During the Harlem Renaissance, jazz and blues became popular. The music was sung by Bessie Smith and played by Louis Armstrong and Duke Ellington. In the jazz clubs of Harlem, music filled the air. Audiences were thrilled when the beat began to <u>throb</u>.

<u>Theaters</u> on and off Broadway presented musical and dramatic works that were written and produced by African Americans. Shows featured black musicians, singers, dancers, and actors.

Two important writers of the time were Langston Hughes and Zora Neale Hurston. In their works, Hughes and Hurston addressed a <u>lifetime</u> of <u>memories</u> of the African American experience.

A notable artist of the Harlem Renaissance was Aaron Douglas. Douglas used a "primitive" style and worked African images into his paintings. The <u>swirling</u> colors of some of his works create the effect of motion.

During the 1930s, the Great Depression made life hard throughout the United States. Because of the Depression, and for a variety of other reasons, the Harlem Renaissance lost its <u>brilliance</u>. Still, the era lives on. It has had an important influence on modern African American writers and artists. In addition, its works continue to be appreciated and studied by all Americans.

1. Underline the words that tell what kind of <u>treasure</u> was produced during the Harlem Renaissance. What is a *treasure* to you?

2. Underline the words that give clues to the meaning of <u>commence</u>. What does *commence* mean?

3. Underline the words that tell how audiences reacted when the beat of a song began to <u>throb</u>. Define *throb*.

4. Underline the words that tell what was presented in the <u>theaters</u>. Use *theaters* in a sentence.

5. Underline the words that describe the <u>lifetime</u> and <u>memories</u> that Hughes and Hurston wrote about. Write a sentence about a *memory* from your *lifetime*.

6. Describe how <u>swirling</u> colors might look. Define *swirling*.

7. Underline the words that explain why the Harlem Renaissance lost its <u>brilliance</u>. Define *brilliance*.

3

"The Treasure of Lemon Brown" by Walter Dean Myers
Reading Warm-up B

Read the following passage. Pay special attention to the underlined words. Then, read it again, and complete the activities. Use a separate sheet of paper for your written answers.

Christina had heard the expression "you don't know what you've got till it's gone." She had not thought it applied to her, however.

That changed the day her mother asked her to baby-sit for her brother. Jeffrey was four years old and always wanted to copy Christina. She thought he was annoying.

That day, Christina's mother beckoned to her and said, "I'm taking Grandma to the doctor. Will you watch Jeffrey?"

Christina saw the expression on her mother's face. She knew what awaited her if she refused the request. She imagined the brittle tones of her mother's voice. She imagined that her mother would be lecturing her all evening. So Christina agreed to watch Jeffrey.

Christina and her brother played ball in the yard for a while. Then they played in the sandbox. Jeffrey asked question after question. Christina thought Jeffrey's questions were extremely annoying.

When she heard the phone ring, Christina scooted inside to answer it. She was gone only a minute, but when she returned, she could not find Jeffrey. She searched every corner of the yard, but the youngster was not to be found. Then she noticed that the gate was open. An ominous feeling settled over her. She rushed down the street, calling, "Jeffrey! Jeffrey!" As she called, she remembered all the endearing things about her brother. She remembered how she had helped her mother bathe him when he was a baby. She remembered his little voice calling her when he wanted to show her something. Now that voice seemed precious, not annoying.

As she hurried along the sidewalk, Christina heard a noise from behind a shrub. Could it be Jeffrey? The suspense seemed overwhelming. She parted the branches and revealed her brother. On his lap was a kitten. "Look what I found!" He beamed.

"Yes," she answered, "and look what I found!" She gathered him into her arms and hugged him tightly.

1. How might Christina's mother have beckoned to Christina? Define *beckoned*.

2. Underline the words that tell what awaited Christina if she refused her mother's request. What has ever *awaited* you?

3. Underline the words that tell what sounded brittle. Define *brittle*.

4. Why did Christina imagine that her mother would be lecturing her? Define *lecturing*.

5. What is a synonym for youngster? Use *youngster* in a sentence.

6. Circle the word that ominous describes. What does *ominous* mean?

7. Why did Christina find the suspense overwhelming? Tell about a time you felt *suspense*.

8. Underline the words that tell what Christina revealed. Define *revealed*.

Walter Dean Myers
Listening and Viewing

Segment 1: Meet Walter Dean Myers
- Why was it important for Walter Dean Myers to write about his community?
- What would you write about your community?

_____

_____

_____

Segment 2: The Short Story
- Why would a scrapbook be a good basis for a short story?
- In what ways might Myers's short stories serve as his own scrapbook?

_____

_____

_____

Segment 3: The Writing Process
- What does Myers use for inspiration for his characters?
- Would that method help you develop characters? Why or why not?

_____

_____

_____

Segment 4: The Rewards of Writing
- What does Walter Dean Myers mean when he says, "Reading can make you more"?
- How has reading made you "more"?

_____

_____

_____

Unit 2
Learning About Short Stories

The **short story** is a form of fiction. Certain elements are common to short stories. For example, all short stories contain **characters,** the people or animals in the story. The reasons that explain why characters act as they do are called their **motivation.** The way in which a writer reveals a character's personality and qualities is called **characterization.** There are two kinds of characterization:

- Through **direct characterization,** the writer *tells* what the character is like.
- Through **indirect characterization,** the writer *shows* what the character is like. That is, the reader must draw conclusions about the character's personality and qualities based on the character's appearance, words, and actions and what other characters say about him or her.

The **plot** is the series of events in a short story. A plot usually has five parts:

1. The **exposition** introduces the **setting** (the time and place of the story), the characters, and the basic situation.
2. The **rising action** introduces, develops, and deepens the **conflict,** or problem.
3. The **climax** is the point of highest tension, the turning point. During the climax, the characters confront the conflict.
4. During the **falling action,** the characters solve the problem, and the tension eases.
5. The **resolution** is the conclusion, when the conflict is settled and the outcome of the story is revealed.

The **theme** is a central message about life. A **universal theme** is one that is expressed in many cultures and time periods. It reflects basic human values. An example is "Crime does not pay."

A. DIRECTIONS: *On the line, write the letter of the short story element that each sentence illustrates.*

_____ 1. "Experience is a great teacher."
    A. conflict   B. theme

_____ 2. "He was a clever man."
    A. direct characterization   B. indirect characterization

_____ 3. "It was a cold winter's night."
    A. setting   B. plot

_____ 4. "Jake couldn't hold on to the rocky ledge any longer. He started to fall."
    A. resolution   B. climax

_____ 5. "Once the fire was out, we found a safe place to lie down and rest."
    A. rising action   B. falling action

B. DIRECTIONS: *On a separate sheet of paper, write the exposition of a short story. In your exposition, introduce the setting, a main character, and a basic situation. Use indirect characterization to show what your main character is like.*

"The Treasure of Lemon Brown" by Walter Dean Myers

Model Selection: Short Story

The characters in short stories are driven by **motivations**—reasons, needs, and feelings that cause them to act the way they do.

Characterization is the way in which a writer reveals a character's traits, or personal qualities. Through **direct characterization,** the writer *tells* what the character is like. Through **indirect characterization,** the writer *shows* what the character is like. With indirect characterization, the reader must draw conclusions about the character based on the character's appearance, words, and actions, as well as what other characters say about him or her.

A. DIRECTIONS: *Answer these questions about the plot, characters, characterization, and setting of "The Treasure of Lemon Brown."*

1. In the exposition, Greg is angry. What basic situation has caused his anger?

   _____

2. Describe the traits, or personal qualities, of Lemon Brown.

   _____

   _____

3. Lemon Brown says, "Hard times caught up with me." What does he mean? Is this an example of direct or indirect characterization? Explain your answer.

   _____

   _____

4. What conflict do Greg and Lemon Brown face?

   _____

   _____

5. How do Greg and Lemon Brown behave at the climax of the story?

   _____

B. DIRECTIONS: *The **theme** of a story is its message about life. A **universal theme** reflects basic human values in many cultures. An example is "Hard work pays off." Answer these questions about the theme of "The Treasure of Lemon Brown."*

1. What might be the theme of "The Treasure of Lemon Brown"? Support your answer by citing details from the story.

   _____

   _____

2. Is the theme you stated universal? Explain why or why not.

   _____

   _____

Name _____ Date _____

"The Treasure of Lemon Brown" by Walter Dean Myers
Selection Test A

Learning About Short Stories *Identify the letter of the choice that best answers the question.*

___ 1. What is a character's motivation?
   A. the way a character looks in certain situations
   B. the reasons a character acts in certain ways
   C. what a character says about another character
   D. the point when a character solves a problem

___ 2. Honesty and fairness might illustrate which element of a short story?
   A. character traits
   B. the theme
   C. the setting
   D. the exposition

___ 3. What is a universal theme?
   A. a message about friendship
   B. a message about the author's life
   C. a message about life that many cultures express
   D. a message about the world that the author expresses

___ 4. Which short story element names the problem that one or more characters face?
   A. resolution
   B. exposition
   C. theme
   D. conflict

___ 5. What is the climax of a short story?
   A. the moment when the problem is solved
   B. the turning point or moment of greatest tension
   C. the point at which the setting is introduced
   D. the point at which the main character appears

Critical Reading

___ 6. Who is the main character in "The Treasure of Lemon Brown"?
   A. Greg
   B. Greg's father
   C. Lemon Brown
   D. the thieves

_____ 7. As "The Treasure of Lemon Brown" opens, what problem does Greg face?

   A. He cannot go home because it is raining.

   B. He has been suspended from his basketball team.

   C. He cannot find Lemon Brown's treasure.

   D. He cannot play basketball because he is failing math.

_____ 8. Which statement is an example of direct characterization?

   A. "Don't try nothin' 'cause I got a razor."

   B. "What you doing here?"

   C. The figure shuffled forward again.

   D. He was an old man.

_____ 9. What conflict occurs while Greg is with Lemon Brown?

   A. Lemon Brown gives up his career as a blues singer.

   B. Lemon Brown's wife becomes sick and dies.

   C. Thieves try to rob Lemon Brown's treasure.

   D. Lemon Brown's son dies while fighting in a war.

_____ 10. What is Lemon Brown's treasure?

   A. a gold razor

   B. a bag of gold coins

   C. a harmonica and some news clippings

   D. some news clippings and a picture of his son

_____ 11. Why does Lemon Brown give the treasure to his son?

   A. He wants him to be a blues singer.

   B. He is afraid someone will steal it.

   C. He wants his son to feel safe.

   D. He wants his son to be proud of him.

_____ 12. What happens to Lemon Brown's son?

   A. He is killed in a war.

   B. He is attacked by thieves.

   C. He dies in an abandoned tenement.

   D. He becomes a basketball player.

_____ 13. When does Lemon Brown feel proud and happy?

   A. when Greg understands that he was a great blues singer

   B. when he realizes that his son treasured the things he had given him

   C. when Greg realizes that he will be all right in east St. Louis

   D. when he frightens away the thieves and knows his treasure is safe

____ **14.** What is the setting of most of the action of "The Treasure of Lemon Brown"?
   A. Greg's apartment
   B. a sidewalk in Greg's neighborhood
   C. an abandoned tenement
   D. the Community Center

____ **15.** Which statement best expresses Greg's feelings at the end of the story?
   A. He is worried that Lemon Brown will not be all right.
   B. He feels that Lemon Brown's treasure is worthless.
   C. He wants to help Lemon Brown find a place to live.
   D. He has developed a new appreciation for his father.

Essay

16. The theme of a short story is its message about life. In an essay, tell what you think is the theme of "The Treasure of Lemon Brown." Support your opinion by citing at least two details from the story.

17. Why might Greg smile at the end of the story? Does the smile relate to his meeting with Lemon Brown? In an essay, discuss Greg's smile. Cite three details from the story to support your points.

Name _____ Date _____

Learning About Short Stories *Identify the letter of the choice that best completes the statement or answers the question.*

_____ 1. The part of a short story in which the main character and setting are introduced is called the
   A. resolution.
   B. exposition.
   C. motivation.
   D. theme.

_____ 2. The reasons why a character in a short story acts in certain ways are called the
   A. characterization.
   B. resolution.
   C. conflict.
   D. motivation.

_____ 3. Which of the following is an example of indirect characterization?
   A. "Help yourself to more cookies," she said with a smile.
   B. My brother Paul is thirteen years old.
   C. Jacob was a very tall man.
   D. Aunt Hilda had a great job, working at a pet store.

_____ 4. Which statement is always true of a universal theme?
   A. It involves friendship.
   B. It is directly stated by the author.
   C. It is directly stated by one of the characters.
   D. It has to do with values shared by most people and cultures.

_____ 5. Which of the following is *not* one of the five parts of a plot?
   A. motivation
   B. exposition
   C. climax
   D. resolution

_____ 6. The part of a short story that comes directly after the climax is the
   A. exposition.
   B. rising action.
   C. falling action.
   D. resolution.

Critical Reading

_____ 7. In the exposition of "The Treasure of Lemon Brown," Greg is in trouble because
   A. he is in danger of failing math.
   B. he has made friends with Lemon Brown.
   C. he has missed basketball practice.
   D. he has been playing basketball.

____ 8. Why does Greg enter the building where Lemon Brown is staying?
   A. He is curious about Lemon Brown's treasure.
   B. He knows his father will lecture him when he goes home.
   C. He wants to join the checkers tournament.
   D. He wants to avoid some thugs who are on the sidewalk.

____ 9. Lemon Brown says, "Every man got a treasure. You don't know that, you must be a fool!" What aspect of the story is brought out by those lines?
   A. the setting
   B. direct characterization
   C. the theme
   D. the conflict

____ 10. What conflict do Greg and Lemon Brown share?
   A. They fear they will lose their treasure.
   B. They must find a safe place to live.
   C. They must face a group of thugs.
   D. They have lost people they loved.

____ 11. The climax of the story occurs when
   A. Greg learns that Lemon Brown's treasure is a harmonica.
   B. Greg decides not to tell his father about Lemon Brown.
   C. One of the thugs starts climbing the stairs toward Lemon Brown.
   D. Greg howls, and Lemon Brown hurls himself down the stairs.

____ 12. What motivates the thugs?
   A. They think that Lemon Brown's treasure is worth a lot of money.
   B. They know that Lemon Brown was once a famous blues singer.
   C. They believe that Lemon Brown has reported them to the police.
   D. They think that Lemon Brown's harmonica is made of solid gold.

____ 13. Lemon Brown gave the harmonica and news clippings to his son because he wanted his son to
   A. become a great blues singer.
   B. guard his treasure.
   C. return from the war safely.
   D. know about his father's achievements.

____ 14. Lemon Brown tells Greg that his heart was broken when
   A. he found out that his son had been killed in the war.
   B. he found out that his son did not appreciate his treasure.
   C. he realized that he was not talented enough to be a great blue singer.
   D. he realized that his son did not value the harmonica as much as he did.

____ 15. Lemon Brown is surprised and pleased to learn that
   A. Greg was interested in learning to play the harmonica.
   B. Jesse was going to find a place for him to live in east St. Louis.
   C. Jesse treated the harmonica and clippings as if they were treasures.
   D. Greg was going to try to do better in math so that he could play basketball.

____ 16. Lemon Brown tells Greg about Jesse during the story's
   A. exposition.
   B. rising action.
   C. falling action.
   D. resolution.

____ 17. During the story, Greg's feelings for Lemon Brown change from
   A. fear to curiosity to respect.
   B. curiosity to horror to acceptance.
   C. fear to friendship to alarm.
   D. concern to fear to friendship.

____ 18. Which statement is true of "The Treasure of Lemon Brown"?
   A. Most of the action takes place on a city street.
   B. Most of the action takes place inside an abandoned building.
   C. Most of the action takes place in Greg's apartment.
   D. Most of the action takes place early in the Community Center.

____ 19. Greg most likely decides not to tell his father about Lemon Brown because
   A. he does not want to get a lecture about being out after dark on a school night.
   B. he is afraid that his father will think Lemon Brown's treasure is silly.
   C. he wants to help Lemon Brown find a new place to live.
   D. he wants to respect Lemon Brown's privacy.

____ 20. Which statement best expresses the theme of "The Treasure of Lemon Brown"?
   A. The life of a blues singer can be extremely difficult.
   B. People should respect what their fathers say and do.
   C. The value of a treasure may be unrelated to its monetary value.
   D. To play sports, you must work hard in school and get good grades.

Essay

21. In an essay, discuss what Greg learns about fathers from Lemon Brown. Consider how that lesson might affect Greg's relationship with his own father. Support your points by citing at least two details from "The Treasure of Lemon Brown."

22. In an essay, state what you think is the theme of "The Treasure of Lemon Brown." Support your opinion by citing at least two details from the story. Then, tell whether or not the theme you stated is a universal theme, and explain why it is or is not.

23. A character's traits—revealed through his appearance, words, and actions—help readers understand the character and his or her actions. A character acts in certain ways because of his or her motives. In an essay, discuss what Lemon Brown's character traits tell you about him and his actions. In particular, tell what motives lead him to act as he does.

Name _____

Unit 2: Short Stories
Part 1 Concept Map

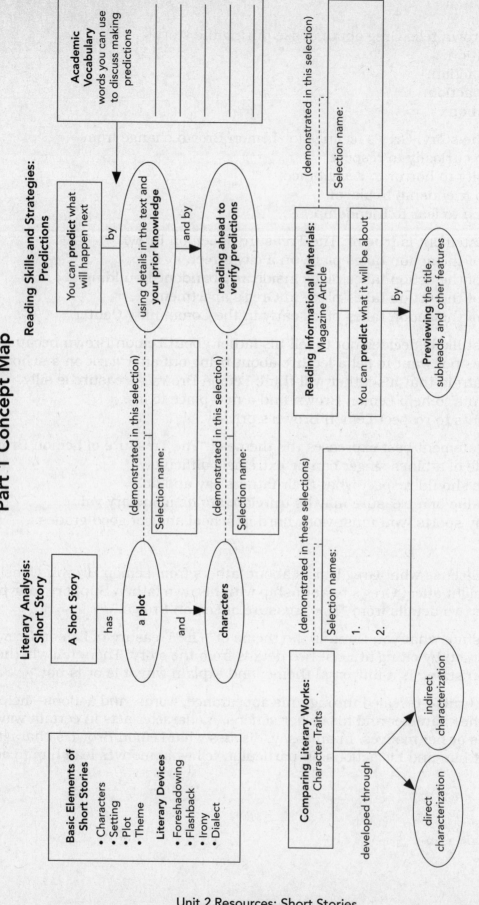

Academic Vocabulary words you can use to discuss making predictions

Reading Skills and Strategies: Predictions

You can **predict** what will happen next

by

using details in the text and **your prior knowledge**

and by

reading ahead to verify predictions

Reading Informational Materials: Magazine Article

(demonstrated in this selection)

Selection name:

You can **predict** what it will be about

by

Previewing the title, subheads, and other features

Literary Analysis: Short Story

A Short Story

has

a plot

and

characters

(demonstrated in this selection)

Selection name:

(demonstrated in this selection)

Selection name:

Basic Elements of Short Stories
• Characters
• Setting
• Plot
• Theme

Literary Devices
• Foreshadowing
• Flashback
• Irony
• Dialect

Comparing Literary Works: Character Traits

(demonstrated in these selections)

Selection names:
1.
2.

developed through

indirect characterization

direct characterization

Part 1 Student Log

Complete this chart to track your assignments.

Writing	Extend Your Learning	Writing Workshop	Other Assignments

14

Unit 2: Short Stories
Part 1 Diagnostic Test 3

MULTIPLE CHOICE

Read the selection. Then, answer the questions that follow.

In colonial America, apprenticeship was a common way for a boy to learn a trade. He would sign an indenture, or contract, with a master, who would train him in all aspects of his livelihood.

A boy could train to be a baker or a blacksmith, a cooper (barrel maker) or a chandler (candle maker). Boys with more education and a love of learning might apprentice in a printer's shop or in a merchant's office.

The period of service was usually five or seven years. No money changed hands until the final year. All the same, it was costly to the master. He had to provide his apprentice with room and board. Sometimes he also taught the boy how to read, write, and keep the business's accounts.

A master could be a tyrant or a gentle teacher, stingy or generous. Some masters criticized their apprentices constantly, while others taught with praise. No matter what, a boy was expected to obey his master's wishes.

When his apprenticeship ended, the young man set out with a little money in his pocket to make his way in the world. He was called a *journeyman*. That's because he often had to journey from place to place to find employment. Usually, he hoped to save enough money to start his own business.

1. What did a master receive in return for teaching an apprentice?
   A. the gratitude of the community
   B. a letter of thanks from the governor
   C. free labor for the term of apprenticeship
   D. increased business from the boy's family

2. On what was the relationship between a master and his apprentice based?
   A. mutual respect and sympathy
   B. a contract signed by both parties
   C. the U.S. Constitution
   D. the English educational system

3. Why did money change hands during the final year of the apprenticeship?
   A. The apprentice repaid the loan his master had given him.
   B. The master lent the journeyman a small amount of money.
   C. The journeyman received a small salary from the apprentice.
   D. The master paid the apprentice a small salary.

4. What was likely to happen if a master ordered an apprentice to work long hours seven days a week?
   A. The boy would refuse to work on Sunday.
   B. The boy would complain to the local authorities.
   C. The boy would do whatever his master told him to do.
   D. The boy would leave his apprenticeship.

5. How do a journeyman and an apprentice differ?
   A. in their natural abilities and intelligence
   B. in their experience and training
   C. in their interests and ambitions
   D. in their personality and character

6. On the basis of this passage, what can you conclude about girls and women?
   A. They served as masters but not apprentices.
   B. They served as apprentices but not masters.
   C. They had no part in the apprenticeship system.
   D. They had their own apprenticeship system.

7. Today, some jobs still require a period of apprenticeship. Which of the following jobs requires a novice to learn skills and techniques from a master craftsman?
   A. fine cabinet-making
   B. truck driver
   C. elected official
   D. college professor

Read the selection. Then, answer the questions that follow.

The Statue of Liberty is perhaps the world's most famous birthday gift. The French government arranged for the sculptor Frédéric-Auguste Bartholdi to create a statue to honor the friendship between France and the United States. The statue was supposed to be completed in 1876 to celebrate the 100th anniversary of the Declaration of Independence, in 1776.

The actual completion of the statue took a bit longer. Because the copper statue was to be so tall, Bartholdi had to find someone to help him design a steel support system for it. That job was done by Alexandre-Gustave Eiffel, who later designed the famous Eiffel Tower in Paris.

The Statue of Liberty was finished in France in 1884. It was then taken apart into 350 individual pieces and shipped in crates to the United States. The statue would stand on a stone pedestal, which was being built on an island in New York harbor. Finally, the statue was put back together and dedicated on October 22, 1886. The final structure is just over 305 feet tall. Each eye is two and a half feet wide, and each hand is 16 feet long. In 1986, the statue's 100th anniversary party was attended by millions, who watched spectacular fireworks and sang "Happy Birthday" to Lady Liberty.

8. When was the Statue of Liberty dedicated?
   A. 1876
   B. 1986
   C. 1889
   D. 1886

9. What material is the outer "skin" of the statue made of?
   A. copper
   B. bronze
   C. stone
   D. steel

10. A *pedestal* is something that
    A. sits on top of something else.
    B. surrounds a work of art.
    C. supports something else.
    D. is used to move something else.

11. Why was the Statue of Liberty built?
    A. to welcome immigrants
    B. to compete with the Eiffel Tower
    C. to honor French-American friendship
    D. to represent democracy and justice

12. The height of the Statue of Liberty is about equal to the length of
    A. a schoolbus.
    B. 10 people who are six feet tall each.
    C. a 100-yard football field.
    D. a mile.

13. What does *spectacular* mean?
    A. very small but loud
    B. strange
    C. very distant
    D. large and impressive

14. About how long did it take the Statue of Liberty to be built and installed?
    A. 100 years
    B. ten years
    C. two years
    D. five years

15. What did millions of people celebrate in 1986?
    A. the anniversary of the signing of the Declaration of Independence
    B. the friendship between France and the United States
    C. the 100th anniversary of the Statue of Liberty
    D. the 150th anniversary of the Statue of Liberty

Vocabulary Warm-up Word Lists

Study these words from "The Bear Boy." Then, apply your knowledge in the activities that follow.

Word List A

lance [LANS] *n.* a long spear
The knight aimed the deadly <u>lance</u> at his enemy.

lodge [LAHJ] *n.* a small house
Kuo-Haya lived in an adobe <u>lodge</u> built into the mountainside.

neglected [ni GLEKT id] *v.* failed to do something
Sara <u>neglected</u> to water her plants, so they soon wilted.

preparations [prep uh RAY shunz] *n.* the work involved in making something ready
The <u>preparations</u> for the wedding included choosing flowers.

result [ri ZUHLT] *n.* something that happens because of something else
As a <u>result</u> of the new policy, students can take classes online.

timid [TIM id] *adj.* shy; not brave or confident
Cameron felt <u>timid</u> when he spoke before a large audience.

weapons [WEP uhnz] *n.* things used to fight with
International law prohibits the use of nuclear <u>weapons</u>.

wrestling [RES uh ling] *adj.* struggling and holding
The children <u>wrestling</u> outside are just playing.

Word List B

encourage [en KUR ij] *v.* to support and give confidence
My parents <u>encourage</u> me to pursue my dreams.

guidance [GY duhns] *n.* helpful advice or counsel
Ms. Tillman's students seek her <u>guidance</u> when they want to improve their grades.

initiation [i NISH ee ay shun] *n.* introduction into a group or club
The new members prepared for their <u>initiation</u> into the fellowship.

manhood [MAN hood] *n.* the state of being an adult man rather than a boy
Mark felt he had entered <u>manhood</u> when he took over the family business.

powerful [POW er fuhl] *adj.* having great strength or authority
The singer's <u>powerful</u> voice was heard clearly in the last row of the huge auditorium.

relatives [REL uh tivz] *n.* members of your family
Aunt Mary and Uncle John are my favorite <u>relatives</u>.

responsibility [ri spahn suh BIL uh tee] *n.* a duty or job
Logan accepted the <u>responsibility</u> of being class president.

violence [VY uh luhns] *n.* physical force that is capable of hurting others
Disagreements that become physical result in <u>violence</u>.

"The Bear Boy" by Joseph Bruchac
Vocabulary Warm-up Exercises

Exercise A *Fill in each blank in the paragraph below with an appropriate word from Word List A. Use each word only once.*

The abandoned building had once been a replica of an adobe [1] _____.
The money to maintain it had run out. As a [2] _____, it had been
[3] _____ for years. Inside on a worn blanket lay someone's
[4] _____ for a meal, the food now covered in dust. The collection of
[5] _____ hanging on the wall, including a [6] _____,
seemed out of place. The Pueblos were not a [7] _____ people, but neither were they warriors. On one wall hung pictures of Pueblo children
[8] _____ with one another.

Exercise B *Answer the questions with complete explanations.*

Example: If a person acts <u>immaturely</u>, is he or she acting like an adult?
No; immaturely means "lacking the characteristics of an adult," so someone who is acting immaturely is not acting like an adult.

1. When you <u>encourage</u> someone, are you being helpful?
   _____

2. If you view a scene of <u>violence</u>, is it a pleasant sight?
   _____

3. When you go through an <u>initiation</u> into a club, have you become a member of
   the club?
   _____

4. Do a person's <u>relatives</u> include everyone in his or her neighborhood?
   _____

5. If you fulfill a <u>responsibility</u>, are you likely to feel good about what you have done?
   _____

6. If someone has a <u>powerful</u> personality, would he or she stand out in a group?
   _____

7. Do boys enter <u>manhood</u> when they graduate from sixth grade?
   _____

8. Would you be pleased if someone offered you <u>guidance</u>?
   _____

Name _____   Date _____

"The Bear Boy" by Joseph Bruchac
Reading Warm-up A

Read the following passage. Pay special attention to the underlined words. Then, read it again, and complete the activities. Use a separate sheet of paper for your written answers.

Gluskonba was a hero of the Abenaki people. Long ago three men asked Gluskonba to grant each of them a wish. They were not <u>timid</u> men. They had survived cold and hunger to get to Gluskonba's island. People had seen them <u>wrestling</u> strong animals. Gluskonba greeted them, saying, "You are brave men. For that reason I will grant each of you your wish."

The first man, who was greedy, wished for many fine possessions. The second man, who was proud, wished to outlive all other men. The third man, who was neither greedy nor proud, wished to be a better hunter so that he could provide food for his people. Gluskonba smiled at him, for his was a worthy wish.

Gluskonba gave each man a buckskin pouch. He warned each man not to open his pouch until he was home and inside his own <u>lodge</u>. The men agreed and left the island, each going his own way.

The first man walked and wondered about the objects in his pouch. He imagined buckskin clothing and fine <u>weapons</u>, such as a strong <u>lance</u> for the hunt. At last his excitement grew too great. He peeked inside the pouch. Instantly, all the fine possessions flew out and smothered him.

After many miles, the man who had wished to outlive everyone else decided to open his pouch. "How could it hurt me?" he thought. "I'm going to live forever anyway." He peeked inside, and immediately he turned into a giant boulder.

On his way home, the third man thought only about the duties he had <u>neglected</u> while away from his people. When he reached his lodge and opened the pouch, he discovered that it was empty. Disappointed, he went about his business. Slowly, however, he came to understand certain things. He understood how to make <u>preparations</u> for the hunt respectfully and how to show respect for the animals he hunted. As a <u>result</u>, he got his wish: He became the best hunter among his people.

1. Underline the words that show that the men were not <u>timid</u>. How might a *timid* person behave?

2. Circle the words that tell what the men were seen <u>wrestling</u> with. Use *wrestling* in a sentence.

3. Circle the word whose meaning is similar to <u>lodge</u>. In your own words, tell what each man was supposed to do once he was in his *lodge*.

4. Circle the word that names one of the <u>weapons</u> the first man hoped he would find in his pouch. What other *weapons* might he have wanted?

5. Circle the words that tell what a <u>lance</u> is used for. Describe a *lance*.

6. Circle the word that tells what the third man had <u>neglected</u>. Use *neglected* in a sentence.

7. Write a sentence describing how a hunter might respectfully make <u>preparations</u> for the hunt. Define *preparations*.

8. Underline the words that tell the <u>result</u> of the man's understanding. Tell why his understanding had that *result*.

"The Bear Boy" by Joseph Bruchac
Reading Warm-up B

Read the following passage. Pay special attention to the underlined words. Then, read it again, and complete the activities. Use a separate sheet of paper for your written answers.

Children of the Cheyenne enjoyed the loving <u>guidance</u> of their parents and other <u>relatives</u> from birth to maturity. During a child's earliest years the mother provided for his or her wellbeing, giving the child much love and attention. Life on the Great Plains was uncertain and difficult, however, so children had to grow up quickly.

Like most youngsters, the Cheyenne children played games. Still, life was not all play. The children had their chores. Girls learned to bead and sew. They helped their mothers collect and prepare food. Boys helped care for the tribe's horses and learned to make weapons and musical instruments. To <u>encourage</u> a boy to master horsemanship, a father might give his son a pony.

Unlike other tribes, the Cheyenne did not have a formal <u>initiation</u> welcoming a boy into <u>manhood</u>. Instead, a boy became a man by showing that he was <u>powerful</u>: Only after he had killed a buffalo and survived the <u>violence</u> of a raiding party was a boy considered a man.

As Cheyenne girls grew up, they continued to perform domestic tasks: preparing food and sewing and adorning clothes with beadwork. The last skill a girl learned before getting married was how to tan and prepare animal hides.

A young woman had the right to choose the man she would marry. Nevertheless, the young man had to prove himself worthy before she would accept him. A courtship might go on for years. Once married, however, a couple accepted full <u>responsibility</u> for their lives; they left childhood behind.

1. Underline the sentence that tells how a mother provided <u>guidance</u>. What other kind of *guidance* might a mother give?

2. Circle the kinds of <u>relatives</u> mentioned in the first paragraph. Name some other *relatives*.

3. In your own words, explain how giving a boy a pony could <u>encourage</u> him to master horsemanship.

4. What word describes the kind of <u>initiation</u> into manhood that the Cheyenne did *not* have? What is an *initiation*?

5. Describe an event in which a boy enters *manhood*.

6. Underline the words that show how a Cheyenne proved he was <u>powerful</u>. Use *powerful* in a sentence of your own.

7. Circle the words that name an event in the life of the Cheyenne that involved <u>violence</u>. Give an antonym of *violence*.

8. What <u>responsibility</u> did a married couple accept? What might have been involved in that *responsibility*?

"The Bear Boy" by Joseph Bruchac
Reading: Use Prior Knowledge to Make Predictions

Predicting means making an intelligent guess about what will happen next in a story based on details in the text. You can also **use prior knowledge to make predictions.** For example, if a character in a story notices animal tracks in the snow, you can predict that the animal will play a part in the story because you know from prior knowledge that animal tracks mean that the animal is nearby.

DIRECTIONS: *Fill in the following chart with predictions as you read "The Bear Boy." Use clues from the story and your prior knowledge to make predictions. Then, compare your predictions with what actually happens. An example is shown.*

Story Details and Prior Knowledge	What I Predict Will Happen	What Actually Happens
People said that someone who followed a bear's tracks might never come back, but Kuo-Haya had never been told that. I know that if people are not warned of a danger, they may do something dangerous.	Kuo-Haya will see and follow a bear's tracks.	Kuo-Haya sees and follows a bear's tracks and finds some bear cubs.

"The Bear Boy" by Joseph Bruchac
Literary Analysis: Plot

Plot is the related sequence of events in a short story and other works of fiction. A plot has the following elements:

- **Exposition:** introduction of the setting (the time and place), the characters, and the basic situation
- **Rising Action:** events that introduce a **conflict,** or struggle, and increase the tension
- **Climax:** the story's high point, at which the eventual outcome becomes clear
- **Falling Action:** events that follow the climax
- **Resolution:** the final outcome and tying up of loose ends, when the reader learns how the conflict is resolved

In a story about a race, for example, the exposition would probably introduce the runners. The rising action might include a description of a conflict between two of the runners and some information about the start of the race. The climax might be the winning of the race by one of the runners. The falling action might include a meeting between the two runners, and the resolution might describe the end of their conflict.

DIRECTIONS: *Answer the following questions about the plot elements of "The Bear Boy."*

1. The exposition of "The Bear Boy" introduces characters and describes a setting. Who are the characters, and what is the setting?

   _____

   _____

2. How do you know that the father's neglect of Huo-Kaya is part of the rising action?

   _____

   _____

3. What happens in the climax of "The Bear Boy"?

   _____

   _____

4. Describe one event in the falling action of the story.

   _____

   _____

5. What happens in the resolution of "The Bear Boy"?

   _____

   _____

Name _____ Date _____

"The Bear Boy" by Joseph Bruchac
Vocabulary Builder

Word List

| timid | initiation | neglected |

A. DIRECTIONS: *Use each vocabulary word by following the instructions below. Use the words in the same way they are used in "The Bear Boy," and write sentences that show you understand the meaning of the word.*

1. Use the word *timid* in a sentence about a rabbit.

_____

_____

2. Use the word *initiation* in a sentence about a ceremony.

_____

_____

3. Use the word *neglected* in a sentence about a garden.

_____

_____

B. DIRECTIONS: *On each line, write the letter of the word that is a synonym for the vocabulary word.*

____ 1. initiation
   A. question   C. ceremony
   B. performance   D. hunt
____ 2. neglected
   A. tended   C. hurt
   B. afraid   D. ignored
____ 3. timid
   A. shy   C. restless
   B. helpless   D. worried

"The Bear Boy" by Joseph Bruchac
Support for Writing an Informative Article

Use the graphic organizer below to record details from each section of "The Bear Boy." Your details should tell *when, how much, how often,* or *to what extent.*

Introduction

Details:

↓

Body

Details:

↓

Conclusion

Details:

Now, use your notes to write an informative article telling how mother bears care for their cubs. Write for an audience of third-graders.

"The Bear Boy" by Joseph Bruchac

Support for Extend Your Learning

Research and Technology

Use the chart below to list the steps in the bees' honey-making process. Write the steps in order.

How Bees Make Honey

Step	Process
1	
2	
3	
4	
5	

Then, use your notes to create a diagram of the process. Use arrows to show the order in which the process takes place.

Listening and Speaking

Across the top of this T-chart, write your opinion of the training of wild animals. Then, record several reasons for your opinion. For each reason, write a fact that supports it. At the bottom of the page, write a sentence summarizing your viewpoint.

My Viewpoint:

Reasons	Facts

Summary: _____

_____

_____

"The Bear Boy" by Joseph Bruchac
Enrichment: Initiation Into Adulthood

In "The Bear Boy," Kuo-Haya stays with the bears in order to learn the things he must know to become a man. In many cultures around the world, young people go through initiation ceremonies to become adults. They learn lessons and often have to pass a test of some kind to become full members of their society.

A. DIRECTIONS: *List eight things young people should know before they become adults in our society.*

1. _____
   _____

2. _____
   _____

3. _____
   _____

4. _____
   _____

5. _____
   _____

6. _____
   _____

7. _____
   _____

8. _____
   _____

B. DIRECTIONS: *Now, write three responsibilities that adults in our society have.*

1. _____
   _____

2. _____
   _____

3. _____
   _____

"The Bear Boy" by Joseph Bruchac
Selection Test A

Critical Reading *Identify the letter of the choice that best answers the question.*

____ 1. In "The Bear Boy," why doesn't Kuo-Haya's father spend time with his son?

   A. He does not like Kuo-Haya.

   B. He blames Kuo-Haya for his wife's death.

   C. He is sad about the death of his wife.

   D. He is busy doing other things.

____ 2. Why does Kuo-Haya follow the bear tracks?

   A. He does not know that it is dangerous to do so.

   B. He wants to find and kill a bear to prove his strength.

   C. He wants to get away from his father.

   D. He is lost and wants to find his way home.

____ 3. What fact helps you predict that the mother bear will come when Kuo-Haya is playing with the cubs?

   A. Mother bears usually stay close to their cubs.

   B. Bears live in large family groups.

   C. Bears are not afraid of humans.

   D. The cubs have called loudly for their mother.

____ 4. Which of the following choices would best help you predict what will happen in a story?

   A. the climax of the plot

   B. the name of the author

   C. the names and ages of the characters

   D. story details and your prior knowledge

____ 5. In "The Bear Boy," what does the mother bear do to Kuo-Haya?

   A. She attacks him.

   B. She encourages him to play with her cubs.

   C. She teaches him to run.

   D. She helps him get back together with his father.

____ 6. Using your prior knowledge and the following quotation, what can you predict that Kuo-Haya's father will do?

> Although the father tried to follow, the mother bear stood up on her hind legs and growled. She would not allow the father to come any closer.

   A. He will give up and go home.
   B. He will try another way to get his son.
   C. He will struggle with the bear.
   D. He will beg the bear to let his son go.

____ 7. What does Kuo-Haya's father show about himself when he leaves gifts for the bees?
   A. He is learning to use love.
   B. He is smarter than the bears.
   C. He is learning from the medicine man.
   D. He understands what bears like.

____ 8. What happens in the rising action of "The Bear Boy"?
   A. Kuo-Haya comes back to the village.
   B. Kuo-Haya's father teaches his son.
   C. Kuo-Haya becomes a great runner.
   D. Kuo-Haya's father talks to the medicine man.

____ 9. What happens in the climax of "The Bear Boy"?
   A. Kuo-Haya's father gathers his weapons.
   B. The medicine man tells Kuo-Haya's father that he has behaved badly.
   C. The mother bear growls at the trackers.
   D. Kuo-Haya's father figures out how to get his son back.

____ 10. What promise does Kuo-Haya's father make to his son?
   A. He will teach him to wrestle and run.
   B. He will bring the bears honey
   C. He will be friends with the bears.
   D. He will respect the medicine man.

____ 11. What lesson have the bears taught Kuo-Haya's father?
   A. He should treat his son well.
   B. He should give gifts to animals.
   C. He should be fierce and cruel.
   D. He should wrestle like a bear.

_____ 12. Why is Kuo-Haya's story told now?

A. It warns people about the dangers of bears.

B. It shows people how to treat wild animals.

C. It reminds parents to show love for their children.

D. It explains how Kuo-Haya became a great wrestler and runner.

Vocabulary and Grammar

_____ 13. Which of the following events from "The Bear Boy" shows Kuo-Haya being timid?

A. Kuo-Haya calls to the bears in a friendly tone and tells them he will not hurt them.

B. Kuo-Haya is a great wrestler and the greatest runner in his community.

C. Kuo-Haya looks down and slips away when other boys race or wrestle.

D. Kuo-Haya looks at his father and walks away when his father calls to him.

_____ 14. In which sentence is the word *neglected* used correctly?

A. Kuo-Haya's father neglected the bees by leaving them a gift.

B. The neglected boy was happy with the attention he was receiving.

C. Kuo-Haya's father neglected his son, and the boy felt lonely.

D. The medicine man was pleased when Kuo-Haya's father neglected his son.

_____ 15. Which verb in this passage from "Bear Boy" is a linking verb?

He did not teach his boy how to run. He did not show him how to wrestle. He was always too busy.

A. teach

B. run

C. show

D. was

Essay

16. In "The Bear Boy," Huo-Kaya's father sees a bee and gets an idea. Did you predict that he would take the bees' honey and use it to get his son back? In an essay, explain whether or not you predicted that would happen. If you did predict it, tell what prior knowledge you used to make the prediction. If you did not predict it, explain what you thought would happen and why.

17. Consider the five basic plot elements of "The Bear Boy": exposition, rising action, climax, falling action, and resolution. In an essay, describe an event from the story that illustrates each element. Then, tell whether you think that the elements work together to create a satisfying story. Explain your answer.

"The Bear Boy" by Joseph Bruchac
Selection Test B

Critical Reading *Identify the letter of the choice that best completes the statement or answers the question.*

____ 1. In "The Bear Boy," why does Kuo-Haya's father neglect his son?
   A. He believes that raising a son is not a father's responsibility.
   B. He blames Kuo-Haya for the death of his wife.
   C. He is mourning the death of his wife.
   D. He is preoccupied with wrestling and running.

____ 2. Why does Kuo-Haya follow the tracks of the bear?
   A. He has not heard what the villagers say about the bears.
   B. He wants to find and kill the bear to prove his courage.
   C. He wants to escape from his father and the other villagers.
   D. He is lost and hopes the tracks will lead him home.

____ 3. What prior knowledge about bears suggests that the mother bear will come when Kuo-Haya is playing with her cubs?
   A. Mother bears stay close to their cubs.
   B. Bears live in large family groups.
   C. Bears are not afraid of human beings.
   D. Cubs call loudly for their mother.

____ 4. In what part of the story's plot does this event occur?
   Kuo-Haya looked up and saw the mother bear standing above him.

   A. the exposition
   B. the rising action
   C. the falling action
   D. the resolution

____ 5. Which of the following choices would best help you predict what will happen in a story?
   A. the climax of the plot
   B. the exposition and rising action
   C. the names and ages of the characters
   D. story details and prior knowledge

____ 6. In "The Bear Boy," how does the mother bear treat Kuo-Haya?
   A. She attacks him and wounds him.
   B. She teaches him to run.
   C. She urges him to play with her cubs.
   D. She helps him reunite with his father.

____ 7. Kuo-Haya does not try to return to the village because
   A. he is happy with the bears.
   B. he hates his father.
   C. he is afraid of the bears.
   D. he is afraid of the villagers.

____ 8. Using prior knowledge about human behavior and the information in the following passage, what can you predict will happen in "The Bear Boy"?

Although the father tried to follow, the mother bear stood up on her hind legs and growled. She would not allow the father to come any closer.

A. Kuo-Haya's father will kill the bear with his bow and arrow and his lance.
B. Kuo-Haya's father will allow nature to show him the solution.
C. Kuo-Haya's father will befriend the cubs and reason with the mother bear.
D. Kuo-Haya's father will reason with his son and promise to teach him to wrestle.

____ 9. When he leaves gifts for the bees, Kuo-Haya's father reveals that he is changing. What does his action show?
A. He is learning to use love to get his son back.
B. He has become smarter than the bears.
C. He has become smarter than the medicine man.
D. He understands what bears like.

____ 10. Which event is part of the rising action of "The Bear Boy"?
A. Kuo-Haya returns to the village.
B. Kuo-Haya's father teaches his son.
C. Kuo-Haya becomes a great runner and wrestler.
D. Kuo-Haya's father talks to the medicine man.

____ 11. The climax of "The Bear Boy" occurs when
A. the mother bear threatens the trackers.
B. the medicine man criticizes Kuo-Haya's father's behavior.
C. Kuo-Haya's father figures out how to get his son back.
D. Kuo-Haya's father promises to be friends with the bears.

____ 12. The resolution of "The Bear Boy" occurs when
A. the mother bear defends Kuo-Haya and outwits Kuo-Haya's father.
B. Kuo-Haya returns to the village and shows that he is no longer timid.
C. Kuo-Haya's father promises that he will always be friends with the bears.
D. Kuo-Haya follows the bear tracks and finds happiness with the bears.

____ 13. From the bears, Kuo-Haya's father has learned
A. to treat his son well.
B. to be fierce and cruel.
C. to give gifts to animals.
D. to wrestle like a bear.

____ 14. Why has Kuo-Haya's story become a legend?
A. It warns people about the dangers of bears.
B. It shows parents how to help their children become adults.
C. It reminds parents to show love for their children.
D. It explains how Kuo-Haya became a great wrestler and runner.

Vocabulary and Grammar

____ 15. Which of the following events in "The Bear Boy" demonstrates that Huo-Kaya is timid?
A. Kuo-Haya reaches the age when he will be initiated into manhood.
B. Kuo-Haya learns from his father how to become a great runner.
C. Kuo-Haya looks down and slips away when other boys race or wrestle.
D. Kuo-Haya walks into the bears' cave when his father calls to him.

____ 16. In which sentence is the word *neglected* used correctly?
A. Kuo-Haya's father neglected that his son preferred to live with the bears.
B. The neglected trail was well marked and easy for Kuo-Haya to follow.
C. Kuo-Haya's father neglected his son, and so the boy felt unloved.
D. Neglected, Kuo-Haya knew that he should follow the bears' tracks.

____ 17. Which verb in the following sentence from "The Bear Boy" is a linking verb?
"You are right," he said. "I will go and bring back my son."

A. are
B. said
C. go
D. bring

____ 18. Which choice includes all of the action verbs in the following passage from "The Bear Boy"?
So Kuo-Haya's father went back to his home. He was angry now. . . . But the medicine man came to his lodge and showed him the bear claw that he wore around his neck.

A. went, came
B. showed, wore
C. went, came, showed, wore
D. went, was, came, showed, wore

Essay

19. In "The Bear Boy," Kuo-Haya's father sees a bee and gets an idea. Did you predict that he would take the bees' honey and use it to distract the bears? In an essay, explain how easy or difficult it was to predict the outcome of the story. What prior knowledge does a reader need? What details in the story must a reader be aware of?

20. Many legends tell a story that teaches a lesson. In a brief essay, explain what lesson "The Bear Boy" teaches readers. What do the characters learn in the story? What should readers learn from the characters? Use examples from the tale to support your answer.

Vocabulary Warm-up Word Lists

Study these words from "Rikki-tikki-tavi." Then, complete the activities.

Word List A

balancing [BAL uhns ing] *v.* keeping steady and not falling over
  The acrobat was <u>balancing</u> a chair on his chin.

bred [BRED] *v.* raised
  Ms. Cochrane <u>bred</u> English terriers for show.

brood [BROOD] *n.* all the young in one family
  The hen led her <u>brood</u> of chicks into the barn.

clenched [KLENCHT] *v.* held or squeezed
  Chelsea <u>clenched</u> the bat and swung hard at the fast ball.

fraction [FRAK shuhn] *n.* a small portion or small amount
  At discount stores, you may pay a <u>fraction</u> of an item's value.

peculiar [pi KYOOL yer] *adj.* strange or odd
  The strangely dressed performers were a <u>peculiar</u> sight.

splendid [SPLEN did] *adj.* beautiful or impressive; brilliant
  From the mountaintop at dawn, we saw a <u>splendid</u> sunrise.

thickets [THIK its] *n.* thick growths of plants or bushes
  The rabbit hid in the <u>thickets</u> that grew along the trail.

Word List B

bungalow [BUHNG uh loh] *n.* a small house
  The <u>bungalow</u> was large enough to house just the two of them.

inherited [in HE ri tid] *v.* had a trait passed down from one family member to another
  My brothers and I <u>inherited</u> our mother's long, straight nose.

paralyzed [PA ruh lyzd] *v.* made someone or something helpless and unable to function
  The venom of the black mamba temporarily <u>paralyzed</u> its prey.

revived [ri VYVD] *v.* brought someone or something back to consciousness
  The paramedic <u>revived</u> the accident victim.

savagely [SAV ij lee] *adj.* fiercely; violently
  The lion roared <u>savagely</u> before disappearing into the jungle.

scornfully [SKAWRN fuh lee] *adv.* expressing something in a way that shows dislike or disrespect
  The unhappy employee spoke <u>scornfully</u> of the new manager.

scuttled [SKUHT uhld] *v.* ran or moved quickly with short steps
  The little dog <u>scuttled</u> across the slippery floor.

valiant [VAL yuhnt] *adj.* brave or courageous
  We honor the country's <u>valiant</u> soldiers on Veteran's Day.

Name _____ Date _____

"Rikki-tikki-tavi" by Rudyard Kipling
Vocabulary Warm-up Exercises

Exercise A *Fill in each blank in the paragraph below with an appropriate word from Word List A. Use each word only once.*

The fox led her [1] _____ of pups into the den before returning to the

riverbank. She smelled a [2] _____ odor. It was odd—not the odor of

another animal. She was [3] _____ to be cautious, so she stayed

deep in the [4] _____, well out of sight. Soon she saw a boy. He was

[5] _____ on a stone as he tried to cross the narrow river. He

[6] _____ a fishing rod tightly in one hand. The fox slunk back just a

[7] _____ of an inch and then turned and ran. The boy caught sight of

the impressive animal. "What a [8] _____ fox!" he cried just as he lost

his footing and splashed into the river.

Exercise B *Answer the questions with complete explanations.*

Example: If you are <u>hurrying</u>, are you taking your time?
No; hurrying means "rushing," so I would not be taking my time.

1. If someone spoke <u>scornfully</u> to you, would you be pleased?

   _____

2. If you <u>inherited</u> your father's looks, would you resemble your father?

   _____

3. If your jaw were <u>paralyzed</u>, would you be able to open your mouth?

   _____

4. If you lived in a <u>bungalow</u>, would you have room for a lot of guests?

   _____

5. If a friend did something <u>valiant</u>, would you admire her?

   _____

6. If someone <u>scuttled</u> away, would you think he or she was in no hurry?

   _____

7. If the wind was said to be blowing <u>savagely</u>, would you go outside?

   _____

8. If someone has been <u>revived</u>, is he or she asleep?

   _____

"Rikki-tikki-tavi" by Rudyard Kipling
Reading Warm-up A

Read the following passage. Pay special attention to the underlined words. Then, read it again, and complete the activities. Use a separate sheet of paper for your written answers.

The Indian mongoose has a <u>splendid</u> reputation for bravery. That reputation dates back to ancient Egypt, where the weasel-like creature scouted out crocodiles and ate their eggs or their newly hatched <u>brood</u>. The ancient Egyptians called the mongoose pharaoh's mouse, but that name is misleading. The mongoose is no mouse.

The Indian mongoose lives in fields or in heavy brush: tangled <u>thickets</u> and hedges. It eats rats, mice, snakes, lizards, the eggs of those creatures, and insects. It usually hunts at night. Most important, the mongoose can move like lightning. Its speed is a great advantage when it does the thing for which it is most famous: killing cobras and other snakes native to India. The mongoose is a snake's worst enemy.

In some ways the mongoose has an advantage over the snake. Its thick hide and long thick hair act as armor, protecting it from the snake's poisonous fangs. In addition, it takes a lot of cobra venom to kill an adult mongoose. The young mongoose is at risk, however, because its body is less tolerant of the venom. Many young mongooses die of snakebites before they can become skilled fighters.

The mongoose's snake dance is dazzling to behold. The mongoose is <u>balancing</u> lightly on its feet. In a <u>fraction</u> of a second, it leaps in any direction. By the time the snake strikes, the mongoose has already moved. When the snake grows exhausted, the mongoose leaps onto its back. At last the mongoose has <u>clenched</u> the snake's head between its sharp teeth, and it snaps the snake's spine.

Some species of mongooses are <u>bred</u> as pets. A mongoose may seem like a <u>peculiar</u> pet, but the animal is both intelligent and entertaining. If you happen to be in India, one may even save your life.

1. Underline the words that tell what is <u>splendid</u> about the mongoose. Give an antonym of *splendid*.

2. Circle the words that describe the crocodiles' <u>brood</u>. In your own words, rewrite the sentence, using a synonym for *brood*.

3. Circle the words that give a clue to the meaning of <u>thickets</u>. Use *thickets* in a sentence.

4. Underline the words that tell how the mongoose is <u>balancing</u>. Define *balancing*.

5. Underline the words that tell what happens in a <u>fraction</u> of a second. Tell about something else that can happen in a *fraction* of a second.

6. Circle the words that tell what the mongoose has <u>clenched</u> between its teeth. Rewrite the sentence, using a synonym for *clenched*.

7. Circle the words that tell what some mongooses are <u>bred</u> for. Name another animal that is *bred* for a special purpose.

8. Circle the words that tell what may seem like a <u>peculiar</u> pet. Write a sentence explaining why it is not really *peculiar*.

"Rikki-tikki-tavi" by Rudyard Kipling
Reading Warm-up B

Read the following passage. Pay special attention to the underlined words. Then, read it again, and complete the activities. Use a separate sheet of paper for your written answers.

Heather was <u>paralyzed</u> by the heat and humidity. She could not move, so she sat on the porch of the <u>bungalow</u>, sipping lemonade while the sun's heat beat <u>savagely</u> down on the tile roof. The doors and windows stood wide open, welcoming every wayward breeze. That did not help much, though. There was hardly a breath of air. Occasionally, a beetle <u>scuttled</u> across the porch, but mostly the insects remained silent and still in the heat of the burning sun.

"So this is India," thought Heather.

The bungalow in which she was staying belonged to her grandparents. Three days before, she had arrived for a month-long vacation. The house was near Calcutta, India's largest city, a teeming hive of activity. Heather had never been to India before, but she had <u>inherited</u> her grandfather's love of travel. She longed to see it all, from the parched desert to the snow-covered mountains. Still, she knew that the country was too vast to be seen in a lifetime, let alone a month's vacation.

Heather's family had lived here for generations. They had lived here when Great Britain ruled the country. Those days were long over, however. India gained its independence in the 1940s, after a <u>valiant</u> struggle against colonial rule. Many British politicians had <u>scornfully</u> predicted that India would not be able to rule itself, but they were wrong. The country is strong and thriving. Now the British return as guests, not as rulers.

Heather gazed from the porch that encircled the house, watching dark clouds blowing in from the Bay of Bengal. It would start to rain soon. Just the thought of rain <u>revived</u> her energy. Perhaps she would drive to Calcutta and explore the city. It was time to learn more, to see more.

1. Tell what <u>paralyzed</u> Heather. Circle the words that give the meaning of *paralyzed*.

2. Circle the phrase that tells where in the <u>bungalow</u> Heather is sitting. Write a sentence describing where you might see a *bungalow*.

3. Tell what beat <u>savagely</u> down on the roof. Use *savagely* in a sentence of your own.

4. Circle the word that tells what kind of insect <u>scuttled</u> across the porch. What is a synonym for *scuttled*?

5. Underline the phrase that tells what Heather <u>inherited</u>. Name something else that might be *inherited*.

6. Circle the word that tells what India gained after a <u>valiant</u> struggle. Write the meaning of *valiant*.

7. Underline the words that tell what was <u>scornfully</u> predicted. Use *scornfully* in a sentence.

8. Circle the words that tell what <u>revived</u> Heather's energy. Tell what has *revived* your energy on a hot day.

Name _____   Date _____

"**Rikki-tikki-tavi**" by Rudyard Kipling
Reading: Use Prior Knowledge to Make Predictions

Predicting means making an intelligent guess about what will happen next in a story based on details in the text. You can also **use prior knowledge to make predictions.** For example, if a story introduces a mongoose and a snake and you know that mongooses and snakes are natural enemies, you can predict that the story will involve a conflict between the two animals.

DIRECTIONS: *Fill in the following chart with predictions as you read "Rikki-tikki-tavi." Use clues from the story and your prior knowledge to make predictions. Then, compare your predictions with what actually happens. An example is shown.*

Story Details and Prior Knowledge	What I Predict Will Happen	What Actually Happens
Teddy's mother says, "Perhaps he isn't really dead." I know that Rikki-tikki is the hero of the story, and heroes rarely die during a story.	The mongoose will live.	The mongoose lives.

"Rikki-tikki-tavi" by Rudyard Kipling
Literary Analysis: Plot

Plot is the related sequence of events in a short story and other works of fiction. A plot has the following elements:

- **Exposition:** introduction of the setting (the time and place), the characters, and the basic situation
- **Rising Action:** events that introduce a **conflict,** or struggle, and increase the tension
- **Climax:** the story's high point, at which the eventual outcome becomes clear
- **Falling Action:** events that follow the climax
- **Resolution:** the final outcome and tying up of loose ends, when the reader learns how the conflict is resolved

For example, in a story about a battle, the exposition would introduce the contestants. The rising action might explain the conflict between the contestants and describe events leading up to the battle. The climax might be the winning of the battle by one of the contestants. The falling action could include a celebration of the victory, and the resolution might tell about events that took place in the years following the battle.

DIRECTIONS: *Answer the following questions about the plot elements of "Rikki-tikki-tavi."*

1. Who are the characters, and what is the setting described in the exposition?

   _____

   _____

2. How do you know that the appearance of Nag is part of the rising action?

   _____

   _____

3. What happens in the climax of "Rikki-tikki-tavi"?

   _____

   _____

4. Describe one event in the falling action of the story.

   _____

   _____

5. What happens in the resolution of "Rikki-tikki-tavi"?

   _____

   _____

"Rikki-tikki-tavi" by Rudyard Kipling
Vocabulary Builder

Word List

> revived   immensely   consolation

A. DIRECTIONS: *Use each vocabulary word by following the instructions below. Use the words in the same way they are used in "Rikki-tikki-tavi," and write sentences that show you understand the meaning of the word.*

1. Use the word *revived* in a sentence about a bird.

   _____

   _____

2. Use the word *consolation* in a sentence about a race.

   _____

   _____

3. Use the word *immensely* in a sentence about an activity.

   _____

   _____

B. DIRECTIONS: *On each line, write the letter of the word or phrase that is a synonym for the vocabulary word.*

____ 1. immensely
   A. mildly
   B. greatly
   C. immediately
   D. loudly

____ 2. revived
   A. continued to live
   B. relaxed in a reclining position
   C. returned to consciousness
   D. fell asleep again

____ 3. consolation
   A. confusion about a loss
   B. assurance of victory
   C. confidence in victory
   D. comfort after a disappointment

"Rikki-tikki-tavi" by Rudyard Kipling
Support for Writing an Informative Article

Use the graphic organizer below to record details from each section of "Rikki-tikki-tavi." Your details should tell *when, how much, how often,* or *to what extent.*

Introduction

Details:

Body

Details:

Conclusion

Details:

Now, use your notes to write a short informative article about mongooses. Write for an audience of third-graders.

"Rikki-tikki-tavi" by Rudyard Kipling
Support for Extend Your Learning

Research and Technology

Use this chart to make notes about the countries on each continent that have cobras. If no countries on a continent have cobras, write *None*. You also might note any details about the places where cobras live—for example, the climate or the terrain.

Continent	Countries With Cobras
South America	
North America	
Europe	
Asia	
Africa	
Australia	

Then, use your notes to make a diagram of the places in the world where cobras live.

Listening and Speaking

Across the top of this T-chart, write your opinion about mongooses and cobras, stating which animal you find more interesting. Then, record several reasons for your opinion. For each reason, write a fact that supports it. At the bottom of the page, write a sentence summarizing your viewpoint.

My Viewpoint:

Reasons	Facts

Summary: _____

_____

_____

"Rikki-tikki-tavi" by Rudyard Kipling
Enrichment: Real-Life Animals

Kipling's story, though fictional, is based on facts about mongooses and cobras. For example, mongooses are known for their ability to kill snakes and rodents, and cobras are the natural enemies of mongooses. If you research other facts about these two animals, you will see how true to life Kipling's fictional tale is.

DIRECTIONS: *Complete the following chart about the mongoose and the cobra. Use science books or other reliable resources to find the information. Create an additional category to add to the chart, and add the information needed to complete it.*

Characteristics	Mongoose	Cobra
Physical features		
Where it lives		
What it eats		
Its defense weapons		

Name _____ Date _____

"The Bear Boy" by Joseph Bruchac
"Rikki-tikki-tavi" by Rudyard Kipling
Build Language Skills: Vocabulary

The Root -dict-

The word *predict* comes from the root *-dict-*, meaning "to speak," and the prefix *pre-*, meaning "before" or "in front of." When you *predict* something, you *speak* about what might happen *before* you know for sure what will happen.

A. DIRECTIONS: *Look up each word in a dictionary, and write its meaning on the line following the word. Then, explain how the meaning of the root -dict- ("to speak") is contained in the word's meaning.*

1. *diction:* _____

   Explanation: _____

2. *dictionary:* _____

   Explanation: _____

Academic Vocabulary Practice

anticipate	indicate	plot	predict	verify

B. DIRECTIONS: *Use an Academic Vocabulary word from the box in your answer to each question. Answer the question in a full sentence, and use each word only once.*

1. A friend has told you that a movie is very good. Do you consider seeing it? Why or why not?

   _____

2. Think of a story or movie you liked. What did you like about its sequence of events?

   _____

3. You are reading a suspenseful story. Before it is over, do you say or think about what is going to happen? Why or why not?

   _____

4. You are shopping for something that is in a display case, and you would like to take a closer look at it. How do you tell the salesperson which item you would like to see?

   _____

5. Your friend insists that your favorite movie was made in 1992, but you are sure it was made in 1994. How do you find out which date is correct?

   _____

"The Bear Boy" by Joseph Bruchac
"Rikki-tikki-tavi" by Rudyard Kipling
Build Language Skills: Grammar

Action Verbs and Linking Verbs

Verbs are words that express an action (for example, *swim* and *throw*) or a state of being (for example, *am, is, was,* and *seemed*). The verbs that express an action are called *action verbs.*

   Jessica *climbed* a mountain.

   The verbs that express a state of being are called *linking verbs.* Linking verbs join the subject of a sentence with a word or expression that describes or renames the subject.

   Jessica *seems* strong.

   Jessica *is* a mountain climber.

   Besides forms of *be* and *seem,* other verbs that can describe or rename a subject are *appear, look,* and *sound.*

A. PRACTICE: *Underline the verbs in each sentence. On the line, identify each verb as an* action verb *or a* linking verb.

1. Rikki-tikki-tavi is a brave little mongoose. _____

2. Mongooses seem harmless, but they fight bravely. _____,
   _____

3. Rikki-tikki lives with a human family, and they love him. _____,
   _____

4. A snake threatens the family, and Rikki-tikki is furious. _____,
   _____

5. Rikki-tikki defeats the snake, and the family is very happy. _____,
   _____

B. Writing Application: *Write a paragraph about a time when you or someone you know was in danger. Use at least three action verbs and three linking verbs. Underline each action verb once and each linking verb twice.*

_____

_____

_____

_____

_____

_____

_____

_____

Name _____   Date _____

"Rikki-tikki-tavi" by Rudyard Kipling
Selection Test A

Critical Reading *Identify the letter of the choice that best answers the question.*

_____ 1. What kind of animal is Rikki-tikki-tavi?
   A. a cat
   B. a muskrat
   C. a weasel
   D. a mongoose

_____ 2. In "Rikki-tikki-tavi," a flood takes Rikki-tikki from his home to the care of an English family. In what part of the plot does the flood take place?
   A. during the climax
   B. during the resolution
   C. during the falling action
   D. during the exposition

_____ 3. Based on this quotation and your prior knowledge, what can you predict will happen?
   "No," said his mother; "let's take him in and dry him. Perhaps he isn't really dead."
   A. Rikki-tikki will soon die.
   B. Rikki-tikki will probably live.
   C. The mother will become Rikki-tikki's only friend.
   D. Rikki-tikki will fight Nag and Nagaina.

_____ 4. At the beginning of "Rikki-tikki-tavi," which characteristic does Rikki-tikki display as soon as he has warmed up?
   A. greed
   B. bravery
   C. curiousity
   D. laziness

_____ 5. Based on the following passage, what do you think it means when the tail of an animal like Rikki-tikki grows "bottlebrushy"?
   "This is a splendid hunting ground," [Rikki-tikki] said, and his tail grew bottlebrushy at the thought of it.
   A. The animal is happy and excited.
   B. The animal is hungry.
   C. The animal is lost and afraid.
   D. The animal is alert.

____ 6. When Rikki-tikki first comes to the garden, a conflict is introduced. Whom is the conflict between?
   A. Nag and Nagaina
   B. Rikki-tikki and Nag
   C. Rikki-tikki and Darzee
   D. Darzee and Darzee's wife

____ 7. Who is Nagaina?
   A. Nag's wife
   B. Nag's father
   C. Nag's sister
   D. Nag's mother

____ 8. After Rikki-tikki kills Karait, how does he feel?
   A. confident
   B. annoyed
   C. jealous
   D. defeated

____ 9. What prediction can you make based on your prior knowledge and this quotation from "Rikki-tikki-tavi"?

   "Teddy's safer with that little beast than if he had a bloodhound to watch him. If a snake came into the nursery now—"

   A. The snakes are not a threat to Teddy.
   B. Rikki-tikki will fail to protect Teddy from a snake attack.
   C. Rikki-tikki will protect Teddy from a snake attack.
   D. Rikki-tikki will attack Teddy.

____ 10. The birds and frogs rejoice and sing, "*Ding-dong-tock!* Nag is dead!" In what part of the plot does this event take place?
   A. during the rising action
   B. during the falling action
   C. during the exposition
   D. during the climax

____ 11. Which statement best describes Rikki-tikki's character?
   A. He is cautious and selfish.
   B. He is fierce and bloodthirsty.
   C. He is brave and loyal.
   D. He is loving and shy.

Vocabulary and Grammar

____ 12. In which sentence about "Rikki-tikki-tavi" is *immensely* used correctly?

A. Darzee's wife takes great pride in her immensely eggs and cares for them.

B. Once Teddy's family gets used to living in the bungalow, they like it immensely.

C. The Coppersmith, the town crier of every garden, spreads the word immensely.

D. Fearful that Nagaina will turn and strike at him, Rikki-tikki holds on immensely.

____ 13. In which sentence about "Rikki-tikki-tavi" is *revived* used correctly?

A. The garden Rikki-tikki entered revived lime and orange trees.

B. Teddy's father revived Nag by shooting him with his rifle.

C. Teddy's family was revived to know that Nagaina was dead.

D. After Rikki-tikki revived, he thought how lucky he was to be alive.

____ 14. Which word in this passage is a linking verb?

Teresa was on the phone when Megan arrived to pick her up.

A. was

B. when

C. arrived

D. pick

____ 15. Which word in this passage from "Rikki-tikki-tavi" is an action verb?

"Who is Nag?" he said. "I am Nag."

A. Who

B. is

C. said

D. am

Essay

16. Did you predict the result of the battle between Rikki-tikki-tavi and Nagaina? In an essay, explain how easy or difficult it is for readers to predict the outcome of "Rikki-tikki-tavi." Name the events in the story that might help the reader to predict the outcome. Name any events that might make it difficult for the reader to predict the outcome.

17. Consider the five basic plot elements: exposition, rising action, climax, falling action, and resolution. In an essay, describe an event in "Rikki-tikki-tavi" that illustrates each element. Then, explain why you think the plot elements do or do not create a satisfying story.

"Rikki-tikki-tavi" by Rudyard Kipling
Selection Test B

Critical Reading *Identify the letter of the choice that best completes the statement or answers the question.*

____ 1. Read the following quotation from "Rikki-tikki-tavi." Then, based on the quotation and your prior knowledge, choose the most likely outcome from the choices below.

"No," said his mother; "let's take him in and dry him. Perhaps he isn't really dead."

A. Rikki-tikki will soon die.
B. Rikki-tikki will survive.
C. Rikki-tikki will survive and attack the boy's mother.
D. The mother will become Rikki-tikki's only friend.

____ 2. After Teddy's father beats the dead Karait, Rikki-tikki thinks, "What is the use of that? . . . I have settled it all." This thought shows that Rikki-tikki feels
A. proud.
B. annoyed.
C. jealous.
D. defeated.

____ 3. Using prior knowledge and the information contained in the following passage from "Rikki-tikki-tavi," what can you predict will happen?

Darzee and his wife only cowered down in the nest without answering, for from the thick grass at the foot of the bush there came a low hiss.

A. Rikki-tikki will run away.
B. Darzee will be killed.
C. A snake will appear.
D. Rikki-tikki will be killed.

____ 4. Using prior knowledge and the information contained in the following passage from "Rikki-tikki-tavi," what can you predict will happen?

Though Rikki-tikki had never met a live cobra before, his mother had fed him on dead ones, and he knew that all a grown mongoose's business in life was to fight and eat snakes. Nag knew that, too, and at the bottom of his cold heart he was afraid.

A. Rikki-tikki will return to his mother and again eat dead cobras.
B. Nag will defeat Rikki-tikki in battle.
C. Rikki-tikki will defeat Nag in battle.
D. Rikki-tikki and Nag will settle their differences peacefully.

____ 5. The central conflict in "Rikki-tikki-tavi" is between
A. the English family and the snakes.
B. Darzee and the cobras.
C. Rikki-tikki and the cobras.
D. Rikki-tikki and Karait.

___ 6. During what part of the plot do Nag and Nagaina talk about their plan?
   A. during the climax
   B. during the falling action
   C. during the rising action
   D. during the exposition

___ 7. Why do Nag and Nagaina want to do away with the entire English family?
   A. They resent the English as conquerors of their land.
   B. They believe that once the family is gone, Rikki-tikki will leave and they will be safe.
   C. They know how much Rikki-tikki loves the English family and hope to break his spirit.
   D. They hope to deprive Rikki-tikki of his main source of food.

___ 8. The climax of "Rikki-tikki-tavi" occurs when
   A. Rikki-tikki saves Teddy from Karait's attack.
   B. Rikki-tikki fights with Nag.
   C. Rikki-tikki fights with Nagaina.
   D. Rikki-tikki makes sure another cobra never enters the garden.

___ 9. Rikki-tikki's main reason for hunting down Nagaina is that
   A. Rikki-tikki is still hungry and wants Nagaina's eggs.
   B. Nagaina's eggs are about to hatch, and the newborn snakes will need food.
   C. Rikki-tikki knows that he must kill Nagaina and destroy her eggs to protect the family.
   D. Rikki-tikki feels that he still has something to prove to the family.

___ 10. Rikki-tikki's main helper in his fight with Nagaina is
   A. Darzee.
   B. Darzee's wife.
   C. Teddy.
   D. Teddy's father.

___ 11. Which of the following events occurs during the resolution of "Rikki-tikki-tavi"?
   A. Darzee's wife fools Nagaina.
   B. Rikki-tikki cracks all of Nagaina's eggs except one.
   C. The birds and the frogs announce Rikki-tikki's victory.
   D. Rikki-tikki makes sure that a cobra never again enters the garden.

___ 12. What information about snakes does the reader *not* learn from "Rikki-tikki-tavi"?
   A. A snake's eyes never change their expression no matter what the snake is thinking.
   B. If a bird looks into a snake's eyes, the bird will become frightened and unable to move.
   C. The bite of a mongoose will kill a snake.
   D. Snakes' eggs are enclosed in a shell.

____ 13. Which characteristics most help Rikki-tikki defeat the snakes?
   A. his fear and his hatred
   B. his courage and his stubbornness
   C. his anger and his strength
   D. his cleverness and his speed

____ 14. Which of the following statements best describes Rikki-tikki's character?
   A. He is cautious and loyal.
   B. He is brave and loyal.
   C. He is bloodthirsty and loyal.
   D. He is loving and shy.

Vocabulary and Grammar

____ 15. If Rikki-tikki fears the cobra *immensely,* he fears it
   A. a little bit.
   B. a great deal.
   C. only for a moment.
   D. only at first.

____ 16. Someone who needs *consolation* is probably
   A. happy.
   B. puzzled.
   C. sad.
   D. confident.

____ 17. Which of the following sentences from "Rikki-tikki-tavi" contains a linking verb?
   A. Darzee, the tailorbird bird, helped him.
   B. Chuchundra the muskrat . . . gave him advice.
   C. He was a mongoose, rather like a little cat in his fur and his tail.
   D. One day, a high summer flood washed him out of the burrow.

____ 18. Which of the following sentences from "Rikki-tikki-tavi" contains an action verb?
   A. "All mongooses are like that."
   B. "There are more things to find out about in this house."
   C. He spent all that day roaming over the house.
   D. It was a large garden, only half cultivated.

Essay

19. Did you predict the outcome of the battle between Rikki-tikki and Nagaina? In an essay, explain how easy or difficult it is for readers to predict the outcome of "Rikki-tikki-tavi." What prior knowledge do they need? What events in the story help the reader predict the outcome? What events, if any, might make it difficult for the reader to predict the outcome?

20. In "Rikki-tikki-tavi," a story of conflict between natural enemies, the animals have personalities and demonstrate character traits that are very human. In an essay, analyze how traits such as loyalty, bravery, and selfishness drive the action of the story. Illustrate your points with examples of events in the story. For example, Rikki-tikki's curiosity leads him to explore the garden; Nag's fear causes him to plot against Rikki-tikki.

Vocabulary Warm-up Word Lists

Study these words from Letters from Rifka. *Then, complete the activities.*

Word List A

bales [BAYLZ] *n.* large bundles of something, usually bound up
   The field was full of <u>bales</u> of hay.

belongings [bee LAWNG ingz] *n.* things that belong to someone
   My most important <u>belongings</u> are in a special place.

details [dee TAYLZ] *n.* the small parts that go into making up something
   Many <u>details</u> went into the planning of our winter vacation.

flickering [FLICK er ing] *adj.* twinkling
   From afar, the city lights look like <u>flickering</u> candles.

huddled [HUHD uhld] *v.* hunched, or pulled oneself up or together
   Vanessa <u>huddled</u> under the blanket to keep warm.

peasants [PEZ uhntz] *n.* poor laborers who work on farms
   The <u>peasants</u> worked for weeks harvesting the corn.

regiment [REJ i muhnt] *n.* a military unit made up of two or more battalions
   The soldiers in the <u>regiment</u> marched in unison.

vanished [VAN isht] *v.* disappeared or went suddenly from sight
   It seemed as if the magician's rabbit <u>vanished</u> into thin air.

Word List B

boxcar [BAHX cahr] *n.* a car on a freight train that holds goods that are being transported
   The <u>boxcar</u> bound from Florida was loaded with grapefruit.

burlap [BER lap] *adj.* made from burlap, a rough material woven from fiber
   The potatoes were packaged in a <u>burlap</u> bag.

candlesticks [KAN duhl stiks] *n.* holders for candles
   The silver <u>candlesticks</u> shone in the light of the candles.

dimpled [DIM puhld] *adj.* having dimples, small, natural dents of the skin
   The doll had <u>dimpled</u> cheeks.

filthy [FIL thee] *adj.* extremely dirty or disgusting
   At the end of the day, the auto mechanic's overalls were <u>filthy</u>.

precaution [pree CAW shun] *n.* something done ahead of time to prevent a danger
   As a <u>precaution</u>, we locked the windows before leaving on vacation.

rucksack [RUHK sak] *n.* a sack strapped over the shoulders; a knapsack or backpack
   The hiker's <u>rucksack</u> contained her lunch and a change of clothes.

vultures [VUHL cherz] *n.* large scavenging birds; also, greedy persons who prey on others
   Like <u>vultures</u>, the thieves emptied the dresser draws in their search for valuables.

from **Letters from Rifka** by Karen Hesse
Vocabulary Warm-up Exercises

Exercise A *Fill in each blank in the paragraph below with an appropriate word from Word List A. Use each word only once.*

During the American Revolution one of the most difficult times was the winter at Valley Forge. The soldiers in General Washington's [1] _____ had few supplies. The farmers who lived nearby were not [2] _____, but they were not wealthy either. They lived simply and had few [3] _____. They had little to share with the soldiers. Washington's men suffered from the cold. They stuffed their ragged boots with hay they tore from the [4] _____ they found in nearby fields. They [5] _____ around the fire's [6] _____ flames to warm themselves. Some men, deserters, [7] _____. Meanwhile, Washington mapped out a strategy, working out the [8] _____ of a bold plan to win the war.

Exercise B *Revise each sentence so that the underlined vocabulary word is used in a logical way. Be sure to keep the vocabulary word in your revision.*

Example: We cried when we read the <u>humorous</u> story.
We laughed when we read the <u>humorous</u> story.

1. Everyone admired the child's <u>dimpled</u> eyes.

   _____

2. The crowded <u>boxcar</u> was full of passengers.

   _____

3. We placed new light bulbs in the <u>candlesticks</u>.

   _____

4. As a <u>precaution</u>, we left our umbrellas behind.

   _____

5. The hiker explained that a <u>rucksack</u> is a kind of blanket.

   _____

6. Because the children were not hungry, they devoured their lunch like <u>vultures</u>.

   _____

7. The <u>burlap</u> felt comfortable against his skin.

   _____

8. The house was sparkling clean; even the curtains were <u>filthy</u>.

   _____

53

from Letters from Rifka by Karen Hesse
Reading Warm-up A

Read the following passage. Pay special attention to the underlined words. Then, read it again, and complete the activities. Use a separate sheet of paper for your written answers.

Fiddler on the Roof, a Broadway play, first opened in 1964. It is based on a collection of short stories by a Russian Jewish writer who called himself Sholom Aleichem. The play, a musical, was made into a movie in 1971. *Fiddler* was one of the first Broadway musicals to deal with serious issues, such as persecution and poverty.

The story is set in 1905 in Russia. The characters are Jewish <u>peasants</u>. The main character is Tevye, a poor dairy farmer. During the story, each of Tevye's daughters comes to him. Each daughter asks him to allow her to break with tradition so that she can marry the man she loves. The story is both humorous and sad. It deals with Tevye's struggle to hang on to tradition in the face of a changing world.

In fact, the early twentieth century—when *Fiddler* takes place—was a difficult time for Jews living in Russia. Persecution and violence were common. In the play, soldiers from the local Russian <u>regiment</u> make an appearance. They make the audience aware of the dangers that Tevye and his family face.

In one scene, Tevye tends to the <u>details</u> of his work caring for the animals in the barn. When he is finished, he is <u>huddled</u> among the <u>bales</u> of hay, daydreaming of how different things would be if he were rich. He sings "If I Were a Rich Man."

In another scene, the Jewish tradition of lighting candles and reciting blessings is portrayed. Music and <u>flickering</u> candlelight play on the faces of the children, creating a beautiful scene.

By the end of the play, many changes have taken place in Tevye's family and village. Tevye realizes that the family is in danger. They must pack a few <u>belongings</u> and flee. Although their traditions remain with them, the life they knew has <u>vanished</u>.

1. Circle the words that tell where the <u>peasants</u> lived. Define *peasants*.

2. Circle the word that gives a clue about what a <u>regiment</u> is. What is a *regiment*?

3. Underline the words that tell something about the <u>details</u> of Tevye's work. Use *details* in a sentence.

4. Underline the words that tell what Tevye is doing when he is <u>huddled</u> among the <u>bales</u> of hay. Define the word *huddled*. Tell what *bales* are.

5. Circle the word that tells what was <u>flickering</u>. What does *flickering* mean?

6. What sort of <u>belongings</u> do you think Tevye's family packed? Define *belongings*.

7. Underline the words that tell what has <u>vanished</u>. Use *vanished* in a sentence.

from **Letters from Rifka** by Karen Hesse
Reading Warm-up B

Read the following passage. Pay special attention to the underlined words. Then, read it again, and complete the activities. Use a separate sheet of paper for your written answers.

The U.S. Holocaust Memorial Museum opened in 1993 in Washington, D.C. It honors the memory of the millions of Jews and other people who were exterminated by the Nazis during World War II.

The collection includes films, oral histories, artifacts, and photographs that document the horrors of the Holocaust. One may view the beautiful candlesticks that Jewish families used to celebrate the Sabbath. Those and other valuables were taken from the families by German soldiers. The soldiers were in charge of rounding up the Jews. They shipped the Jews to ghettos. Then, they shipped them to concentration camps. The camps were prisons where inmates were forced to work. Eventually, the Nazis executed millions of Jews and others in the camps.

In the museum's collection of photographs are heartbreaking pictures of adults and young children. The children, dressed in filthy ragged clothing, stare back at the camera. Their once round and dimpled cheeks are thin and hollow. Some of the adults carry a rucksack or just a sack made of burlap, which holds the few possessions they have left. The rest of their valuables had been taken from them by the Nazis—much as vultures might prey on the remains of helpless creatures. Other photographs show groups of prisoners. They have been rounded up like cattle, to be placed on one boxcar after another. Trains of boxcars transported the victims to the concentration camps.

In films and oral histories, survivors of the camps tell their experiences. As conditions got worse, some families tried to take the precaution of sending members of the family away before they could be captured. Others tried to find places to hide.

The Holocaust Memorial Museum serves as an important source of information about this painful and terrible period of history.

1. Underline the words that tell what the candlesticks were used for. What are *candlesticks*?

2. Circle the words that tell what was filthy. What is an antonym of *filthy*?

3. Describe how the dimpled cheeks of children look. Define *dimpled*.

4. Underline the words that tell what some people carried in a rucksack. What is a *rucksack*?

5. Circle the words that tell what is made of burlap. What might *burlap* be used for?

6. Why were the Nazis like vultures? What are *vultures*?

7. Who was loaded into the boxcar of a train? What is a *boxcar*?

8. Underline the words that tell what some people tried to do as a precaution. Define *precaution*.

Name _____ Date _____

from *Letters from Rifka* by Karen Hesse
Reading: Read Ahead to Verify Predictions and Reread to Look for Details

A **prediction** is an informed guess about what will happen. Use details in the text and your own knowledge and experience to make predictions as you read. Then, **read ahead to verify predictions,** to check whether your predictions are correct.

- As you read, ask yourself whether new details support your predictions. If they do not, revise your predictions based on the new information.
- If the predictions you make turn out to be wrong, **reread to look for details** you might have missed that would have helped you make a more accurate prediction.

If it had not been for your father, though, I think my family would all be dead now: Mama, Papa, Nathan, Saul, and me.

Details in this passage can help you predict that the narrator will reveal that Rifka has escaped a dangerous situation. You can read further in the excerpt from *Letters from Rifka* to check this prediction.

DIRECTIONS: *Complete the following chart. If a prediction in the second column is correct, write* Correct *in the third column. If a prediction is wrong, write* Incorrect *in the third column. Then, in the fourth column, describe what does happen, and include a detail that would have allowed an accurate prediction. The first item has been completed as an example.*

Detail in *Letters from Rifka*	Prediction	Verification of Prediction	Event in Selection and Additional Detail
1. Tovah's father helps Rifka's family.	Tovah's father is in danger.	Incorrect	Tovah's father makes it home safely: "I am sure you and Cousin Hannah were glad to see Uncle Avrum come home today."
2. Rifka is not sure she will be able to distract the guards.	Rifka will not succeed.		
3. Nathan deserts the army.	Soldiers will look for Nathan.		
4. Rifka says, "Don't we need papers?"	Papa will find the papers.		

from *Letters from Rifka* by Karen Hesse
Literary Analysis: Character

A **character** is a person or an animal that takes part in the action of a literary work.

- A **character's motives** are the emotions or goals that drive him or her to act one way or another. Some powerful motives are love, anger, and hope.
- **Character traits** are the individual qualities that make each character unique. These may be things such as stubbornness, sense of humor, or intelligence.

Characters' motives and qualities are important because they influence what characters do and how they interact with other characters. As you read, think about what the characters are like and why they do what they do. For example, consider this passage:

> I am sure you and Cousin Hannah were glad to see Uncle Avrum come home today. How worried his daughters must have been after the locked doors and whisperings of last night.

This passage illustrates Rifka's character traits: her caring nature and concern for others. It also suggests a motive for her actions: She wants her family to be safe.

A. DIRECTIONS: *After each character's name, write as many adjectives as you can think of that describe that character's traits.*

1. **Rifka:** _____

   _____

   _____

2. **Papa:** _____

   _____

   _____

B. DIRECTIONS: *Each quotation on the right states or hints at a motive for one of the actions on the left. On the line before each action, write the letter of the quotation that provides the motive.*

___ 1. Rifka writes to Tovah.

___ 2. Nathan deserts the army.

___ 3. Rifka distracts guards.

___ 4. Mama insists on taking candlesticks.

___ 5. Avrum helps the family escape.

A. "I've come," he said, "to warn Saul."

B. "Soon enough they will sweep down like vultures to pick our house bare."

C. "We made it!"

D. "If it had not been for your father, . . . my family would all be dead now."

E. "I knew, no matter how frightened I was, I must not let them find Nathan."

from *Letters from Rifka* by Karen Hesse
Vocabulary Builder

Word List

distract	emerged	huddled

A. DIRECTIONS: *Think about the meaning of the underlined word in each of these sentences. Then, answer the question.*

1. What might Rifka have done to <u>distract</u> the guards?

   _____

   _____

2. If Nathan had <u>emerged</u> from under the burlap bags, what might have happened?

   _____

   _____

3. Why had the family <u>huddled</u> in Tovah's cellar through the night?

   _____

   _____

B. DIRECTIONS: *Write the letter of the word or phrase that can replace the Word List word in each sentence.*

____ 1. Rifka tried to <u>distract</u> the guards from finding Nathan by talking to them about Pushkin.
   A. play a trick on   C. draw attention away from
   B. frighten   D. entertain

____ 2. The travelers <u>emerged</u> from the train looking tired and pale.
   A. ran away   C. fell
   B. got onto   D. came into view

____ 3. To keep warm, the family <u>huddled</u> together.
   A. crowded   C. slept
   B. fought   D. hid

Name _____ Date _____

from *Letters from Rifka* by Karen Hesse
Support for Writing a Journal Entry

For your **journal entry,** put yourself in the place of the character you have chosen. Write that character's name on the line. Then, imagine what you see and what you feel on the night of the escape, and record those ideas on this chart.

My character: _____

Event	Details from My Point of View	My Feelings About the Escape
Nathan's arrival home		
The plan to escape		
Hiding on the train		
Rifka's distraction		

Now, use your notes to write a journal entry about the night of the escape.

Name _____ Date _____

from *Letters from Rifka* by Karen Hesse
Support for Extend Your Learning

Research and Technology

Use this chart to record information for your **outline** of findings about the persecution of Jews in Russia in the early twentieth century.

Russia in the Early Twentieth Century	Jewish Persecution in Early-Twentieth-Century Russia

Listening and Speaking

Answer these questions to organize your thoughts in preparation for a **discussion** of Nathan's motives for deserting the army and the risks his action involved.

1. What reason does Nathan give for leaving his regiment? For what other reasons might he have left?

   _____

   _____

2. What might have happened to Nathan as a consequence of his desertion?

   _____

3. What might have happened if Nathan had not deserted?

   _____

   _____

4. Do you think that Nathan should have deserted? Why or why not?

   _____

   _____

   _____

from *Letters from Rifka* by Karen Hesse
Enrichment: Aleksandr Pushkin

On her flight from Russia, Rifka carries a book by Aleksandr Pushkin that her cousin Tovah has given her. Pushkin was a Russian writer who lived from 1799 to 1837. Many critics consider him the greatest Russian poet. He also wrote plays, novels, and essays. In his writing, he used the common speech of Russians. That style influenced many other Russian writers.

DIRECTIONS: *Read this poem by Pushkin. Then, answer the questions that follow.*

A Little Bird

In alien lands devoutly clinging
To age-old rites of Russian earth,
I let a captive bird go winging
To greet the radiant spring's rebirth.

My heart grew lighter then: why mutter
Against God's providence, and rage,
When I was free to set aflutter
But one poor captive from his cage!

1. What might the speaker mean by "alien lands"?

   _____

   _____

   _____

2. Whom or what might the speaker mean when he talks about the "captive bird"?

   _____

   _____

   _____

3. How is Rifka like the bird, "set aflutter" in freedom? Explain your ideas.

   _____

   _____

   _____

   _____

   _____

from *Letters from Rifka* by Karen Hesse
Selection Test A

Critical Reading *Identify the letter of the choice that best answers the question.*

_____ 1. Where are Rifka and her family heading as she writes her letter?
   A. to Russia
   B. to Poland
   C. to prison
   D. back home

_____ 2. Which family member in *Letters from Rifka* does not know about the escape?
   A. Uncle Avrum
   B. Hannah
   C. Tovah
   D. Bubbe Ruth

_____ 3. How does Rifka feel about Uncle Avrum?
   A. She is angry with him.
   B. She is jealous of him.
   C. She is grateful to him.
   D. She is scornful of him.

_____ 4. Which detail in *Letters from Rifka* helps you predict that guards will come to the railroad station?
   A. It is so dark that Rifka cannot see Nathan's eyes.
   B. Rifka hides her mother's candlesticks in her rucksack.
   C. At dawn, Rifka stands alone outside a boxcar.
   D. Nathan asks Rifka whether she can distract the guards.

_____ 5. Which word best describes Nathan's action of returning home to warn Saul in *Letters from Rifka*?
   A. brave
   B. cowardly
   C. boastful
   D. cruel

_____ 6. Why is Rifka at first happy to think that Saul will go into the army?
   A. He is cruel to her and often violent.
   B. He has always wanted to join the army.
   C. He will make the family proud.
   D. He teases her and drives her crazy.

____ **7.** In *Letters from Rifka*, why does the family decide to leave their home?

    A. Family members have sent them the fare to America.

    B. They do not have enough food to survive the winter in Russia.

    C. They want to save Nathan's life and keep Saul out of the army.

    D. Their neighbors have betrayed them to the soldiers.

____ **8.** Why does Rifka's mother take the candlesticks?

    A. She does not want the peasants to steal them.

    B. She hopes to use them as a weapon.

    C. They were a gift from her beloved sister.

    D. They belong to Uncle Avrum.

____ **9.** What can you predict about Rifka's family from this quotation?

    They bring him back and kill him in front of his regiment as a warning to the others. Those who have helped him, they also die.

    A. The whole family will die.

    B. The whole family is in danger.

    C. Only Rifka's father is in danger.

    D. Only Nathan is in danger.

____ **10.** In *Letters from Rifka*, what does Papa's decision to leave show about him?

    A. He hates the Russian government.

    B. He cares deeply about his family.

    C. He is desperate for money.

    D. He has given in to despair.

____ **11.** In *Letters from Rifka*, why isn't Tovah allowed to hear the plans for escape?

    A. She is unable to keep a secret.

    B. She is too young to understand.

    C. The family wants to keep her from worrying.

    D. The family wants to keep her out of danger.

____ **12.** Which phrase best describes Rifka's relationship with Tovah?

    A. competitive and jealous

    B. friendly but distant

    C. warm and loving

    D. cold and uncaring

Vocabulary and Grammar

____ **13.** In which of these sentences about *Letters from Rifka* is the word *distract* used correctly?

    A. Rifka's letter was written to distract Tovah's worry.

    B. Papa had to distract his family to leave.

    C. Rifka had to distract the guards from their search.

    D. Uncle Avrum returned home to distract his daughters.

____ **14.** In *Letters from Rifka*, when the guards *emerged* from the shelter, what happened?

    A. They became difficult to see.

    B. They came into view.

    C. They dried off.

    D. They yielded to other guards.

____ **15.** In which of the following sentences about *Letters from Rifka* is the verb irregular?

    A. Rifka and her family are on their way to Poland.

    B. Hannah drapes a shawl over Rifka's shoulders.

    C. At the train station, Papa whispers to Rifka.

    D. Rifka packs Mama's candlesticks in her rucksack.

Essay

16. Rifka's life is about to change completely. In an essay, describe three ways in which her life may be different. Consider what you know about Rifka's life. When does the story take place? Where has she been living? Where does Papa say they are going? Use details from *Letters from Rifka* to make your predictions.

17. Rifka and Nathan have character traits that will help them face the dangers and hardships of their journey. In an essay, describe those character traits. Explain how they will help Rifka and Nathan. Use details from *Letters from Rifka* to support your answer.

from _Letters from Rifka_ by Karen Hesse
Selection Test B

Critical Reading _Identify the letter of the choice that best completes the statement or answers the question._

____ 1. Rifka is grateful to Uncle Avrum because
    A. he gave her family money.
    B. he helped her family plan their escape.
    C. he distracted the guards.
    D. he hid Nathan from the guards.

____ 2. Nathan asks Rifka to distract the guards because
    A. they are not likely to suspect her.
    B. he does not think the family will escape.
    C. Papa is not brave enough to do it.
    D. she is the smartest one in the family.

____ 3. Rifka agrees to try to distract the guards because
    A. she does not fear them.
    B. she is the youngest.
    C. she does not want to disappoint Nathan.
    D. she wants to prove her courage to Tovah.

____ 4. Which detail in _Letters from Rifka_ helps you predict that guards will come to the railroad station?
    A. There had been locked doors and whispering the night before.
    B. At dawn, Rifka stands alone outside a boxcar in the train station.
    C. The members of the family hide in different cars of the train.
    D. Nathan asks Rifka whether she can distract the guards.

____ 5. What can the reader predict about the guards from this line from _Letters from Rifka_?
    They [the guards] did not notice me at first.
    A. The guards will not notice Rifka.
    B. The guards will soon notice Rifka.
    C. The guards will keep Rifka from leaving.
    D. The guards will try to help Rifka.

____ 6. If Rifka is not successful at distracting the guards, what is likely to happen?
    A. The family will escape without her.
    B. The family will be killed.
    C. Saul will enlist in the army.
    D. Uncle Avrum will be imprisoned.

____ 7. In _Letters from Rifka_, Nathan's life is in danger because
    A. he has refused to fight in battle.
    B. he has refused to join the army.
    C. he is a Jew and a deserter.
    D. he was not born in Russia.

_____ 8. In *Letters from Rifka*, what character trait does Nathan display by deserting?
   A. cowardice
   B. uncertainty
   C. obedience
   D. courage

_____ 9. What can the reader predict about Rifka's family from this quotation?

   They bring him back and kill him in front of his regiment as a warning to the others. Those who have helped him, they also die.

   A. The whole family is in danger.
   B. Both Saul and Nathan are in danger.
   C. Only Saul is in danger.
   D. Only Nathan is in danger.

_____ 10. Why is Rifka ashamed of her reaction when she hears that Saul must join the army?
   A. She knows that Saul will probably be killed.
   B. She realizes that they are all in danger.
   C. She thinks that her father feels the same way.
   D. She knows that Saul is fond of her.

_____ 11. What is the meaning of this passage from *Letters from Rifka*?

   "Don't we need papers?" I asked.

   Papa looked from Nathan to Saul. "There is no time for papers," he said.

   A. The family will leave the country without the government's permission.
   B. The family cannot wait until the next day's newspapers are published.
   C. The family will not have time to look for their birth certificates.
   D. The family will have to leave all their paper goods behind.

_____ 12. In *Letters from Rifka*, Papa's motive for leaving his home is
   A. his hatred of the Russian government.
   B. his desire to live in America.
   C. his concern for his family.
   D. his concern for Rifka's safety.

_____ 13. Rifka's family plans to go to America because
   A. they have relatives there.
   B. Papa knows he can find work there.
   C. it is the only country that will accept them.
   D. it is the closest country.

_____ 14. The phrase that best describes Rifka's relationship with Tovah is
   A. competitive and jealous.
   B. friendly but distant.
   C. warm and sisterly.
   D. sweet but shallow.

Vocabulary and Grammar

_____ 15. In *Letters from Rifka*, the word *huddled* best describes
A. the way the guards walk on the train platform.
B. the way Nathan leaves the army.
C. the way Rifka's family hides in the basement.
D. the way Saul acts toward Rifka.

_____ 16. In which sentence about *Letters from Rifka* is the word *emerged* used correctly?
A. The family emerged from their hiding place after dark.
B. Nathan emerged from the boxcar so that no one would see him.
C. Rifka emerged her book in her rucksack.
D. The family emerged together to board the train.

_____ 17. In which of these sentences about *Letters from Rifka* is the verb regular?
A. Rifka writes a letter to her cousin Tovah.
B. Rifka's grandmother will hear of the escape.
C. Rifka has a copy of a book by Pushkin in her hand.
D. Rifka will distract the guards at the railroad station.

_____ 18. Which of these sentences about *Letters from Rifka* contains a past participle?
A. Rifka is writing to her cousin Tovah as the story opens.
B. Rifka agrees that she will be able to distract the guards.
C. Rifka admits that she would have liked to fly away.
D. Rifka writes that her family huddled in the cellar.

_____ 19. What is the principal part of the italicized verb in this sentence from *Letters from Rifka*?

Papa said we must tell no one we were *leaving*, not even Bubbe Ruth.

A. present
B. present participle
C. past
D. past participle

Essay

20. Rifka and Nathan have character traits that will help them face the dangers and hardships ahead of them on their journey. In an essay, describe those character traits. Which traits do they share? How will their character traits help them? Use two or three examples from *Letters from Rifka* to support your answer.

21. Rifka accepts the responsibility of distracting the guards at the train station. What motives and character traits does she possess that might help her perform this dangerous job? In an essay, explain why you think she succeeds. Use three details from *Letters from Rifka* to support your answer.

Vocabulary Warm-up Word Lists

Study these words from "Two Kinds." Then, complete the activities.

Word List A

arched [AHRCHT] *adj.* having an arch or curved shape with space below it
　　Beth reached up and touched the <u>arched</u> ceiling.

assured [uh SHOORD] *v.* promised confidently
　　The doctor <u>assured</u> Ann that she would soon feel better.

exist [eg ZIST] *v.* to have reality; to be
　　Does the Loch Ness monster really <u>exist</u>?

nervousness [NER vuhs nes] *n.* uneasiness or worry about something
　　Evan's <u>nervousness</u> about his new job soon went away.

regret [ri GRET] *n.* a troubled feeling over something that happened
　　Sue remembered with <u>regret</u> that awful day when she embarrassed her best friend, Beth.

sulky [SUHL kee] *adj.* ill-humored or gloomy
　　He gave her a <u>sulky</u> look when she refused to accompany him.

talented [TAL uhn tid] *adj.* gifted or having natural ability
　　The <u>talented</u> singer amazed the audience with the range of her voice.

uneven [uhn EE vuhn] *adj.* rough or irregular
　　The hem of the skirt was <u>uneven</u>.

Word List B

assortment [uh SAWRT muhnt] *n.* a collection or variety
　　Sam chose a praline from the <u>assortment</u> of candy.

fascinated [FAS uh nay tid] *v.* intently interested by something
　　Chris was <u>fascinated</u> by the novel.

heaving [HEEV ing] *v.* rising and falling
　　After lifting the heavy table, her chest was <u>heaving</u>.

images [IM uh jiz] *n.* mental pictures of something
　　Many <u>images</u> came to mind when she thought about the holidays.

miniature [MIN ee uh cher] *adj.* very small
　　The dollhouse contained <u>miniature</u> furniture.

petals [PET uhlz] *n.* the colored parts of a flower that are shaped like leaves
　　The rose <u>petals</u> were a pretty shade of yellow.

purely [PYOOR lee] *adv.* entirely
　　We met <u>purely</u> by accident.

throughout [throo OWT] *adv.* in or during every part of; from start to finish
　　There was lively conversation <u>throughout</u> dinner.

"Two Kinds" by Amy Tan
Vocabulary Warm-up Exercises

Exercise A *Fill in each blank in the paragraph below with an appropriate word from Word List A. Use each word only once.*

Delia was in a pouty, [1] _____ mood. It was the day she was supposed to take pictures for the yearbook, but nothing was going right. Her camera was out of film, and her alarm clock had not sounded on time. When she looked in the mirror, she saw that her bangs were [2] _____. All these problems added to the [3] _____ she was feeling. She began to think she would remember this day with [4] _____. What had she been thinking about when she volunteered for this job? When she got to school and walked under the [5] _____ gates, she saw her friend Gary. He told her not to worry. "You are one of the most [6] _____ photographers ever to [7] _____ around here," he [8] _____ her with a smile.

Exercise B *Decide whether each statement below is true or false. Circle T or F. Then, explain your answer.*

1. Artists usually do not have many mental <u>images</u> when they paint.
   T / F _____

2. If you are breathing heavily, your chest may be <u>heaving</u>.
   T / F _____

3. If a library has a large <u>assortment</u> of books, it does not have much to read.
   T / F _____

4. *Bored* is the opposite of <u>*fascinated*</u>.
   T / F _____

5. An adult can sit comfortably on a <u>miniature</u> chair.
   T / F _____

6. If you leave a performance early, you will have stayed <u>throughout</u> it.
   T / F _____

7. If something happens <u>purely</u> by design, it was completely planned.
   T / F _____

8. Most flowers do not have colorful <u>petals</u>.
   T / F _____

"Two Kinds" by Amy Tan
Reading Warm-up A

Read the following passage. Pay special attention to the underlined words. Then, read it again, and complete the activities. Use a separate sheet of paper for your written answers.

Julie and her teammates thought their soccer team was the pits. The Hawks had been playing together for a while, but the results of their efforts were <u>uneven</u> at best. Once the other team scored a goal, the Hawks would stop trying. It was as if their efforts had failed to <u>exist</u> at all.

One day something happened, and that something was Coach Mary Michaels. Coach Michaels made the Hawks practice every day. The girls were in a <u>sulky</u> mood at first, but that did not bother the coach. She just kept them running, drilling, and practicing plays. Coach told them, "You are already <u>talented</u> athletes. All you need is lots of practice and belief in yourselves."

Then, a miracle happened. The Hawks won a game! The more they believed they could win, the more games they won. The Hawks made it into the county champion-ship finals.

On a cold October day, the girls faced their biggest challenge—the Rockets, one of the highest rated teams. Julie began to feel her old feeling of <u>nervousness</u>, and she sensed it in her teammates, too. The Hawks took the field. The teams were evenly matched. The Hawks scored a goal, and their spirits soared. Then, near the end of the second half, the Rockets scored. The game was tied.

The Hawks faltered. Julie felt it, that feeling of giving up before it was over. The coach talked to them as she rotated the players. "Don't give up," she said. "If you lose without trying, it will be a <u>regret</u> you'll always have." The Hawks kept trying. Then, at the last minute, a Rocket forward landed a goal in the <u>arched</u> net. The whistle blew, and the game was over.

Julie and her teammates hung their heads, but to their surprise Coach Michaels greeted them with a smile. "Sure, we like to win games," she <u>assured</u> them, "but that is not the only way to measure victory. Today you won something more important: self-respect." Julie would always remember those words.

1. Underline the words that tell what was <u>uneven</u>. Define *uneven*.

2. Underline the words that explain why it seemed that the team's efforts did not <u>exist</u> at all. Use *exist* in a sentence.

3. Circle the word that <u>sulky</u> describes. How would a person with a *sulky* expression look?

4. Underline the words that tell the two things the coach told the players they needed, in addition to being <u>talented</u>. Define *talented*.

5. Underline the words that give a clue to the meaning of <u>nervousness</u>. What is *nervousness*?

6. Underline the words that tell what <u>regret</u> the team would always have, according to the coach. Use *regret* in a sentence.

7. Circle the word that tells what was <u>arched</u>. What does an *arched* object look like?

8. Underline the words that tell what the coach <u>assured</u> the players. What does *assured* mean?

Name _____ Date _____

Read the following passage. Pay special attention to the underlined words. Then, read it again, and complete the activities. Use a separate sheet of paper for your written answers.

Chinatown, in San Francisco, is one of the largest communities of Chinese Americans and Asian Americans in the United States. Chinese immigrants have been settling there since the 1850s. One of its famous sights is the Gateway to China. Built in the 1970s, the gateway is known <u>throughout</u> the world as a symbol of San Francisco's Chinatown.

As you walk along the streets of Chinatown, your senses are bombarded by an <u>assortment</u> of smells, sounds, and sights. Flower markets catch the eye. The <u>petals</u> of red, yellow, pink, and white flowers create a dazzling splash of color.

Strollers are <u>fascinated</u> by the many objects in souvenir shops. <u>Miniature</u> statues of animals, paper fans, umbrellas, jade jewelry, and silk dresses are just some of the shops' treasures. Pieces of furniture painted with dragons, butterflies, and flowers are <u>purely</u> imaginative works of art.

Many of the buildings in San Francisco's Chinatown are banks or offices. They were built to look like traditional Chinese buildings, however. They bring to mind <u>images</u> of Asian culture.

Perhaps most important, visitors breathe deeply of the delicious smells that waft from the restaurants. If you enjoy spicy food, this is the place to find it. If you do not like spicy food, be careful. More than one diner has experienced a <u>heaving</u> chest after tasting a bit of red pepper. There is mild food, too, however. At the end of the meal comes the fortune cookie. The little piece of rolled-up paper inside the cookie may contain a prediction about the future.

Chinatown is also known for its colorful parades, with dancing dragons and fireworks, especially during the Chinese New Year's celebration. San Francisco's Chinatown is an intriguing neighborhood with a population, culture, and history all its own.

1. The gateway is a symbol of Chinatown throughout the world. What is another word for <u>throughout</u>? Use *throughout* in a sentence.

2. Underline the words that tell what <u>assortment</u> of things bombard the senses. What is an *assortment*?

3. Underline the words that give clues to the meaning of the word <u>petals</u>. What is your favorite flower, and what color is its *petals*?

4. Underline the words that tell what the strollers are <u>fascinated</u> by. Define *fascinated*.

5. Circle the words that tell what kind of <u>miniature</u> objects are sold in the souvenir shops. Name some other *miniature* objects that are sold in stores.

6. What is a synonym for <u>purely</u>? Use *purely* in a sentence.

7. Circle the words that tell what <u>images</u> are brought to mind. Define *images*.

8. What food may bring about a diner's <u>heaving</u> chest? What does *heaving* mean?

"Two Kinds" by Amy Tan

Reading: Read Ahead to Verify Predictions and Reread to Look for Details

A **prediction** is an informed guess about what will happen. Use details in the text and your own knowledge and experience to make predictions as you read. Then, **read ahead to verify predictions,** to check whether your predictions are correct.

- As you read, ask yourself whether new details support your predictions. If they do not, revise your predictions based on the new information.
- If the predictions you make turn out to be wrong, **reread to look for details** you might have missed that would have helped you make a more accurate prediction.

"Of course you can be prodigy, too," my mother told me when I was nine. "You can be best anything."

Details in this passage can help you predict that the narrator's mother will encourage her to become a prodigy. You can read further in "Two Kinds" to check this prediction.

DIRECTIONS: *Complete the following chart. If a prediction in the second column is correct, write* Correct *in the third column. If a prediction is wrong, write* Incorrect *in the third column. Then, in the fourth column, describe what does happen, and include a detail that would have allowed an accurate prediction. The first item has been completed as an example.*

Details in "Two Kinds"	Prediction	Verification of Prediction	Event in Selection and Additional Detail
1. The mother wants her daughter to be "a Chinese Shirley Temple."	The daughter will become the Chinese Shirley Temple.	Incorrect	The narrator fails at being Shirley Temple. "We didn't immediately pick the right kind of prodigy."
2. The daughter begins to think thoughts with "won'ts."	The daughter will rebel against her mother.		
3. The narrator must perform a simple piece "that sounded more difficult than it was."	She will perform well.		
4. The daughter sees her mother's offers of the piano "as a sign of forgiveness."	The daughter will take the piano.		

"Two Kinds" by Amy Tan
Literary Analysis: Character

A **character** is a person or an animal that takes part in the action of a literary work.

- A **character's motives** are the emotions or goals that drive him or her to act one way or another. Some powerful motives are love, anger, and hope.
- **Character traits** are the individual qualities that make each character unique. These may be things such as stubbornness, sense of humor, or intelligence.

Characters' motives and qualities are important because they influence what characters do and how they interact with other characters. As you read, think about what the characters are like and why they do what they do. For example, consider this passage:

> She had come here in 1949 after losing everything in China: her mother and father, her family home, her first husband, and two daughters, twin baby girls. But she never looked back with regret. There were so many ways for things to get better.

This passage illustrates the mother's character traits: her strength and courage. It also suggests a motive for her actions: She wants things to get better.

A. DIRECTIONS: *After each character's name, write as many adjectives as you can think of that describe that character's traits.*

1. **The daughter:** _____

_____

_____

2. **The mother:** _____

_____

_____

B. DIRECTIONS: *Each quotation on the right states or hints at a motive for one of the actions on the left. On the line before each action, write the letter of the quotation that provides the motive.*

___ 1. Daughter wants to become a prodigy.

___ 2. Mother pushes her daughter to be a prodigy.

___ 3. Daughter refuses to play the piano.

___ 4. Mother offers her daughter the piano.

___ 5. Daughter begins to resist her mother's efforts to make her a prodigy.

A. I could sense her anger rising to its breaking point. I wanted to see it spill over.

B. I was filled with a sense that I would soon become *perfect*. My mother and father would adore me.

C. I saw the offer as a sign of forgiveness, a tremendous burden removed.

D. I won't let her change me, I promised myself. I won't be what I'm not.

E. "Only ask you be your best. For your sake."

"Two Kinds" by Amy Tan
Vocabulary Builder

Word List

reproach	conspired	devastated

A. DIRECTIONS: *Think about the meaning of the underlined word in each of these sentences. Then, answer the question.*

1. Would the daughter have been beyond reproach if she had become a prodigy? Why or why not?

   _____

   _____

2. How would the daughter have felt when her mother's expression devastated her?

   _____

   _____

3. If the mother and Old Chong conspired to hold a talent show, whose idea was it? How do you know?

   _____

   _____

B. DIRECTIONS: *Write the letter of the word or phrase that can replace the Word List word in each sentence.*

____ 1. The parents conspired to show off their children's talents.
  A. talked eagerly   C. worked together
  B. made contacts   D. revealed the plans

____ 2. The conflict between mother and daughter might have devastated their relationship for good.
  A. renewed   C. eliminated
  B. destroyed   D. restored

____ 3. The daughter knew that her attitude toward practicing for the recital was worthy of reproach.
  A. praise   C. enthusiasm
  B. perfection   D. blame

"Two Kinds" by Amy Tan
Support for Writing a Journal Entry

For your **journal entry,** put yourself in the narrator's place after the piano recital. Imagine your thoughts and your feelings, and record them on this chart.

Event	Details from My Point of View	My Feelings About the Piano Recital
Members of the Joy Luck Club comment on the recital.		
I travel home on the bus with my parents.		
My mother says nothing and goes to her bedroom.		
I think about the day.		

Now, use your notes to write a journal entry describing the narrator's thoughts and feelings at the end of the day of the piano recital.

"**Two Kinds**" by Amy Tan
Support for Extend Your Learning

Research and Technology

Use this chart to record information for your **outline** of findings about traditional Chinese beliefs and customs concerning the relationship between parents and children.

Father's Role	Mother's Role	Daughter's Role	Son's Role
_____	_____	_____	_____
_____	_____	_____	_____
_____	_____	_____	_____
_____	_____	_____	_____
_____	_____	_____	_____
_____	_____	_____	_____
_____	_____	_____	_____
_____	_____	_____	_____

Listening and Speaking

Answer these questions to organize your thoughts in preparation for a **discussion** of Henri Frédéric Amiel's statement.

1. What is your definition of *talent*? _____

_____

2. What prior knowledge or experience supports your definition?

_____

_____

3. What is your definition of *genius*? _____

_____

4. What prior knowledge or experience supports your definition?

_____

_____

5. Do you agree with Amiel's definitions? Explain.

_____

_____

Name _____ Date _____

"**Two Kinds**" by Amy Tan
Enrichment: Performing Arts

"Two Kinds" suggests that there are three ingredients necessary to succeed as a performer: talent, interest, and commitment. Have you ever thought of performing? Here are some questions to think about:

- Can I learn the skill on my own, or will I need to take lessons?
- Does my school offer lessons, or will I have to find instruction outside school?
- Can I take group lessons, or are individual lessons necessary?
- Does my school provide a list of instructors? Should I ask others for recommendations? Should I check a phone directory or Internet listing?
- Do I have time for this commitment? Can I balance it with my other responsibilities?

A. DIRECTIONS: *Think of a performing art that interests you. It might be ballet, singing, acting, playing an instrument, stand-up comedy, or some combination of these. Then, answer these questions.*

1. What is the performing art in which I am interested? _____

2. What would be my first step in acquiring the skill needed to practice this art?

_____

3. What other steps should I take to develop my skill in this art?

_____

_____

B. DIRECTIONS: *Find out from an instructor or from someone who is involved in the art how many hours each week you will need to set aside for practice. Then, use this chart to budget your time. Assume that you will have sixteen hours each day for all of your activities, or 112 hours per week.*

Activity	M	Tu	W	Th	F	Sat	Sun	Total hours/ week (112 total)
School								
Homework								
Sports								
Chores								
Leisure								
Other								
Practice								

from *Letters from Rifka* by Karen Hesse
"Two Kinds" by Amy Tan
Build Language Skills: Vocabulary

The Roots -*dict*- and -*ver*-

The word *predict* comes from the root *dict-*, meaning "to speak," and the prefix *pre-*, meaning "before" or "in front of." When you *predict* something, you *speak* about what might happen *before* you know for sure what will happen.

The word *verify* contains the root -*ver*-, meaning "true." When you read ahead to *verify* a prediction, you check to see whether the prediction will turn out to be *true*.

A. DIRECTIONS: *Rewrite each sentence, replacing the italicized word or phrase with one of these words:* predict, verify, verdict.

1. The meteorologists *say that in the future* it will rain heavily.

   _____

2. The scientists conducted a study to *find out whether* their theory *was true*.

   _____

3. The jurors delivered their *judgment* solemnly.

   _____

Academic Vocabulary Practice

anticipate	indicate	plot	predict	verify

B. DIRECTIONS: *Follow the instructions to write sentences using each Academic Vocabulary word.*

1. Use *indicate* in a sentence about getting lost.

   _____

2. Use *anticipate* in a sentence about tryouts for a play.

   _____

3. Use *plot* in a sentence about a movie.

   _____

4. Use *predict* in a sentence about taking a test.

   _____

5. Use *verify* in a sentence about a science experiment.

   _____

from *Letters from Rifka* by Karen Hesse
"Two Kinds" by Amy Tan
Build Language Skills: Grammar

Regular and Irregular Verbs

Most verbs are *regular*; that is, they form their tenses in a predictable way.

I *climb* that mountain every day.

Last month Michael *climbed* that mountain.

Jessica *has* often *climbed* that mountain.

Verbs that are *irregular* do not follow a predictable pattern.

I *am* a mountain climber.

Michael *was* a mountain climber before he broke his leg.

Jessica *has been* a mountain climber since she learned to walk.

There are four main forms of every verb, called the principal parts. Each principal part indicates when something happens. The principal parts are **present, present participle, past,** and **past participle.**

A. PRACTICE: *Underline the verbs in each sentence. On the line, identify each verb as* regular *or* irregular. *Then, identify the principal part of each verb. The principal part will be* present, present participle, past, *or* past participle.

1. Her brother ran away from the army.

   Regular/Irregular: _____; **Principal part:** _____

2. The whole family fled from their home and is starting a new life.

   Regular/Irregular: _____; **Principal part:** _____

   Regular/Irregular: _____; **Principal part:** _____

3. Rifka was courageous, and she saved her family.

   Regular/Irregular: _____; **Principal part:** _____

   Regular/Irregular: _____; **Principal part:** _____

B. Writing Application: *Write a paragraph about a time when you or someone you know faced a frightening situation. Use at least three regular verbs and three irregular verbs. Underline each regular verb once and each irregular verb twice.*

_____

_____

_____

_____

_____

"Two Kinds" by Amy Tan
Selection Test A

Critical Reading *Identify the letter of the choice that best answers the question.*

___ 1. In "Two Kinds," how does the mother feel about life in America?
   A. She is depressed and bitter.
   B. She is fearful and nervous.
   C. She is resentful and angry.
   D. She is optimistic and expectant.

___ 2. In "Two Kinds," why does the mother take her daughter to get her hair curled?
   A. She wants her daughter to look more grown-up.
   B. She wants her daughter to look taller.
   C. She wants her daughter to look like Shirley Temple.
   D. She wants her daughter to be a child model.

___ 3. What detail in "Two Kinds" helps you predict that the daughter will not become the next Shirley Temple?
   A. She is unable to learn to dance.
   B. She tells her mother she does not want to perform.
   C. Her hair does not curl like Shirley Temple's.
   D. She tells her mother she hates Shirley Temple.

___ 4. In "Two Kinds," why is the daughter at first excited about her mother's ambitions for her?
   A. She identifies with the child star Shirley Temple.
   B. She hopes that she will win her parents' approval.
   C. She wants to prove that she has more talent than Waverly.
   D. She is bored and hopes to find an outlet for her talent.

___ 5. Which choice best sums up the daughter's attitude toward her mother's quizzes in "Two Kinds"?
   A. She is eager to please.
   B. She wishes to perform perfectly.
   C. She enjoys them endlessly.
   D. She is impatient and bored.

____ 6. In "Two Kinds," what does the daughter realize after she becomes angry at her reflection in the mirror?
   A. If she becomes a prodigy, she will be be a sad, unpleasant girl.
   B. If she does not become a prodigy, she will not succeed at anything.
   C. She has the power to decide for herself who she will be.
   D. She can be the prodigy her mother wants her to be.

____ 7. What best describes how the daughter and Waverly feel about each other in "Two Kinds"?
   A. warm and sisterly
   B. friendly but distant
   C. cold and uncaring
   D. jealous and competitive

____ 8. What detail from "Two Kinds" helps you predict that the daughter might not do well at her recital?
   A. She does not practice carefully.
   B. She refuses to practice at all.
   C. She refuses to perform.
   D. She gets sick beforehand.

____ 9. In "Two Kinds," how does the daughter feel before her performance at the talent show?
   A. fearful
   B. confident
   C. nervous
   D. bored

____ 10. In "Two Kinds," how does the mother act after the piano recital?
   A. She shouts at her daughter.
   B. She cries and cannot be comforted.
   C. She pretends it did not matter.
   D. She is quiet and keeps to herself.

____ 11. In "Two Kinds," what character trait do the daughter and her mother share?
   A. sensitivity
   B. stubbornness
   C. playfulness
   D. calmness

_____ 12. What is the central idea of "Two Kinds"?

    A. If you do not succeed at first, try again.

    B. A happy family requires obedient children.

    C. An important part of growing up is discovering one's own goals and desires.

    D. Parents who expect a lot will inspire high levels of achievement in their children.

Vocabulary and Grammar

_____ 13. The following sentence from "Two Kinds" suggests what meaning of *devastated*?

    But my mother's expression was what devastated me: a quiet, blank look that said she had lost everything.

    A. failed

    B. surprised

    C. destroyed

    D. impressed

_____ 14. In "Two Kinds," when Old Chong and the mother *conspired* to have the daughter play in a talent show, what did they do?

    A. they worked separately

    B. they planned together secretly

    C. they asked the daughter

    D. they studied a great deal

_____ 15. In which of the following sentences about "Two Kinds" is the verb irregular?

    A. The narrator's mother gets an idea about Shirley Temple.

    B. The narrator's mother presents her daughter with tests.

    C. The narrator's mother watches *The Ed Sullivan Show*.

    D. The narrator's mother conspires to hold a talent show.

Essay

16. Generations of immigrants to America have dealt with the confusions and conflicts that come from adjusting to a new culture. In an essay, describe the problems that the daughter and her mother face in "Two Kinds." How is the mother's process of adjustment different from the daughter's? Use events and details from the story to support your response.

17. The daughter and her mother in "Two Kinds" are alike in certain ways and different in other ways. Write an essay comparing and contrasting their characters. Describe two similarities and two differences, and use events and details from the story to support your opinion.

"**Two Kinds**" by Amy Tan
Selection Test B

Critical Reading *Identify the letter of the choice that best completes the statement or answers the question.*

____ 1. In "Two Kinds," why does the mother take her daughter to the Mission district to get her hair curled?
   A. She wants her daughter to look more sophisticated.
   B. She wants her daughter to look more American.
   C. She wants her daughter to look like a Chinese Shirley Temple.
   D. She wants her daughter to look like a model in a magazine.

____ 2. In "Two Kinds," the mother's schemes for promoting her daughter's career as a "prodigy" are best described as
   A. sensitive and warm.
   B. lighthearted and joyous.
   C. insensitive and unrealistic.
   D. well planned and carefully thought out.

____ 3. In "Two Kinds," what changes the daughter's attitude about becoming a prodigy?
   A. She sees her mother's disappointment after she fails a test.
   B. She realizes that she will have to learn to play the piano.
   C. She realizes that Waverly has a natural talent for chess.
   D. She understands that she has the talent to become a writer.

____ 4. When the daughter in "Two Kinds" looks in the mirror and begins thinking "thoughts filled with lots of won'ts," the reader can predict that she will
   A. do what her mother wants her to do.
   B. begin to rebel against her mother.
   C. try harder to do well on the tests.
   D. perform poorly at the piano recital.

____ 5. In "Two Kinds," when the mother criticizes the girl's performance on *The Ed Sullivan Show*, the reader can predict that she will
   A. buy her daughter a dress like the one the girl wears.
   B. teach her daughter to play the piano.
   C. find the girl and criticize her performance.
   D. insist that her daughter learn to play the piano.

____ 6. In "Two Kinds," the feeling of the daughter's account of her piano lessons with Mr. Chong is
   A. angry.
   B. comical.
   C. sad.
   D. bitter.

_____ 7. In "Two Kinds," the daughter's behavior before the recital helps the reader predict that she will
   A. do well at her piano recital.
   B. do badly at her piano recital.
   C. play with feeling at her piano recital.
   D. play confidently at her piano recital.

_____ 8. In "Two Kinds," the daughter's performance at the talent show is
   A. the only time she disappoints her mother.
   B. a painful memory that will always haunts her.
   C. the first of many times she disappoints her mother.
   D. the first time she makes her mother proud.

_____ 9. In "Two Kinds," why does the daughter mention her mother's dead daughters when her mother insists that she practice the piano after the recital?
   A. She wants to hurt and defy her mother.
   B. She feels bad that she is an only child.
   C. She wants her mother to love her.
   D. She is jealous of their talent.

_____ 10. When the daughter in "Two Kinds" is grown up, her mother offers to give her the piano for her birthday. This act shows that the mother
   A. still believes that her daughter can become a great pianist.
   B. wants to remind her daughter that she disappointed her parents.
   C. wants her daughter to know that she has gotten over her disappointment.
   D. continues to feel bitter and never wants to see the piano again.

_____ 11. In "Two Kinds," in which way are the daughter and her mother alike?
   A. Neither is strong willed.
   B. Neither is stubborn.
   C. Neither is sensitive.
   D. Neither is hopeful.

_____ 12. The titles of the piano pieces the daughter plays at the end of "Two Kinds" are "Pleading Child" and "Perfectly Contented." These titles represent
   A. the daughter's feelings about her mother.
   B. Schumann's understanding of children and the piano.
   C. the daughter's feelings about learning to play the piano.
   D. the difficulty of becoming a talented pianist.

_____ 13. What is the theme, or central idea, of "Two Kinds"?
   A. Persistence is the key to success.
   B. High expectations are the key to success.
   C. Discovering one's own goals and desires is an important part of growing up.
   D. A family cannot be happy unless the children obey and respect their parents.

Vocabulary and Grammar

____ 14. In which of the following sentences is the word *conspired* used correctly?
   A. The daughter conspired to do better than Waverly at the piano recital.
   B. The mothers in Chinatown conspired to show off their children's talent.
   C. The mother was conspired by her daughter's piano recital.
   D. The daughter felt conspired as she walked onstage and began to play.

____ 15. As it is used in "Two Kinds," the word *devastated* best describes
   A. the daughter after her mother offers her the piano.
   B. Mr. Chong during the daughter's lessons.
   C. the mother after the piano recital.
   D. the girl on *The Ed Sullivan Show*.

____ 16. In which sentence about "Two Kinds" is the word *reproach* used correctly?
   A. The mother would often reproach her with a new plan for fame.
   B. Mr. Chong's reproach to the piano was based on keeping the rhythm.
   C. The daughter felt reproach when she watched *The Ed Sullivan Show*.
   D. Waverly Jong's behavior as a Chinese daughter was beyond reproach.

____ 17. What is the principal part of the italicized verb in this sentence?
   It was being *pounded* out by a little Chinese girl, about nine years old.

   A. present
   B. present participle
   C. past
   D. past participle

Essay

18. Consider this line from "Two Kinds":

   For unlike my mother, I did not believe I could be anything I wanted to be. I could only
   be me.

In an essay, explain how those words describe the conflict between the daughter and
her mother. How is the conflict resolved? Use events and details from the story to support your explanation.

19. The title "Two Kinds" refers to the statement by the mother that there are only two
kinds of daughters:

   "Those who are obedient and those who follow their own mind!"

At the end of "Two Kinds," the daughter puts the title in a different light when she realizes that the titles "Pleading Child" and "Perfectly Contented" are "two halves of the
same song." In an essay, describe the connection between these two titles and the "two
kinds" of daughters. Refer to events and details in the story to support your response.

Vocabulary Warm-up Word Lists

Study these words from "Seventh Grade" and "Stolen Day." Then, complete the activities.

Word List A

affects [uh FEKTS] *v.* influences or changes someone or something
Cheap motor oil badly <u>affects</u> how a car engine runs.

bustled [BUHS uhld] *v.* rushed around being busy
The woman <u>bustled</u> around reorganizing the shelves.

confusing [kuhn FYOOZ ing] *adj.* difficult to understand
Einstein's theory of relativity is <u>confusing</u> to most people.

conviction [kuhn VIK shuhn] *n.* a strong belief or opinion
He voted with <u>conviction</u> for his party's presidential candidate.

formed [FAWRMD] *v.* made or organized
The freezing rain <u>formed</u> icicles on the trees.

provide [proh VYD] *v.* to give or supply something to someone
We <u>provide</u> childcare services to working mothers.

squirmed [SKWERMD] *v.* wriggled about uncomfortably from embarrassment or shame
Josie <u>squirmed</u> with embarrassment when her friend teased her.

unison [YOO nuh suhn] *n.* acting, speaking, or singing all together in a group
The dancers in the chorus line moved in <u>unison</u>.

Word List B

admiring [ad MYR ing] *v.* thinking how beautiful or impressive someone or something is
I could not help <u>admiring</u> my friend's confidence when she spoke.

afterwards [AF ter wuhrdz] *adv.* later
The couple stopped for dinner; <u>afterwards</u>, they walked in the park.

bluff [BLUHF] *v.* to fake it; act confident; pretend to be sure or positive
The professional spy could <u>bluff</u> her way out of a dangerous situation.

carp [KARP] *n.* a large freshwater fish that is used for food
A traditional Jewish dish, called gefilte fish, is made from <u>carp</u>.

failure [FAYL yer] *n.* lack of success
Mike's <u>failure</u> to make the team forced him to work harder for the next tryouts.

lingered [LING erd] *v.* stayed or waited around
A small group <u>lingered</u> after the party to help clean up.

recent [REE suhnt] *adj.* having happened a short time ago
My nephew's <u>recent</u> visit has left my family exhausted.

solemn [SAHL uhm] *adj.* very serious
My brother's last dinner at home before moving overseas was a <u>solemn</u> occasion.

Name _____ Date _____

"Seventh Grade" by Gary Soto
"Stolen Day" by Sherwood Anderson
Vocabulary Warm-up Exercises

Exercise A *Fill in each blank in the paragraph below with an appropriate word from Word List A. Use each word only once.*

Annie's assignment was to [1] _____ her debating team with an

argument against a new dress code. For days she [2] _____ around the

campus, getting other students' opinions. Many students thought the code was

[3] _____ and made no sense. Finally, Annie had [4] _____

a strong [5] _____ about the issue. During the debate, she

[6] _____ uncomfortably as her opponent argued for the code. When

Annie argued that the dress code badly [7] _____ student morale, the stu-

dents in the audience [8] _____ and applauded.

Exercise B *Revise each sentence so that the underlined vocabulary word is used in a logical way. Be sure to keep the vocabulary word in your revision.*

Example: Because she was <u>curious</u>, Jane did not ask what happened.
Because she was <u>curious</u>, Jane asked what happened.

1. They invited the <u>carp</u> home for dinner.

   _____

2. He cast an <u>admiring</u> glance at the disagreeable clerk.

   _____

3. They attended the play and <u>afterwards</u> went to the theater.

   _____

4. People who <u>bluff</u> their way to success are honest.

   _____

5. He remembered the <u>recent</u> trip he made, the one he went on in 1969.

   _____

6. After he saw his train leave the station, he <u>lingered</u> on the platform, waiting for it to be time to get onboard.

   _____

7. The <u>solemn</u> music made me want to dance.

   _____

8. Their <u>failure</u> to win the game delighted the team.

   _____

Name _____ Date _____

"Seventh Grade" by Gary Soto
"Stolen Day" by Sherwood Anderson
Reading Warm-up A

Read the following passage. Pay special attention to the underlined words. Then, read it again, and complete the activities. Use a separate sheet of paper for your written answers.

There really *is* such a thing as an average seventh grader. This does not mean that all average seventh graders act alike or act together in <u>unison</u>—far from it. The term *average* covers a wide range of individual differences. In general, however, most seventh graders share some common behaviors.

For example, seventh graders are usually enthusiastic about trying new things. If a lesson is interesting, they will plunge right in and have fun while they learn. At the same time, they have greater self-control than they did as sixth graders. Perhaps you remember how as a sixth grader you were always on the move? Remember how you <u>bustled</u> around during class, looking for this, borrowing that? Now you get things done without moving around so much. Do you remember how in sixth grade you fidgeted and <u>squirmed</u> in your seat when you were tired? Now that you have more self-control, you can stay put longer and get down to work. That does not mean you always do, but your teachers are ever hopeful that you will.

Most seventh graders are beginning to explore their identity. If you are a typical seventh grader, you are learning to think for yourself. You have <u>formed</u> opinions and have a growing <u>conviction</u> about who you are. At the same time, you want to fit in with your peers. That means you want to think and act the way your friends do. Trying to be yourself and still be like your friends can be <u>confusing</u>. It <u>affects</u> the way you act from hour to hour. Sometimes you are moody. Sometimes you are bubbling over. That is all right. Eventually your feelings will balance out.

As a seventh grader, there is no merit in having, or not having, these behaviors. Still, knowing about them may <u>provide</u> an understanding of where you are on the path to maturity.

1. Circle the words that are a synonym for <u>unison</u>. Describe something you might do in *unison* with others.

2. Underline the words that describe <u>bustled</u>. Describe someone who acts in the opposite way.

3. Circle the words that mean the opposite of <u>squirmed</u>. Write a synonym for *squirmed*.

4. Circle the word that tells what the average seventh grader has <u>formed</u>. Use the same meaning of *formed* in a sentence of your own.

5. Circle the word that tells what kind of <u>conviction</u> the typical seventh grader has. What is a *conviction*?

6. Underline the phrase that tells what is <u>confusing</u>. Give a synonym for *confusing*.

7. Underline the words that tell how confusion <u>affects</u> a seventh grader. Write a sentence about something else that *affects* behavior.

8. Tell what it is that may <u>provide</u> an understanding. What is a synonym for *provide*?

"Seventh Grade" by Gary Soto
"Stolen Day" by Sherwood Anderson
Reading Warm-up B

Read the following passage. Pay special attention to the underlined words. Then, read it again, and complete the activities. Use a separate sheet of paper for your written answers.

At the aquarium, Melanie went to the freshwater fish exhibit. As she stared into the tank, she noticed a large carp. The carp's big eyes and downturned mouth gave him a solemn, serious look.

Melanie's thoughts drifted back to a recent trip to Mirror Lake, where her family went every summer. On this latest trip, in addition to teaching her to water-ski, her dad had introduced her to fishing.

"This lake is full of carp," he had said. "Sometimes carp will pretend to give up and bluff their way free. You can tell the really clever ones by their size. The largest ones have lived the longest."

"How long do carp live?" Melanie had asked.

"A carp may live fifty years and can weigh over sixty pounds, but that's unusual. The carp in this lake average about eight pounds," her father had explained.

At that moment, Melanie had felt a hard tug on her line. Her dad wrapped his hands around hers, holding the rod as the reel spun freely. "Grab the reel, and click the lock!" he ordered. After one failure, Melanie succeeded in finding the lock, and the line jerked sharply taut. For the next hour she played the line with her dad's help. The fish was still struggling for its life when they finally hauled it aboard.

"Whoa!" exclaimed her dad, admiring the size of the fish. "This guy must be a twenty-pounder!" Then, to her amazement, he removed the hook and tossed the desperate fish back into the lake.

"Right," she had said knowingly, "and may it live to be sixty pounds!" They lingered for a few minutes to watch him swim away. For a long time afterwards, she smiled when she remembered the fish.

1. Circle the words that tell what a carp is. Use *carp* in a sentence.

2. Underline the description that gives clues to the meaning of solemn. Write a word that means the opposite of *solemn*.

3. Circle the word that is a synonym for recent. Write a sentence about a *recent* event in your life.

4. Underline the words that tell how carp will bluff. Write about another animal that will *bluff*. Explain how it will do this.

5. Circle the word that refers to the opposite of failure. Write a sentence that tells about another kind of *failure*.

6. Circle the words that tell what Melanie's dad was admiring about the fish. Tell about someone or something you have been *admiring*.

7. Underline the words that tell how long Melanie and her father lingered. Write a synonym for *lingered*.

8. Underline the words that tell what melanie does afterwards. Which word is a clue that *afterwards* indicates time order?

Name _____ Date _____

"**Seventh Grade**" by Gary Soto
"**Stolen Day**" by Sherwood Anderson
Literary Analysis: Comparing Characters

A **character** is a person or an animal that takes part in the action of a literary work. In literature, you will find characters with a range of personalities and attitudes. For example, a character might be dependable and intelligent but also stubborn. One character might hold traditional values, while another might rebel against them. The individual qualities that make each character unique are called **character traits.**

Writers use the process of **characterization** to create and develop characters. There are two types of characterization:

- **Direct characterization:** The writer directly states or describes the character's traits.
- **Indirect characterization:** The writer reveals a character's personality through his or her words and actions, and through the thoughts, words, and actions of other characters.

DIRECTIONS: *To analyze the use of characterization in "Seventh Grade" and "Stolen Day,"* *complete the following chart. Answer each question with a brief example from the story.* *Write* not applicable *if you cannot answer a question about one of the characters.*

Character	Words that describe the character directly	What the character says and does	How other characters talk about or act toward the character
Victor in "Seventh Grade"			
Teresa in "Seventh Grade"			
The narrator of "Stolen Day"			
The mother in "Stolen Day"			

"**Seventh Grade**" by Gary Soto
"**Stolen Day**" by Sherwood Anderson
Vocabulary Builder

Word List

elective	scowl	conviction	solemn	affects

A. DIRECTIONS: *Think about the meaning of the italicized word in each sentence. Then, answer the question.*

1. Victor might have hoped that math would be an *elective* for seventh-graders. Why? Explain your answer.

   _____

2. Michael has a *conviction* about the benefits of scowling. What does this mean?

   _____

3. The boy was *solemn* after he heard the bad news. How did the boy behave?

   _____

4. A week of rainy weather often *affects* a person's mood. What does the weather have to do with the person's mood?

   _____

5. Mr. Bueller is likely to *scowl* the next time a student speaks nonsense instead of French. How will Mr. Bueller look?

   _____

B. DIRECTIONS: *Write the letter of the word or phrase that is most* similar *in meaning to each Word Bank word.*

____ 1. solemn
   A. joyful   C. serious
   B. silent   D. cheerful

____ 2. scowl
   A. frown   C. shovel
   B. smile   D. boat

____ 3. conviction
   A. prison sentence   C. doctrine
   B. strong belief   D. term

____ 4. elective
   A. optional course   C. dismissal
   B. political process   D. requirement

"Seventh Grade" by Gary Soto
"Stolen Day" by Sherwood Anderson

Support for Writing to Compare Literary Works

Before you **write an essay comparing and contrasting** Victor in "Seventh Grade" with the narrator of "Stolen Day," jot down your ideas in this graphic organizer. In the overlapping section of each set of boxes, write details that are true of both characters. In the sections on the left, write details that describe Victor, and in the sections on the right, write details that describe the boy in "Stolen Day."

What are some of each boy's character traits?

Victor:	Both:	The boy:

What problems does each boy face? How much responsibility does each boy have in creating his problem?

Victor:	Both:	The boy:

What does the character learn from his situation? Which character learns more?

Victor:	Both:	The boy:

Now, use your notes to write an essay that compares and contrasts the two characters.

Name _____ Date _____

Selection Test A

Critical Reading *Identify the letter of the choice that best answers the question.*

____ 1. In "Seventh Grade," why does Victor want to take French as his elective?
   A. He loves foreign languages, and he wants to please his parents.
   B. He might travel to France one day, and a girl he likes is in the class.
   C. It is the only elective that is available by the time he gets to sign up.
   D. It is a way to avoid having to take mathematics, which he dislikes.

____ 2. In "Seventh Grade," Victor and Michael discuss "picking grapes in order to buy their fall clothes." What does this conversation reveal about their characters?
   A. They avoid working.
   B. They are hardworking.
   C. They think picking grapes is messy.
   D. They would rather gossip than work.

____ 3. In "Seventh Grade," how does Victor try to impress Teresa on the first day of French class?
   A. He scowls.
   B. He ignores her.
   C. He asks her about her summer.
   D. He pretends he speaks French.

____ 4. In "Seventh Grade," how does Victor feel about Mr. Bueller after the first French class?
   A. Victor is grateful to him.
   B. Victor is angry with him.
   C. Victor is embarrassed by him.
   D. Victor is confused about him.

____ 5. In "Stolen Day," when do the narrator's legs begin to hurt?
   A. after a long day on the playing field
   B. after an accident at recess
   C. after he sees Walter fishing
   D. after tripping on the way to school

_____ 6. In "Stolen Day," why does the narrator's pain begin to go away as he walks away from the school?

    A. The exercise warms his muscles and eases the stiffness of his joints.

    B. The farther from the school he gets, the less he thinks about his pain.

    C. At first he walks uphill, so when the road levels off, walking becomes easier.

    D. He is trying to be brave, and he is using willpower to make the pain go away.

_____ 7. What does the narrator of "Stolen Day" mean when he describes himself as "pretty sore at Mother"?

    A. He knows that she is in pain.

    B. He loves her and misses her.

    C. He feels hurt because she scolded him.

    D. He is angry with her for ignoring him.

_____ 8. How does the narrator of "Stolen Day" feel after he catches the big carp?

    A. proud

    B. disappointed

    C. ashamed

    D. panicky

_____ 9. The narrator of "Stolen Day" says that his family often laughs at him. How does he react when they do?

    A. He wishes he were an orphan.

    B. He dislikes everyone he knows.

    C. He appreciates the attention.

    D. He dislikes being teased.

_____ 10. What do Victor in "Seventh Grade" and the narrator of "Stolen Day" have in common?

    A. Both want to catch a big fish.

    B. Both want someone's attention.

    C. Both want to learn French.

    D. Both want to impress a girl.

_____ 11. What feeling do both Victor in "Seventh Grade" and the narrator of "Stolen Day" experience?

    A. pleasure

    B. rejection

    C. embarrassment

    D. disappointment

___ **12.** What is similar about the problems faced by Victor in "Seventh Grade" and the narrator of "Stolen Day"?

    A. Both characters face problems that they themselves have created.

    B. Both characters face problems over which they have no control.

    C. Both characters are pressured into making a bad decision.

    D. Both characters make emotional decisions after being teased.

Vocabulary

___ **13.** In which situation would Victor be most likely to *scowl*?

    A. He sees his friend Michael for the first time since last spring.

    B. He learns that the French class Teresa has signed up for is full.

    C. He realizes that math class is not as difficult as he had expected.

    D. He fools Teresa into believing that he can speak some French.

___ **14.** In "Stolen Day," Earl is described as *solemn.* How would he most likely act?

    A. He would lecture his mother and brother.

    B. He would giggle and make a lot of jokes.

    C. He would be serious and quiet.

    D. He would be happy and talkative.

___ **15.** Which of the following situations in "Seventh Grade" describes a *conviction*?

    A. Victor believes that scowling is attractive.

    B. Victor scowls in order to attract girls.

    C. Michael has a crush on Teresa.

    D. Michael embarrasses himself in French class.

Essay

16. The writers of both "Seventh Grade" and "Stolen Day" use direct and indirect characterization to create and develop characters. In an essay, define *direct characterization* and *indirect characterization.* Then, answer these questions for either "Seventh Grade" or "Stolen Day": Other than the main character, which character does the writer develop? Choose one minor character and tell how the writer uses indirect characterization to describe him or her.

17. The writers of both "Seventh Grade" and "Stolen Day" develop the characters of school-age boys. In an essay, describe Victor in "Seventh Grade" and the narrator of "Stolen Day." Begin by telling what each boy is like. Then, consider these questions: What do the boys say? What do they do? How do other characters react to them?

"Seventh Grade" by Gary Soto
"Stolen Day" by Sherwood Anderson

Selection Test B

Critical Reading *Identify the letter of the choice that best completes the statement or answers the question.*

_____ 1. In "Seventh Grade," Michael scowls because
  A. he is angry with Victor.
  B. he is trying to scare some bullies.
  C. he is trying to impress the girls.
  D. he is bitter about being back at school.

_____ 2. In "Seventh Grade," Victor and Michael talk about "picking grapes in order to buy their fall clothes." What does that conversation reveal about their characters?
  A. They are intelligent but irresponsible.
  B. They are hardworking and responsible.
  C. They will do anything to avoid working.
  D. They would prefer talking to working.

_____ 3. What does the following passage from "Seventh Grade" reveal about Victor's character?

  Victor lingered, keeping his head down and staring at his desk. He wanted to leave when she did so he could bump into her and say something clever.

  A. He is proud of his feelings for Teresa.
  B. He thinks he is clever and charming.
  C. He is embarrassed by his feelings.
  D. He likes Teresa a great deal.

_____ 4. How can the reader tell that Victor likes Teresa?
  A. He thinks about her, watches her in homeroom, and looks for her at lunch.
  B. He asks her about her summer and tells her how much he likes her.
  C. He scowls at her and ignores her but later speaks to her about ballet.
  D. He bumps into her after homeroom and offers to tutor her in English.

_____ 5. In "Seventh Grade," how does Mr. Bueller respond when he realizes that Victor pretended to know French to impress Teresa?
  A. He is understanding.
  B. He is mean and spiteful.
  C. He is embarrassed.
  D. He is angry and hurt.

_____ 6. At the end of "Seventh Grade," why does Victor sprint to the library to borrow three French textbooks?
  A. Teresa will speak to him only in French, so Victor wants to learn the language.
  B. Victor likes French so much that he wants to do additional work for the class.
  C. Mr. Bueller is expecting that Victor will be the best student in his class.
  D. Teresa believes Victor can speak French and has asked him to tutor her.

_____ 7. When the narrator of "Stolen Day" observes Walter fishing at the pond, his reaction can best be described as
A. angry
B. sympathetic
C. bitter
D. envious

_____ 8. What does the following passage reveal about the narrator of "Stolen Day"?
It was then that my own legs began to hurt.
A. He lacks physical strength.
B. He may be seriously ill.
C. He has a vivid imagination.
D. He cannot keep from lying.

_____ 9. In "Stolen Day," the relationship between the narrator and his mother can best be described as
A. somewhat distant.
B. extremely tense.
C. somewhat tender.
D. extremely close.

_____ 10. In "Stolen Day," the narrator most likely thinks he has inflammatory rheumatism because
A. he wants to go home from school and go fishing.
B. he feels that his mother is not paying enough attention to him.
C. he believes that he has caught the disease from Walter.
D. he knows a lot about the disease and recognizes the symptoms.

_____ 11. What does this passage from "Stolen Day" reveal about the narrator's character?
"So," I thought, "they'll miss me and there'll be a search made. Very likely there'll be someone who has seen me sitting by the pond fishing, and there'll be a big alarm and all the town will turn out and they'll drag the pond."
A. He loves to pull pranks and play practical jokes.
B. He feels neglected and unappreciated by his family.
C. He needs to be at the center of attention all the time.
D. He hopes to find a good excuse for missing school.

_____ 12. The narrator of "Stolen Day" may best be characterized as someone who
A. is afraid of dying.
B. creates imaginary illnesses.
C. wishes to win sympathy.
D. cannot keep from lying.

_____ 13. Both Victor in "Seventh Grade" and the narrator of "Stolen Day"
A. embarrass themselves.
B. think they are dying.
C. feel confident of their abilities.
D. enjoy themselves at school.

____ 14. Both Victor in "Seventh Grade" and the narrator of "Stolen Day" face a problem. In what way are their problems alike?

A. Both characters are struggling to do well in math.

B. Both characters must compete with their brothers.

C. Both characters want to attract someone's attention.

D. Both characters have no one in whom to confide.

____ 15. In "Seventh Grade," Victor's experience in French class is similar to the experience of the narrator of "Stolen Day" at the dinner table. In what way are the experiences alike?

A. The characters have been unable to control the events that unfold.

B. The characters created the situation that causes them embarrassment.

C. The characters are teased because they were honest about their feelings.

D. The characters feel regret because they have hurt someone they like.

Vocabulary

____ 16. When someone supports a cause with *conviction,*

A. he or she is unsure about it.

B. he or she has no doubts about it.

C. he or she will go to prison for it.

D. he or she does not care about it.

____ 17. How would a *solemn* person most likely act?

A. nervous and fearful

B. serious and quiet

C. loud and excited

D. happy and talkative

____ 18. An *elective* is a class

A. about politics.

B. about electricity.

C. that is optional.

D. that is required.

____ 19. When the father of the narrator of "Stolen Day" says that inflammatory rheumatism *affects* the heart, he means that it

A. improves its condition.

B. causes a change in it.

C. causes it to weaken.

D. makes it beat faster.

Essay

20. The writers of both "Seventh Grade" and "Stolen Day" develop the characters of school-age boys. As the stories unfold, each boy is presented as a believable character. In an essay, compare the characterization of Victor in "Seventh Grade" with the characterization of the narrator of "Stolen Day." Consider these questions as you write your essay: What does the writer of "Seventh Grade" say directly about Victor? What does the narrator of "Stolen Day" reveal about himself through indirect characterization? Cite examples from the stories to support your points. What conclusions about the characterization of the main characters of these stories can you draw?

21. Both Victor in "Seventh Grade" and the narrator of "Stolen Day" face problems. In an essay, compare and contrast the two characters. In writing your essay, consider these questions: What problem does each boy face? How much responsibility does each boy have in creating his problem? Do the boys learn from their experiences? Do the stories end happily? How can you tell?

Writing Workshop—Unit 2, Part 1
Response to Literature: Review of a Short Story

Prewriting: Gathering Details

Use the graphic organizer below to gather details about the various sides of your topic. Write your topic sentence in the top rectangle. Then, while reviewing the story, use the other rectangles provided to record the details you will include in your response.

Narrowed topic sentence:

Detail:	Detail:	Detail:

Detail:	Detail:

Drafting: Providing Elaboration

Use the chart below to list specific examples and direct quotations from the story to support your main ideas.

Questions	Examples and Direct Quotations from the Story
What specific scenes from the story support your main ideas?	
What characters from the story support your main ideas?	
What images from the story support your main ideas?	
What actions in the story support your main ideas?	

Writing Workshop—Unit 2, Part 1
Review of a Short Story: Integrating Grammar Skills

Revising for Correct Verb Tense

Verbs change form to indicate present, past, or future times. The different forms they take to show time are called tenses. Study this chart of the six verb tenses in English.

Tense	What It Shows	What It Usually Looks Like	Examples
Present	happens regularly or generally	main verb	Some coyotes *live* in the desert. A coyote *hunts* by night.
Past	already happened	main verb ending in *-ed*	A coyote *wailed* all night.
Future	going to happen	*will* + main verb	It *will come* again later tonight.
Present Perfect	happened at an indefinite past time or begun in the past and still happening	helping verb *have* or *has* + main verb ending in *-ed*	Sometimes coyotes *have attacked* our goats.
Past Perfect	ended before something else began	helping verb *had* + main verb ending in *-ed*	After they *had killed* two goats, we built a fence.
Future Perfect	will be completed before another	helping verb *will* + *have* + main verb ending in *-ed*	By Tuesday we *will have finished* yet another fence.

A. DIRECTIONS: *One the line before each sentence, identify the tense of the verb in italics.*

_____ 1. In the past, I *have rented* many movies at the video store.

_____ 2. Now I *get* them from the library.

_____ 3. We recently *purchased* a DVD player.

_____ 4. I *will order* that movie tomorrow.

B. DIRECTIONS: *Rewrite these sentences using the correct verb tense.*

1. Yesterday I have borrowed four books from the library.

_____

2. I use the library many times in the past.

_____

3. Yesterday, after I traveled to the library, I walked up to the second floor.

_____

4. I ask the librarian for help but she had ignored me.

_____

Unit 2: Short Stories
Part 1 Benchmark Test 3

MULTIPLE CHOICE

Reading Skill: Predicting

1. Which of the following is an example of a prediction?
   - A. It is a complete surprise that school was cancelled today.
   - B. School will be closed tomorrow because of the snow.
   - C. It is going to snow all night so school might be cancelled.
   - D. School will be closed when there is more than six inches of snow.

2. Which of the following would help you predict what might happen next in a story?
   - A. thinking about what you know about the characters
   - B. looking up unfamiliar words in a dictionary
   - C. asking a friend what they think of the story
   - D. looking carefully at the author's use of language

3. What prediction can you make about the weather based on the following sentence?

   Although it was only noon, the sky began to darken.
   - A. A storm is coming.
   - B. A storm will not arrive.
   - C. A storm will arrive tomorrow.
   - D. The sun is setting early.

4. Which of the following is the best prediction about Joseph?

   Because science is not his best subject, Joseph stayed up very late studying for the test he would be taking the following morning.
   - A. Joseph will be late for school.
   - B. Joseph study more the next evening.
   - C. Joseph will fail his test.
   - D. Joseph will do well on his test.

Read the selection. Then, answer the questions that follow.

Jason woke up to the sound of his mother calling his name. He looked over at his alarm clock and sat up with a jolt. It was 7:55. His bus was going to be there in five minutes! Jason jumped out of bed, threw on his clothes, and ran down the stairs with only a minute to spare before his bus was due to arrive. He was about to walk out the door when he realized that he had forgotten his homework. As he ran up the stairs, he heard the sound of his bus as it drove away without him.

5. What prediction can you make about what Jason will do next?
   - A. Ask his school bus driver to wait.
   - B. Ask someone to take him to school.
   - C. Look all over to find his homework.
   - D. Stay late after school this afternoon.

6. If Jason is late for school what will probably happen to him?
   - A. He will be late again tomorrow.
   - B. He will decide to go home.
   - C. He will be marked as late.
   - D. He will be late again tomorrow.

7. If this text were part of a longer story, how could you verify your prediction?

    A. read ahead

    B. reread the passage

    C. make a Venn diagram of the plot

    D. diagram the character's motives

8. What clues in the text lead you to predict that Jason is going to miss the bus?

    A. His mother woke him up.

    B. Jason jumped out of bed.

    C. He threw on his clothes.

    D. He ran upstairs to get his forgotten homework.

9. Which of the following events contributes to Jason missing the bus?

    A. Jason's mother called his name.

    B. Jason woke up five minutes before his bus was due to arrive.

    C. Jason did his homework the night before.

    D. Jason heard the bus driving away.

Literary Analysis: Plot

10. What is the meaning of the term *plot*?

    A. the final outcome of a story

    B. the high point of a story

    C. the arrangement of events in a story

    D. a guess about what is going to happen next in a story

11. Which of the following will most likely move the action of a story forward?

    A. a unique and interesting title for the story

    B. a happy ending with the issues resolved

    C. the arrival of a character with new information

    D. a friendship between characters that has lasted a long time

12. Identify the climax in the following example.

A boy sees a snake lying still in the road. He bends close to look at it. Suddenly, the snake moves. The boy jumps back.

    A. A boy sees a snake lying in the road.

    B. The snake is lying still in the road.

    C. The boy bends close to look at it.

    D. Suddenly the snake moves.

13. Which of the following best describes the events in a plot?

    A. events that increase the tension or contribute to the resolution

    B. events that are unrelated to the story

    C. events that affect only the internal conflict in the story

    D. events that affect only the external conflict in the story

14. Which of the following would be the best resolution to a short story based on the following event?

A man finds a wrapped package on the ground with both a mailing address and a return address written on the front.

    A. The man takes the package to the post office.

    B. The man burns the package quickly.

    C. The man copies the return address but destroys the package.

    D. The man throws the package away.

15. After three days of being stranded on a mountain ledge, two boys are saved in a dramatic rescue. They are taken to a ranger station, where their parents are waiting for them. The rescue and the return represent which elements of the story?
    A. exposition and conflict
    B. climax and falling action
    C. rising action and resolution
    D. conflict and climax

Literary Analysis: Character

16. Which term refers to how a writer creates and develops characters?
    A. process
    B. outlining
    C. point of view
    D. characterization

17. Which of the following best describes a characteristic of an absent-minded person?
    A. "I wish Jack would hurry. He's always so slow."
    B. "You know Lisa. She gets angry at the smallest thing."
    C. "If I know Lisa, she is still hunting for her shin guards."
    D. "Tell Jack that this is the last time I will help him with his math homework."

18. Which of the following best describes a character who laughs uncertainly and speaks nervously?
    A. The character is confident.
    B. The character is very sad.
    C. The character is joyful.
    D. The character is insecure.

19. Which word best describes a character who cares for an injured bird?
    A. careless
    B. compassionate
    C. hard-working
    D. argumentative

Grammar

20. Which sentence includes a linking verb?
    A. The siren blared.
    B. We heard the wailing siren.
    C. The siren was loud and steady.
    D. Every Tuesday, the fire chief activates the siren.

21. Which sentence includes a linking verb?
    A. Maria's mother called the doctor.
    B. She was very worried.
    C. Maria has a fever.
    D. The doctor will arrive soon.

22. Which word in the following sentence is the main verb in a verb phrase?

    Because she prepared, she is succeeding on the test.

    A. because
    B. is
    C. succeeding
    D. on

23. Which word in the following sentence is a helping verb in a verb phrase?

    Ryan has lost his watch and wants me to help him find it.

    A. has
    B. lost
    C. wants
    D. help

24. Which sentence uses the verb *attend* in the past tense?

    A. He attends an after school program on Tuesdays.
    B. She attended the concert last Saturday.
    C. The two girls had attended the same summer camp.
    D. I have attended this seminar before.

25. Which sentence uses the verb *eat* in the past perfect tense?

    A. Sheila ate her lunch in the cafeteria.
    B. They eat lunch together every day.
    C. Douglas has eaten all the potato chips.
    D. The twins had eaten pizza before they arrived.

26. Which sentence uses the verb *go* in the present perfect tense?

    A. I went to the movies last night.
    B. Jonathan has gone home already.
    C. Liz had gone home before I arrived.
    D. Sara goes to the gym on Thursdays.

27. What tense is the verb *see* in the following sentence?

    Louis did not go to the movies with Jessica because he had seen the film the weekend before.

    A. past tense
    B. past perfect tense
    C. present perfect tense
    D. present tense

Vocabulary: Word Roots

28. What is the meaning of the root shared by *predict* and *dictionary*?
    A. to read
    B. to say
    C. to guess
    D. to write

29. The word root *ver* means "truth." What does it mean to "verify"?
    A. to determine the truth
    B. to retell facts
    C. to tell the story
    D. to guess the future

30. What does the word *veridical* mean?
    A. sincere
    B. standing upright
    C. truthful
    D. fair

31. How would a *dictating machine* be used?
    A. to record pictures
    B. to relay orders
    C. to record speech
    D. to save information

32. What is a *dictum*?
    A. a formal statement
    B. a truthful person
    C. a working plan
    D. a new idea

33. What do Shakespearean characters mean when they say *"Verily"*?
    A. "Absolutely."
    B. "Not a chance."
    C. "Truthfully."
    D. "I don't think so."

ESSAY

Writing

34. On your paper, retell the events from one of the short stories you have read. Organize your retelling in chronological order. Use transitions to make the sequence of events clear.

35. When writing an informative article, it is important to ask questions in order to narrow your focus. Write three questions that you would like to have answered if you were going to write a report about world hunger.

36. Write a paragraph describing a day in your life. Organize your description in time order. Use transitions to indicate the order in which events occurred.

Name _____

Unit 2: Short Stories
Part 2 Concept Map

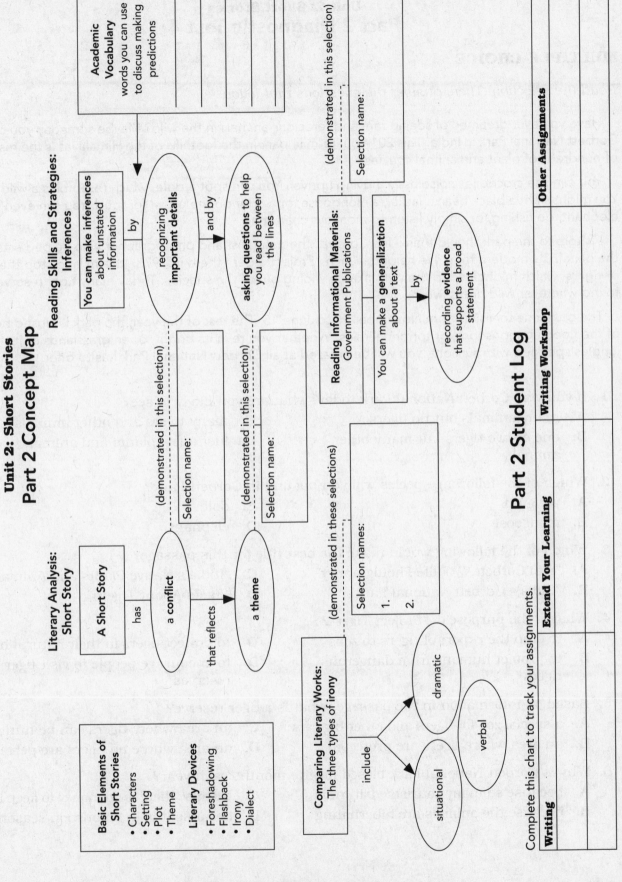

Academic Vocabulary
words you can use to discuss making predictions

_____
_____
_____

Reading Skills and Strategies: Inferences

You can make **inferences** about unstated information

by

recognizing **important details**

and by

asking questions to help you read between the lines

(demonstrated in this selection)

Selection name: _____

(demonstrated in this selection)

Selection name: _____

Literary Analysis: Short Story

A Short Story

has

a conflict

that reflects

a theme

(demonstrated in this selection)

Selection name: _____

Basic Elements of Short Stories

• Characters
• Setting
• Plot
• Theme

Literary Devices

• Foreshadowing
• Flashback
• Irony
• Dialect

Reading Informational Materials:
Government Publications

You can make a **generalization** about a text

by

recording **evidence** that supports a broad statement

Comparing Literary Works:
The three types of irony

(demonstrated in these selections)

Selection names:

1. _____
2. _____

include

dramatic

situational

verbal

Part 2 Student Log

Complete this chart to track your assignments.

Writing	Extend Your Learning	Writing Workshop	Other Assignments

Unit 2: Short Stories
Part 2 Diagnostic Test 4

MULTIPLE CHOICE

Read the selection. Then, answer the questions that follow.

Have you ever dreamed of seeing rare and ferocious animals in the wild? Maybe someday you can visit Corbett National Park in India. This 201-square-mile park in the foothills of the Himalayas is the residence of hundreds of plant and animal species.

You can see crocodiles noiselessly moving upriver. You can spot a dole, which resembles a wild dog. You might sight a black bear, a jackal, a mongoose, or a tiger on the prowl for food. You can even ride an elephant, go fishing, or simply listen to monkeys chattering.

Visitors to the park should thank Jim Corbett, the naturalist and photographer who helped establish the park in its modern form. He helped launch "Project Tiger" there in 1973. Its aim is to stop the killing of tigers, which might lead to the unthinkable wiping out of the species. Today many tiger reserves are found wherever wild tigers live.

The best time to visit is from November 15 to June 15. The rest of the year, the park is closed because of the flooding monsoons, or torrential rains. Whether you're in its bright, open grasslands or its huge jungles speckled with sunlight, you will be amazed at all Corbett National Park has to offer.

1. If you visit Corbett National Park today, what are you likely to see?
   A. many animals but no tigers
   B. one or two tigers but many other animals
   C. many tigers and other animals
   D. just a few plants and animals

2. Which of the following species will you *not* find in Corbett Park?
   A. penguin
   B. mongoose
   C. dole
   D. elephant

3. Which of the following would make the best title for this passage?
   A. "Jim Corbett, Wildlife Photographer"
   B. "India's Corbett National Park"
   C. "India's Native Plants and Animals"
   D. "Facts About Tigers"

4. What is the purpose of "Project Tiger"?
   A. to stop the export of tigers to zoos
   B. to protect humans from dangerous tigers
   C. to protect tigers in their natural habitat
   D. to encourage people to visit tiger reserves

5. Based on information in the passage, what is a tiger reserve?
   A. a special zoo for tigers and other big cats
   B. an area where tigers are protected
   C. an area where tigers can be hunted
   D. an area where no tigers are permitted

6. Why is Corbett National Park closed for five months each year?
   A. because so many tourists visit India
   B. because the animals are hibernating
   C. because there is no money to keep it open
   D. because it is the monsoon season

7. According to this passage, where is Corbett National park located?

A. India   C. Australia

B. Africa   D. Indonesia

Read the selection. Then, answer the questions that follow.

In 1800, pioneers heading west from the thirteen colonies trekked over miles of trails or faced an equally slow boat trip. Flatboats drifted downstream with the current, but going upstream was impossible.

The invention of the steamboat changed water travel forever. It opened up the Midwest to farming, shipping, and industry. It paved the way for America's great westward expansion. Robert Fulton's steamship *Clermont* began operating on the Hudson River in New York in 1807. Boats that used burning fuel to create steam power flourished on the Mississippi River shortly before the Civil War.

A steamboat would chug impressively downriver at eight miles an hour, billows of smoke aloft. Southern dialect met northern accent in the bustle of St. Louis, Missouri, the steamboat capital.

Within a few decades, steamboats became "floating palaces." They could be as long as 300 feet, with five decks. Steamboats could be dangerous, however. Sometimes even a minor blunder would cause a boiler explosion, endangering people's lives and the boat's cargo.

The Civil War halted steamboat traffic on the Mississippi and turned the river into a watery battle route. After the war, steamboat traffic resumed. It was soon overshadowed, however, by the growth of another kind of steam transportation: the railroad.

8. Which of the following events came first?

A. Robert Fulton's *Clermont* sailed on the Hudson.

B. The Civil War interrupted civilian traffic on the Mississippi.

C. St. Louis, Missouri, became a hub for steamboat travel.

D. Flatboats carried passengers down the Mississippi.

9. What type of power made a flatboat move?

A. current in a river

B. burning fuel

C. electricity

D. people rowing

10. According to the passage, which of the following is not an important difference between a flatboat and a steamboat?

A. their source of power

B. their ability to travel downstream

C. their ability to travel upstream

D. their size and design

11. Which of the following best expresses the main idea of this sentence?

Southern dialect met northern accent in the bustle of St. Louis, Missouri, the steamboat capital.

A. People who moved to St. Louis, Missouri, came from all over the United States.

B. St. Louis became the hub of steamboat traffic on the Mississippi River.

C. Many Northerners and Southerners moved to St. Louis, Missouri, when it was founded.

D. St. Louis quickly became the biggest city on the Mississippi River.

12. Why were steamboats on the Mississippi called "floating palaces"?

    A. because of their size and large number of decks

    B. because royalty traveled on them

    C. because of their extraordinary speed

    D. because of the entertainment on board

13. According to the passage, what was the most serious danger aboard a steamship?

    A. The steamship could crash into the shore.

    B. It could crash into another steamship.

    C. It could be overloaded and sink.

    D. It could be set afire by a boiler explosion.

14. Imagine you were a civilian wanting to travel down the Mississippi River on a steamboat during the Civil War. What would happen to you?

    A. You would be unable to find a steamboat to carry you.

    B. You would have to wait until all of the military officers had booked their passage.

    C. You would pay for your passage and have no trouble booking a cabin.

    D. You would be arrested as a spy by the Union army.

15. What permanently ended the golden age of steamboat travel on the Mississippi?

    A. the Civil War

    B. the invention of the flatboat

    C. the invention of steam railroads

    D. the invention of the steam engine

Vocabulary Warm-up Word Lists

Study these words from "The Third Wish." Then, complete the activities.

Word List A

canal [kuh NAL] *n.* a human-made waterway connecting bodies of water
   The Erie <u>Canal</u>, a waterway in New York State was built between Buffalo and Albany.

frantically [FRAN tik lee] *adv.* acting wildly with worry or fear
   Kelly was <u>frantically</u> trying to get her project done before the deadline.

granted [GRANT id] *v.* allowed someone a wish or a favor
   The teacher <u>granted</u> Mike an extra week to catch up on his homework.

occasions [uh KAY zhuhnz] *n.* times when something happens
   My family gathers for special <u>occasions</u>, such as birthdays and weddings.

reflecting [ri FLEKT ing] *v.* thinking carefully and calmly
   Lyle was quietly <u>reflecting</u> on what his friend had told him.

thrashed [THRASHT] *v.* moved from side to side in an uncontrolled way
   The hooked fish <u>thrashed</u> across the deck of the boat.

tremendous [tri MEN duhs] *adj.* enormous; great in amount, size, or power
   Mr. Sutter had <u>tremendous</u> confidence in his students' ability to achieve.

utter [UH tur] *v.* to say something or make a sound
   The puppet's mouth moved but did not <u>utter</u> a word.

Word List B

communicating [kuh MYOO ni kay ting] *v.* expressing thoughts or feelings to someone
   Dave was <u>communicating</u> with his friends on his cell phone.

composure [kuhm POH zhur] *n.* calm; self-control
   Doris defended her actions with <u>composure</u>.

distressed [dis TREST] *adj.* extremely upset or worried
   We were <u>distressed</u> when we heard about the accident.

expression [eks PRESH uhn] *n.* a look on someone's face
   Daniel wore an <u>expression</u> of joy when he received the award.

harsh [HAHRSH] *adj.* unpleasant to the senses
   The actor's <u>harsh</u> laugh spoiled his performance.

prefer [pree FER] *v.* to like or want one thing more than another
   Annie said she would <u>prefer</u> to stay home rather than attend the concert.

rash [RASH] *adj.* done too quickly and without thinking
   Although she was angry, Anna was careful not to make <u>rash</u> accusations.

remote [ri MOHT] *adj.* far away; distant
   The family spent winter vacation at a <u>remote</u> campsite in the mountains.

Name _____ Date _____

Exercise A *Fill in each blank in the paragraph below with an appropriate word from Word List A. Use each word only once.*

Jackie worked [1] _____ to dock the little boat in the

[2] _____ as dark clouds moved across the sky. In a flash, a

[3] _____ wind blew up, and the boat [4] _____ at its

mooring. On [5] _____ such as this, although she was under pressure,

Jackie was carefully [6] _____ on her next move. She knew that boats

like hers were not allowed to dock at the fancy marina, but she requested permission

anyway. Fortunately, the manager [7] _____ her request. Relieved, she

did not [8] _____ another word until she was safely on shore.

Exercise B *Answer each question in a complete sentence. Use a word from Word List B to replace each underlined word or group of words without changing the meaning.*

Example: Where do the hockey players stow their equipment?
(gear) The players keep their gear in the locker room.

1. How might you protect yourself in severe weather?

   _____

2. How might you help a friend who is upset about something?

   _____

3. What would you most like to do on a Saturday night?

   _____

4. What is a faraway place you have visited or would like to visit?

   _____

5. Why would it be reckless for someone to spend all his or her money?

   _____

6. What might be the look on someone's face if he or she has been kept waiting?

   _____

7. How well might someone keep his or her calm in an embarrassing situation?

   _____

8. What is one way of expressing ideas to others?

   _____

"The Third Wish" by Joan Aiken
Reading Warm-up A

Read the following passage. Pay special attention to the underlined words. Then, read it again, and complete the activities. Use a separate sheet of paper for your written answers.

"Be careful what you wish for because your wish might be underline{granted}." I was underline{reflecting} on some of my past wishes and decided that there is truth in that saying.

I used to wish for huge, truly underline{tremendous} things that I thought would make me happy. These were wishes I would never underline{utter} out loud, even to my best friend. They were too outrageous, and I knew they would never come true. There have been underline{occasions} when my wishes have come true, not magically, but when I made them happen. For example, I once wished I could go on a class trip to Washington, D.C. I got a summer job to pay for the trip. I had that same job, selling hot dogs to boaters on the underline{canal}, for the next three summers.

Then there was my wish for a red sports car for my sixteenth birthday. The car I wished for would accelerate to 120 miles per hour in fifteen seconds. I never got that car. When I was sixteen, however, my parents helped me buy a used truck. It was gray. When the speedometer rose above 55, the body underline{thrashed} around like a badly loaded washing machine. Here is the thing about that truck, though: It was tough.

One day the most popular boy in school plowed his fancy wheels into a snow bank. Whom did he underline{frantically} call for help? You guessed it—me! That was sweet.

The money I made at my summer jobs also helped pay for my biggest wish of all, a college education. I guess that is the difference between a wish granted and a wish earned. A wish granted is a nice gift, but a wish earned keeps on giving.

1. Circle the words that tell what might be underline{granted}. What is a synonym for *granted*?

2. Underline the words that tell what the writer was underline{reflecting} on. Use *reflecting* in a sentence.

3. Circle the word that is a synonym for underline{tremendous}. What is the opposite of *tremendous*?

4. Underline the words that tell what the writer would never underline{utter} out loud. Use *utter* in a sentence.

5. On what underline{occasions} did the writer's wishes come true? On what other *occasions* might wishes came true?

6. Circle the word that tells who was on the underline{canal}. What kinds of boats might be used in a *canal*?

7. Underline the phrase that describes how the truck underline{thrashed} around. Use *thrashed* in a sentence.

8. Whom did the popular boy underline{frantically} call? Use *frantically* in a sentence.

"The Third Wish" by Joan Aiken
Reading Warm-up B

Read the following passage. Pay special attention to the underlined words. Then, read it again, and complete the activities. Use a separate sheet of paper for your written answers.

Their names are musical: mute, trumpeter, whistling, and whooper. They can live more than 50 years in the wild. They eat mostly plants that grow in the water. They prefer to fly at night. They are known for having a serene expression as they glide calmly over the water. They are swans, birds of myth and folklore.

One of the more familiar swans is the mute swan. It is a large, all-white bird with a pinkish bill that ends in a black knob. Mute swans are not entirely silent. If you are lucky, you may hear them. They will be communicating with puppylike barking notes or loud, high-pitched purr-ing sounds. These sounds do not travel far, so mute swans appear to be silent. This silence contributes to their supreme composure. It is as if nothing in the world could upset a mute swan. A female mute swan will become distressed, however, if another waterfowl is rash enough to invade her nesting territory. The swan will drive out the offending bird with an angry hiss and a flapping of her wings.

Swans usually mate for life, and they are good parents. The male often takes the firstborn hatchlings swimming to help out the mother while she sits on the remaining eggs. Sometimes you will see chicks riding on the back or under the wings of their parents.

Swans nest in the remote Arctic islands, northern Russia, and as far south as Brazil and Australia. Many migrate to warm climates in winter. Mute swans, how-ever, often move from frozen, freshwater habitats to nearby saltwater habitats.

Swans are one of nature's greatest beauties. To see a swan gliding peacefully on a lake is like a gift. We are instantly drawn into an island of calm far from the harsh clamor of our busy world.

1. Circle the words that tell what swans prefer to do at night. What after-school activities do you **prefer**?

2. Circle the word that tells what kind of expression swans have as they glide over water. What is a synonym for **expression**?

3. Underline the words that tell what sounds the mute swan makes when it is communicating. Use **communicating** in a sentence.

4. Underline the sentence that tells about the swan's composure. In your own words, tell what contributes to this **composure**.

5. Underline the words that tell what the swan does when it is distressed. What might a person do when he or she is **distressed**?

6. Tell what the waterfowl does that is rash. Describe a behavior you think is **rash**.

7. Underline the words that name the remote places where swans nest. Write a word that means the opposite of **remote**.

8. Circle the word that helps to define harsh. Write a sentence that describes a **harsh** sound.

"The Third Wish" by Joan Aiken
Reading: Make Inferences by Recognizing Details

Short story writers do not directly tell you everything there is to know about the characters, setting, and events. Instead, they leave it to you to **make inferences,** or logical guesses, about unstated information.

To form inferences, you must **recognize details** in the story and consider their importance. For example, in "The Third Wish," Mr. Peters finds a swan tangled up in thorns. When he moves closer and tries to free the swan, the swan hisses at him, pecks at him, and flaps its wings in a threatening way. You can use those clues to infer that the swan does not like or trust Mr. Peters.

DIRECTIONS: *The sentences in the left-hand column of this chart offer details about characters in "The Third Wish." (Some of the items are quotations from the story; some are based on the story.) In the right-hand column, describe what the details tell you about the character.*

Detail About a Character	Inference About the Character
1. Presently, the swan, when it was satisfied with its appearance, floated in to the bank once more, and in a moment, instead of the great white bird, there was a little man all in green.	
2. Mr. Peters wishes for a wife "as beautiful as the forest." A woman appears who is "the most beautiful creature he had ever seen, with eyes as blue-green as the canal, hair as dusky as the bushes, and skin as white as the feathers of swans."	
3. But as time went by Mr. Peters began to feel that [Leita] was not happy. She seemed restless, wandered much in the garden, and sometimes when he came back from the fields he would find the house empty. She would return after half an hour with no explanation of where she had been.	
4. After Leita was returned to the form of a swan, she "rested her head lightly against [Mr. Peters's] hand. . . . Next day he saw two swans swimming at the bottom of the garden, and one of them wore the gold chain he had given Leita after their marriage; she came up and rubbed her head against his hand."	

Name _____   Date _____

Most fictional stories center on a **conflict**—a struggle between opposing forces. There are two kinds of conflict:

- When there is an **external conflict,** a character struggles with an outside force, such as another character or nature.
- When there is an **internal conflict,** a character struggles with himself or herself to overcome opposing feelings, beliefs, needs, or desires. An internal conflict takes place in a character's mind.

The **resolution,** or outcome of the conflict, often comes toward the end of the story, when the problem is settled in some way.

A story can have additional, smaller conflicts that develop the main conflict. For example, in "The Third Wish," a small external conflict occurs between Mr. Peters and the swan that is tangled up in the thorns. As Mr. Peters tries to free the bird, the swan looks at him "with hate in its yellow eyes" and struggles with him. In addition, a minor internal conflict that helps to develop the main conflict is Mr. Peters's difficulty in deciding what to do with his three wishes.

DIRECTIONS: *Based on details in each of the following passages from "The Third Wish," identify the conflict as* External *or* Internal. *Then, explain your answer.*

1. [Leita] was weeping, and as he came nearer he saw that tears were rolling, too, from the swan's eyes.

   "Leita, what is it?" he asked, very troubled.

   "This is my sister," she answered. "I can't bear being separated from her."

   Type of conflict: _____

   Explanation: _____

2. "Don't you love me at all, Leita?"

   "Yes, I do, I do love you," she said, and there were tears in her eyes again. "But I miss the old life in the forest."

   Type of conflict: _____

   Explanation: _____

3. She shook her head. "No, I could not be as unkind to you as that. I am partly a swan, but I am also partly a human being now."

   Type of conflict: _____

   Explanation: _____

"The Third Wish" by Joan Aiken
Vocabulary Builder

Word List

```
presumptuous    rash    remote    malicious
```

A. DIRECTIONS: *Think about the meaning of the italicized word in each sentence. Then, in your own words, answer the question that follows, and briefly explain your answer.*

1. The old King knows that most humans make *rash* decisions when they are given permission to make three magical wishes. How much thought do most humans put into their choice of wishes?

_____

2. The old King is *presumptuous* in believing that Mr. Peters will make three foolish wishes. Is the old King overconfident? How do you know?

_____

_____

3. The old King is a *malicious* character. How does he act toward Mr. Peters?

_____

4. Mr. Peters lives in a *remote* valley. Is it close to town? How do you know?

_____

_____

B. DIRECTIONS: *On the line, write the letter of the word whose meaning is* opposite *that of the Word List word.*

___ 1. malicious
    A. wicked   B. tangled   C. sour   D. kind

___ 2. presumptuous
    A. curious   B. modest   C. missing   D. hungry

___ 3. rash
    A. cautious   B. itchy   C. impure   D. hasty

___ 4. remote
    A. casual   B. close   C. faraway   D. controlled

"The Third Wish" by Joan Aiken
Support for Writing an Anecdote

Before writing an **anecdote** using the pattern of three wishes that "The Third Wish" follows, use this graphic organizer. In the first rectangle, briefly describe a wish that a character makes. In the oval below it, describe a problem that the wish might cause. In the square below the oval, describe a way in which your character might solve the problem. Then do the same for the second wish. Finally, complete the information for the third wish.

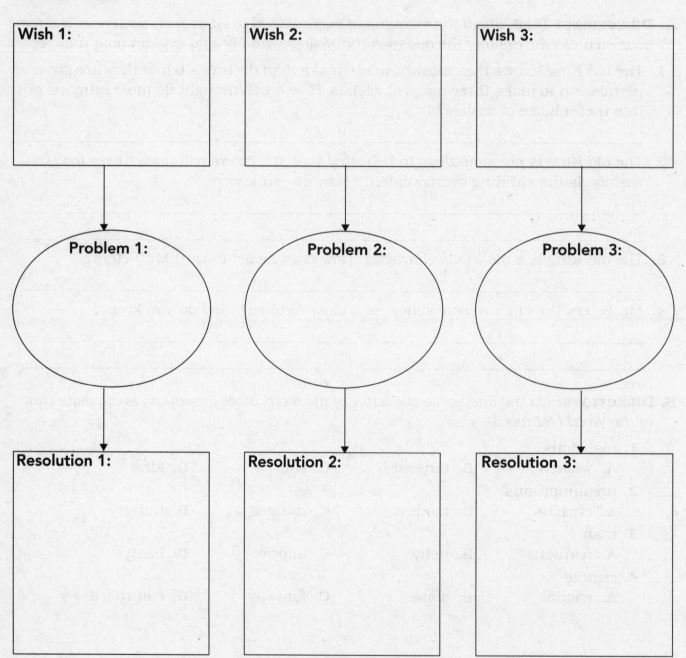

Now, use your notes to write an anecdote using the pattern of three wishes.

Name _____ Date _____

"The Third Wish" by Joan Aiken
Support for Extend Your Learning

Research and Technology

After you have found and read another tale that involves wishes, use this Venn diagram to make notes about how the tale **compares and contrasts** with "The Third Wish."

"The Third Wish"   **Other tale involving three wishes:**
_____

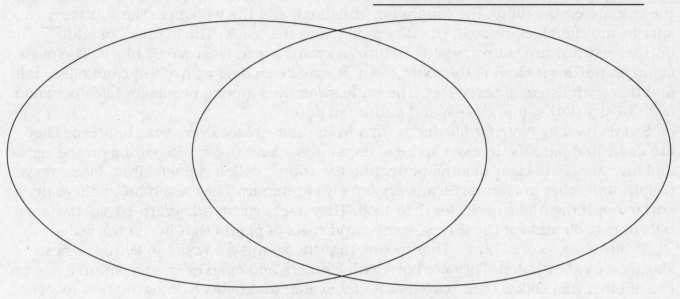

Elements Common to Both Tales

Listening and Speaking

What details from "The Third Wish" support the statement that Mr. Peters was good-natured and a doer of good deeds? List at least three details here:

_____

_____

_____

Now, prepare to write a **news story** announcing the death of Mr. Peters and hailing him as a local hero. Choose a method by which to organize your details (for example, strongest to weakest or least important to most important). Name the method here, and organize your details in the three boxes according to that method.

Method of organization: _____

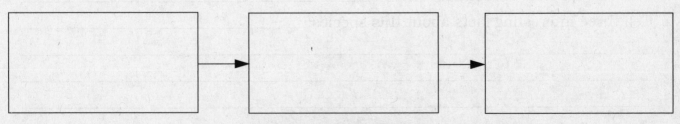

"The Third Wish" by Joan Aiken
Enrichment: A Scientific Look at Swans

In "The Third Wish," Joan Aiken gives the graceful swan magical powers. Throughout history, swans have made appearances in myths, legends, and folk tales. They often symbolize purity, beauty, or innocence.

In the animal world, swans are the largest of the waterfowl, a group that also includes ducks and geese. Worldwide there are seven species of swans, four in the Northern Hemisphere and three in the Southern Hemisphere. The northern species are the trumpeter, the mute, the tundra (or whistling), and the whooper. The southern species are the black-necked, the Coscoroba, and the black. The feathers of adult northern swans are entirely white. Southern swans are at least partly black. The most common northern swan is the mute swan. It may be as long as five feet from bill to tail and has a wingspan of seven feet. The mute swan lives among people and is a common sight in city parks, town lakes, and suburban ponds.

Swans usually mate for life and return to the same place every year to breed. They are dedicated parents. In most species, the adults spend five weeks sitting on the eggs and another six to eight months protecting the young, called *cygnets,* from foxes, dogs, people, and other predators. Swans are largely vegetarian. They reach below the water's surface with their long necks for their food. They use their broad, sharp-edged, flattened bills to tear off and eat the leaves, stems, and roots of plants that live in the water.

Swans are *precocial* birds. That means that the young are ready to leave the nest shortly after they hatch. They are born with feathers and open eyes, and within a day or two of birth they follow their parents into the water, instinctively knowing how to swim.

A. DIRECTIONS: *Answer these questions about swans.*

1. What species of swan is most often found in parks and ponds in North America? What are some of its characteristics?

   _____

   _____

2. What are young swans called? _____

3. How and what do swans eat? _____

   _____

B. DIRECTIONS: *In a library or on the Internet, look up one species of swan, and answer the following questions about that species. Then, share your findings with your class.*

Name of species: _____

Tell three interesting facts about this species: _____

_____

_____

_____

"The Third Wish" by Joan Aiken
Selection Test A

Critical Reading *Identify the letter of the choice that best answers the question.*

____ 1. What information in this passage from "The Third Wish" reveals that there is a conflict between Mr. Peters and the King of the Forest?

> He [the King] had fierce glittering eyes and looked by no means friendly.
> "Well, Sir," he said threateningly.

  A. The King sounds threatening.
  B. The King's eyes are glittering.
  C. The King is usually friendly.
  D. The King calls him "Sir."

____ 2. At the beginning of "The Third Wish," what is the only thing that troubles Mr. Peters?

  A. He is poor.
  B. He has no free time.
  C. He is lonely.
  D. He lives far away.

____ 3. Why does Mr. Peters use only one wish and save the other two?

  A. The King tells him to use only one.
  B. He wants to save two for an emergency.
  C. He is allowed to use only one.
  D. He wants to see if the first one works.

____ 4. When Mr. Peters takes Leita home and shows her all his treasures, what pleases her the most?

  A. the river
  B. the beehives
  C. the flowers
  D. the candlesticks

____ 5. In "The Third Wish," what inference can you make about why Leita is unhappy living with Mr. Peters?

  A. She misses her mother.
  B. She does not like to be inside.
  C. She wishes she were in the city.
  D. She misses her life as a swan.

___ 6. Why does Mr. Peters offer to use a wish to change Leita's sister into a human?
   A. He is angry with Leita.
   B. He wants to make Leita happy.
   C. Leita's sister is sick and needs her help.
   D. Leita wants her sister to be human.

___ 7. Why does Mr. Peters change Leita back into a swan?
   A. She is not nice to him.
   B. She asks him to change her.
   C. She is unhappy as a human.
   D. She no longer pleases him.

___ 8. Mr. Peters uses his second wish to turn Leita back into a swan. How does this action resolve the conflict in the story?
   A. Mr. Peters is happy because he can be alone again.
   B. Leita is with her sister and no longer unhappy.
   C. Mr. Peters had wanted a wife who was not a swan.
   D. Leita had not been nice to him, so he has punished her.

___ 9. After Mr. Peters turns Leita back into a swan, what inference can you make when she rests her head against his hand before flying away?
   A. She is asking him to scratch her head.
   B. She is trying to find a way to bite him.
   C. She is sorry she is a swan again.
   D. She is thanking him for transforming her.

___ 10. Why does Mr. Peters live by the river even when he is old and sick?
   A. He wants to stay near the two swans.
   B. He thinks he is too old to move away.
   C. He cannot afford to move away.
   D. He fears he will miss his neighbors.

___ 11. Why are many people afraid of Mr. Peters when he grows old?
   A. They think he has magical powers.
   B. He never lets people into his house.
   C. He communicates with two swans.
   D. They think he is a thief.

Vocabulary and Grammar

_____ **12.** Based on the way *malicious* is used in this passage from "The Third Wish," what would you say is a characteristic of a *malicious* person?

> He heard a harsh laugh behind him, and turning round saw the old King looking at him with a <u>malicious</u> expression.

    A. He or she is mean.

    B. He or she is talkative.

    C. He or she is curious.

    D. He or she is happy.

_____ **13.** What does the following sentence tell you about the word *remote*?

> Mr. Peters's house is so <u>remote</u> that the nearest neighbor lives miles away, there are no malls nearby, and only sounds of nature can be heard.

    A. It means "unrealistic."

    B. It means "agricultural."

    C. It means "dangerous and untamed."

    D. It means "far from everything else."

_____ **14.** In this sentence, which word does the adjective *gold* modify?

> One of them wore the gold chain he had given Leita after their marriage.

    A. wore

    B. chain

    C. Leita

    D. marriage

_____ **15.** In this sentence, which word is an adjective?

> In his hands were a withered leaf and a white feather.

    A. hands

    B. breast

    C. white

    D. feather

Essay

16. In "The Third Wish," Leita is not happy as Mr. Peters's wife. In an essay, describe Leita's unhappiness. Give three examples of things she says or does that show she is unhappy. Then, explain why she is unhappy and give two examples to support your explanation. Does she care for Mr. Peters? What is making her unhappy?

17. In an essay, explain the central conflict in "The Three Wishes" and the resolution of that conflict. Consider these questions: Who is involved in the conflict? Why is there a conflict? Is the conflict external or internal? How is the conflict resolved?

"**The Third Wish**" by Joan Aiken
Selection Test B

Critical Reading *Identify the letter of the choice that best completes the statement or answers the question.*

____ 1. When the King of the Forest first appears, how do you know that he and Mr. Peters are experiencing an external conflict?
   A. Mr. Peters argues with the King about life as a swan versus life as a human.
   B. Mr. Peters grows mean and threatens the King when he speaks.
   C. The King has fierce eyes, is unfriendly, and speaks threateningly to Mr. Peters.
   D. The King and Mr. Peters get into a fist fight over the three wishes.

____ 2. In "The Third Wish," what can you infer from the following remark by the old King?
   "I have yet to hear of the human being who made any good use of his three wishes—they mostly end up worse off than they started."

   A. The old King is saying that Mr. Peters lacks basic intelligence.
   B. The old King is saying that Mr. Peters will waste the three wishes.
   C. The old King is saying that every human he meets wants three wishes.
   D. The old King is saying that he has granted three wishes to many humans.

____ 3. At the start of "The Third Wish," the only thing troubling Mr. Peters is that
   A. he must make three wishes.
   B. he misses his first wife.
   C. he is somewhat lonely.
   D. he lives in a remote place.

____ 4. In "The Third Wish," Mr. Peters does not use all three of his wishes at once because
   A. the King of the Forest warns him not to.
   B. he wants to save two for an emergency.
   C. the King of the Forest has forbidden him to.
   D. he can think of only one thing to wish for.

____ 5. When Mr. Peters shows Leita all of his treasures, why does the river please her the most?
   A. She likes getting her exercise by swimming.
   B. She will be able to visit with her sister.
   C. She likes to eat fish caught from the river.
   D. She is soothed by the sound of the water.

____ 6. In "The Third Wish," what can you infer about Leita from the time she spends by the river?
   A. She loves nature and the outdoors.
   B. She misses the King of the Forest.
   C. She misses her life as a swan.
   D. She loves watching the flow of water.

_____ 7. Leita tells Mr. Peters not to use his second wish to turn her back into a swan because
   A. she does not want him to use a wish on her.
   B. she feels an obligation to stay with him.
   C. she is getting used to living as a human.
   D. she has fallen in love with him.

_____ 8. Based on this passage, what can you infer from Leita's desire to stay at home?
   Poor Mr. Peters . . . did his best to make her life happier, . . . even suggesting a trip round the world. But she said no to that; she would prefer to stay in their own house near the river.
   A. She does not want to be far from her sister.
   B. She does not care for foreign travel.
   C. She does not like Mr. Peters enough to travel with him.
   D. She does not want to miss her daily swims in the river.

_____ 9. When Mr. Peters comes to bed one night and finds Leita calling out in her sleep, how is her internal conflict revealed?
   A. In her dream, she is talking of her fear of having to leave him.
   B. In her dream, she is afraid of the river and calling for help.
   C. In her dream, she is laughing and playing beside the river.
   D. In her dream, she is crying and calling for her sister to wait for her.

_____ 10. Mr. Peters changes Leita back into a swan because
   A. she does not respect him.
   B. she has begged him to.
   C. she is unhappy as a human.
   D. she has lost hope.

_____ 11. Which statement is the best interpretation of this passage from "The Third Wish"?
   Next day he saw two swans swimming at the bottom of the garden, and one of them wore the gold chain he had given Leita after their marriage; she came up and rubbed her head against his hand.
   A. The swan wishes to return the chain to Mr. Peters.
   B. The chain has gotten tangled around the swan's neck.
   C. The swans have found Leita's gold chain.
   D. The swans are Leita and her sister, Rhea.

_____ 12. Upon his death Mr. Peters is found smiling happily, holding a withered leaf and a white feather. What does that description suggest?
   A. Mr. Peters dies trying to think of a use for the third wish.
   B. Mr. Peters is transformed into a swan before he dies.
   C. Mr. Peters gives his third wish to Leita before he dies.
   D. Mr. Peters never uses the third wish and dies content.

Vocabulary and Grammar

____ 13. In "The Third Wish," Mr. Peters stops himself from making a *rash* decision. Someone who makes a *rash* decision is most likely to be
A. careful.
B. selfish.
C. tired.
D. careless.

____ 14. What is the meaning of the word *malicious* as it is used in this sentence from "The Third Wish"?
He heard a harsh laugh behind him, and turning round saw the old King looking at him with a <u>malicious</u> expression.
A. happy
B. hungry
C. hateful
D. curious

____ 15. Which two words in the following sentence from "The Three Wishes" are adjectives?
Passers-by along the road heard the mournful sound of two swans.
A. along, heard
B. along, mournful
C. mournful, two
D. sound, swans

____ 16. In this sentence about "The Three Wishes," which word does the adjective *restless* modify?
She seemed restless and wandered much in the garden.
A. She
B. seemed
C. wandered
D. much

____ 17. In the following sentence from "The Three Wishes," which three words are adjectives?
There was a little man all in green with a golden crown and long beard.
A. little, all, green
B. little, golden, long
C. green, golden, beard
D. all, green, golden

Essay

18. The King of the Forest claims that he "has yet to hear of the human being who made any good use of his three wishes." In an essay, consider whether Mr. Peters proves the old King wrong. Do Mr. Peters's wishes bring him happiness? Does he put his wishes to good use? Cite two or three events from "The Three Wishes" to support your points.

19. The characters in "The Third Wish" experience both external and internal conflicts. In an essay, define the two types of conflict, and cite an example from the story of each one. Then describe how each conflict is resolved.

Vocabulary Warm-up Word Lists

Study these words from "Amigo Brothers." Then, complete the activities.

Word List A

achieve [uh CHEEV] *v.* to do something successfully after a lot of effort
Paul was proud to <u>achieve</u> his dream of becoming Player of the Year.

barrage [buh RAHZH] *n.* a fast attacking or outpouring that comes all at once
The Web site received a <u>barrage</u> of complaints from angry subscribers.

fitful [FIT fool] *adj.* starting and stopping in an irregular way
Loren had a <u>fitful</u> night's sleep and woke up exhausted.

nimble [NIM buhl] *adj.* able to move quickly and lightly
The gymnast twisted her <u>nimble</u> body into an astounding shape.

opponent [uh POH nuhnt] *n.* a person or team that is against you in a contest
Greta shook hands with her <u>opponent</u> after the tennis match.

shuffle [SHUHF uhl] *n.* a slow walk, with the feet barely leaving the ground
I recognized Vincent's tired <u>shuffle</u> as he came home from work.

style [STYL] *n.* the way in which something is done
Hemingway's <u>style</u> of writing is spare; he says a lot in a few words.

surged [SERJD] *v.* rushed forward with force
The stormy waves <u>surged</u> over the cliffs.

Word List B

challenger [CHAL uhn jer] *n.* someone who competes against a champion
The <u>challenger</u> seemed ready to compete against the chess champion.

clarity [KLAR uh tee] *n.* clearness
Matt spoke with <u>clarity</u> about the techniques of snowboarding.

emerging [ee MERJ ing] *v.* coming out of somewhere
The president's motorcade was <u>emerging</u> from the tunnel.

improvised [IM pruh vyzd] *v.* made up something on the spot
When Sheila forgot her lines she <u>improvised</u> the words.

mild [MYLD] *adj.* moderate; not extreme
Joe Bill enjoys a <u>mild</u> salsa on his tacos.

muscular [mus KYOO ler] *adj.* physically strong with well-developed muscles
Jan needed a <u>muscular</u> skating partner who could lift her easily.

numerous [NOO mer uhs] *adj.* many
<u>Numerous</u> singers auditioned for the popular TV show.

sparring [SPAHR ing] *adj.* using light blows as in a practice boxing match
Rocky's <u>sparring</u> partner delivered a light punch to the jaw.

"Amigo Brothers" by Piri Thomas
Vocabulary Warm-up Exercises

Exercise A *Fill in each blank in the paragraph below with an appropriate word from Word List A. Use each word only once.*

Gladys danced around on her [1] _____ legs. She watched her
[2] _____ arrive. She noticed the girl's weary [3] _____ as she
walked slowly onto the tennis court. At first her opponent's [4] _____ was
inconsistent. Some serves were fast; some were slow. After a few [5] _____
attempts, however, the girl [6] _____ forward with a strong serve. Then both
players sent forth a [7] _____ of hard returns. Gladys had to work hard to
[8] _____ the first win of the match.

Exercise B *Answer the questions with complete explanations.*

Example: If someone is a <u>clumsy</u> player, is he or she skillful?
No; a clumsy player would not be skillful. He or she would trip or bump into other players.

1. If you answer a question with <u>clarity</u>, will people understand your answer?
   _____

2. If a snake is <u>emerging</u> from a pile of leaves, is it likely you have seen its tail?
   _____

3. If you have <u>improvised</u> with a jazz band, is it likely you are a good musician?
   _____

4. If you have <u>numerous</u> things to do, do you have a great deal of free time?
   _____

5. If you are a <u>challenger</u>, are you a champion?
   _____

6. If someone is <u>muscular</u>, can he or she easily lift heavy objects?
   _____

7. If someone takes part in a <u>sparring</u> match, is he or she likely to get seriously injured?
   _____

8. If you have a <u>mild</u> manner, do you get angry often?
   _____

"Amigo Brothers" by Piri Thomas
Reading Warm-up A

Read the following passage. Pay special attention to the underlined words. Then, read it again, and complete the activities. Use a separate sheet of paper for your written answers.

When a little guy wants to <u>achieve</u> something really, really big, he has to work hard, then harder, and harder still. Sal was a little guy who wanted to become a champion middleweight boxer. Sal was 12 years old, stood 4 feet 8 inches tall and weighed in at about 98 pounds. He knew it would be a long, hard road for him to even get inside the ring. If he ever doubted it, his brother, who was known in boxing circles as "The Bruiser," was quick to remind him. Luckily, his brother was a sweet guy despite his crushing name.

"If you want my help, you have to stay steady on the course," his brother had said. "No <u>fitful</u> starts and stops. No 'Today I want it, tomorrow I don't.' Got that?"

"Got it! When do we start?"

"Now," his brother answered as he tossed Sal a pair of training gloves and a helmet. "Gloves up in front of your face and keep your eyes on your <u>opponent</u>. Always keep your eyes on your opponent. No matter what I do, which way I turn, never take your eyes off of me." These primary instructions were delivered as his brother moved around in a <u>nimble</u> dance. He bounced here, now there, never still, never in the same place. Sal wasn't fooled by this quick footwork. He knew his brother's <u>style</u>: tight, controlled, and fast as a viper. Suddenly his brother delivered a <u>barrage</u> of soft jabs. One, two, three, four! Sal was ready for it. He moved his gloves to block the blows then <u>surged</u> forward with a jab to his brother's ribs.

His brother <u>shuffled</u> backward as if dancing on sand. "Good!" he exclaimed. "That's a strong beginning, Bro'. I think we've got something to work with here."

Sal grew six inches taller inside himself. He had taken his first step forward, and it was a good one.

1. Underline the words that tell what Sal wanted to <u>achieve</u>. Write about something you want to *achieve*.

2. Underline the words that mean the opposite of <u>fitful</u>. Write a sentence using the word *fitful*.

3. Circle the word that tells what you should always keep on your <u>opponent</u>. Rewrite the sentence using a synonym for *opponent*.

4. Underline the sentence that describes the brother's <u>nimble</u> dance. Give a synonym for *nimble*.

5. Underline the words that describe the brother's boxing <u>style</u>. Write about another sport that requires a similar *style*.

6. Circle the words that tell what kind of <u>barrage</u> Sal's brother delivered. Use the word *barrage* in a sentence.

7. Underline the words that tell how Sal <u>surged</u> forward. Rewrite the sentence using a synonym for *surged*.

8. Underline the words that that tell how the brother <u>shuffled</u>. Use the same meaning for the word *shuffled* in a sentence.

"Amigo Brothers" by Piri Thomas
Reading Warm-up B

Read the following passage. Pay special attention to the underlined words. Then, read it again, and complete the activities. Use a separate sheet of paper for your written answers.

In early boxing, rules were <u>improvised</u> on the spot. Whatever seemed right at the moment was allowed. Today, there are standard rules for boxing. These rules add <u>clarity</u> to the sport by defining what boxers can and cannot do.

<u>Numerous</u> rules in amateur boxing are different from professional boxing. They are designed to protect the safety of the boxers. For example, professional fighters are rewarded for being forceful. They earn points for knocking down or knocking out their opponents. The objective of amateur boxing is to win points by landing correct blows on the opponent's target area. Knockdowns and knock-outs do not earn points. Amateur rules also apply to women's boxing, an <u>emerging</u> sport.

<u>Mild</u> injuries such as small cuts or slight bruising happen in all boxing events. Even in <u>sparring</u> matches, where the boxers use light blows, injuries sometimes occur. During a professional contest, a fighter's injuries can be extreme. The bout is stopped only when a boxer is knocked out or can no longer continue. In amateur boxing, the rules are more forgiving. For example, the contest ends when bleeding or swelling around the eye limits a boxer's vision.

There is also a difference in the number of rounds allowed. In early boxing, an event could last a long time. It was not unusual for a fight to continue for 30 rounds. In fact, the <u>challenger</u> Paddy Ryan defeated the English champion, Joe Goss, in 1880 after 87 rounds! Today a professional fight is limited to 12 rounds of 3 minutes each. An amateur contest may go up to four 3-minute rounds. Female boxers whose bodies are less <u>muscular</u> are allowed three 2-minute rounds. Contests for boxers under the age of 17 are even shorter.

1. Circle the word that tells what boxers <u>improvised</u>. Use a synonym for *improvised* in a sentence.

2. Underline the words that tell how rules add <u>clarity</u>. Use *clarity* in a sentence.

3. Underline words that tell where <u>numerous</u> rules of professional boxing are different. Rewrite the sentence using a synonym for *numerous*.

4. Underline the words that tell what sport is <u>emerging</u>. Describe another sport that is *emerging*.

5. Underline the words that describe <u>mild</u> injuries. Rewrite the sentence using a synonym for *mild*.

6. Circle the words that describe a <u>sparring</u> match. Write a sentence using *sparring*.

7. Underline the words that tell what the <u>challenger</u> did. Describe a time when your favorite sports team was a *challenger*.

8. Circle the words that identify less <u>muscular</u> boxers. Then describe someone who or something that is *muscular*.

"Amigo Brothers" by Piri Thomas
Reading: Make Inferences by Recognizing Details

Short story writers do not directly tell you everything there is to know about the characters, setting, and events. Instead, they leave it to you to **make inferences,** or logical guesses, about unstated information.

To form inferences, you must **recognize details** in the story and consider their importance. For example, in "Amigo Brothers," the narrator says, "While some youngsters were into street negatives, Antonio and Felix slept, ate, rapped, and dreamt positive." You can use that clue to infer that Felix and Antonio stayed out of trouble.

DIRECTIONS: *The sentences in the left-hand column of this chart offer details about the amigo brothers. In the right-hand column, describe what the details tell you about one or both of these characters.*

Detail About a Character	Inference About the Character
1. "If it's fair, *hermano,* I'm for it." Antonio admired the courage of a tugboat pulling a barge five times its welterweight size.	
2. Tony jogged away. Felix watched his friend disappear from view, throwing rights and lefts. Both fighters had a lot of psyching up to do before the big fight.	
3. Felix did a fast shuffle, bobbing and weaving, while letting loose a torrent of blows that would demolish whatever got in its way. It seemed to impress the brothers, who went about their own business.	
4. [Felix] fought off a series of rights and lefts and came back with a strong right that taught Antonio respect.	
5. The announcer turned to point to the winner and found himself alone. Arm in arm the champions had already left the ring.	

"**Amigo Brothers**" by Piri Thomas
Literary Analysis: Conflict

Most fictional stories center on a **conflict**—a struggle between opposing forces. There are two kinds of conflict:

- When there is an **external conflict,** a character struggles with an outside force such as another character or nature.
- When there is an **internal conflict,** a character struggles with himself or herself to overcome opposing feelings, beliefs, needs, or desires. An internal conflict takes place in a character's mind.

The **resolution,** or outcome of the conflict, often comes toward the end of the story, when the problem is settled in some way.

A story can have additional, smaller conflicts that develop the main conflict. In "Amigo Brothers," for example, a small external conflict occurs one morning as Felix and Antonio work out. There is tension between them, and Felix says, "Let's stop a while, bro. I think we both got something to say to each other." A minor internal conflict occurs when Felix mentions that he has stayed awake at night, "pulling punches" on Antonio. Felix struggles with the conflict between his wish not to harm his friend and his desire to win the fight.

DIRECTIONS: *Based on details in each of the following passages from "Amigo Brothers," identify the conflict as* External *or* Internal. *Then, explain your answer.*

1. He tried not to think of Felix, feeling he had succeeded in psyching his mind. But only in the ring would he really know.

   Type of conflict: _____

   Explanation: _____

2. He walked up some dark streets, deserted except for small pockets of wary-looking kids wearing gang colors. Despite the fact that he was Puerto Rican like them, they eyed him as a stranger to their turf.

   Type of conflict: _____

   Explanation: _____

3. Antonio was passing some heavy time on his rooftop. How would the fight tomorrow affect his relationship with Felix? After all, fighting was like any other profession. Friendship had nothing to do with it. A gnawing doubt crept in.

   Type of conflict: _____

   Explanation: _____

4. Felix and Antonio turned and faced each other squarely in a fighting pose. Felix wasted no time. He came fast, head low, half hunched toward his right shoulder, and lashed out with a straight left.

   Type of conflict: _____

   Explanation: _____

"Amigo Brothers" by Piri Thomas
Vocabulary Builder

Word List

devastating	perpetual	dispelled	evading

A. DIRECTIONS: *Think about the meaning of the italicized word in each sentence. Then, in your own words, answer the question that follows and briefly explain your answer.*

1. The hurricane was *devastating* to the island of Puerto Rico. How did the hurricane affect the island?

   _____

2. When in training, the boxer worked out all day long, her body in *perpetual* motion. How would you describe the boxer when she is in training?

   _____

3. The huge audience that crowded onto the bleachers *dispelled* the rumor that there was little interest in the fight. What happened to the rumor?

   _____

4. The challenger ducked and bobbed, *evading* his opponent's punches. What did the challenger's moves allow him to do?

   _____

B. DIRECTIONS: *On the line, write the letter of the word whose meaning is* opposite *that of the Word List word.*

____ 1. perpetual
   A. permanent   B. temporary   C. strong   D. wide

____ 2. devastating
   A. confusing   B. appearing   C. harmful   D. helpful

____ 3. dispelled
   A. dispersed   B. crumbled   C. gathered   D. hypnotized

____ 4. evading
   A. confronting   B. watching   C. escaping   D. explaining

"Amigo Brothers" by Piri Thomas
Support for Writing an Anecdote

Before writing an **anecdote** that tells what might have happened if one of the "amigo brothers" had been knocked out during the fight, use this graphic organizer. In the rectangle, list details about the fight that you imagine. In the two ovals below it, describe how each boy would feel about the knockout. Then, in the squares below the ovals, describe one way in which the character might act to resolve the conflict.

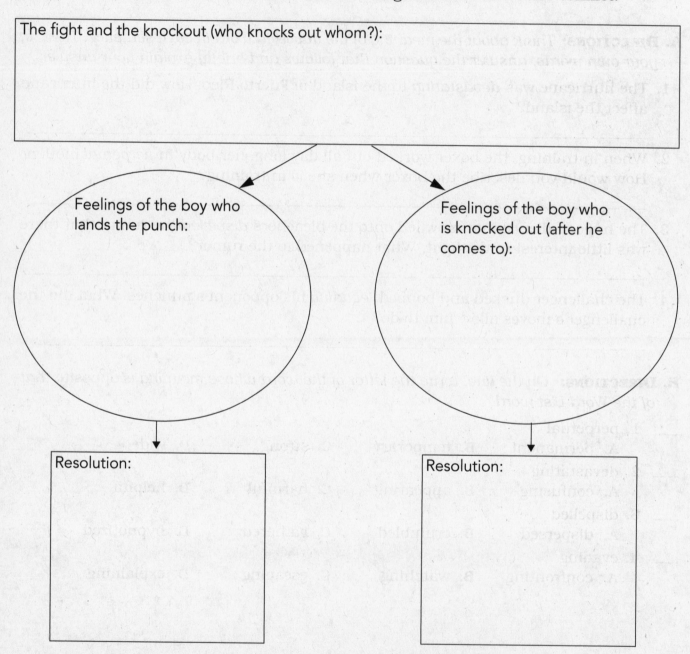

The fight and the knockout (who knocks out whom?):

Feelings of the boy who lands the punch:

Feelings of the boy who is knocked out (after he comes to):

Resolution:

Resolution:

Now use your notes to write an anecdote telling what might have happened if Antonio or Felix had been knocked out. Be sure to tell whether the boys' friendship lasts beyond the fight. How do they act afterward?

"Amigo Brothers" by Piri Thomas
Support for Extend Your Learning

Research and Technology

After you have found sources that describe amateur and professional boxing, use this Venn diagram to make notes showing how the two sports are alike, how they are different, and what elements they have in common.

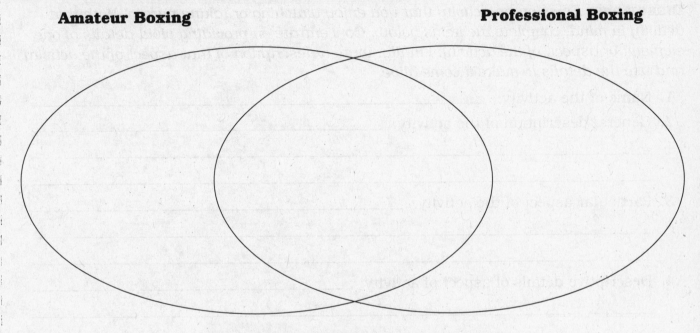

Amateur Boxing   **Professional Boxing**

Elements in Common to Both Sports

Listening and Speaking

In preparation for presenting a **news story** that describes the fight between Antonio and Felix, complete the following items:

Events that take place before the fight: _____

Comment made by Antonio: _____

Comment made by Felix: _____

Events that take place during the fight: _____

Events that take place after the fight: _____

Comment made by Antonio: _____

Comment made by Felix: _____

Name _____ Date _____

"Amigo Brothers" by Piri Thomas
Enrichment: Describing an Activity

In "Amigo Brothers," Felix and Antonio are friends who face each other in a match to determine which of them will represent the Boys Club in the Golden Gloves Championship Tournament. Piri Thomas describes their boxing match in great detail, allowing readers to form a vivid mental image of the fight.

DIRECTIONS: *Envision an activity that you enjoy watching or taking part in. With that activity in mind, complete the items below. Concentrate on providing vivid details of one element, or aspect, of the activity. Finally, write a description of that aspect of the activity and use the details to make it come alive.*

1. Name of the activity: _____

2. General description of the activity: _____
_____
_____

3. Particular aspect of the activity: _____
_____
_____

4. Descriptive details of aspect of activity: _____
_____
_____
_____
_____

5. Detailed description of aspect of activity: _____
_____
_____
_____
_____
_____
_____

"**The Third Wish**" by Joan Aiken
"**Amigo Brothers**" by Piri Thomas
Build Language Skills: Vocabulary

The Prefix *ob-*

The prefix *ob-* generally means "against" or "blocking." The word *object,* which can mean "speak against," begins with the prefix *ob-*. *Ob-* also appears at the beginning of *obstruction, obstacle,* and *obstructive,* which all have meanings related to being blocked, or "not able to continue."

A. DIRECTIONS: *Read the definition of each word that begins with the prefix* ob-*. Then, complete each sentence with the word from the list that makes the best sense. Use each word only once.*

obstacle:	something that stands in the way
obstinate:	sticking to a belief no matter what
obstruct:	to block by putting something in the way
obstructive:	blocking by putting something in the way

1. The jogger had to go around an _____ in the form of a tree that had fallen across her path.

2. That huge satellite dish will _____ my view of the mountain.

3. She was _____ in her views, refusing to change her mind no matter what she read.

4. In the negotiations, one side added so many requirements and was generally so _____ that no settlement could be reached.

Academic Vocabulary Practice

B. DIRECTIONS: *Indicate whether the following sentences make sense if the italicized Academic Vocabulary words are used in the way they are defined in your textbook. Then, explain why each sentence does or does not make sense.*

1. Emily ignored the evidence, relying on her feelings to *conclude* that the man was guilty.

   Yes/No: _____ **Explanation:** _____

2. The witness swore that he had seen the man put an *object* in his pocket.

   Yes/No: _____ **Explanation:** _____

3. The student's paper is well written even though it does not have a *subject.*

   Yes/No: _____ **Explanation:** _____

4. The jurors decided that the woman with a reputation for lying was a *credible* witness.

   Yes/No: _____ **Explanation:** _____

5. A person's *perspective* may be influenced by place of birth, education, and other factors.

   Yes/No: _____ **Explanation:** _____

"The Third Wish" by Joan Aiken
"Amigo Brothers" by Piri Thomas
Build Language Skills: Grammar

Adjectives

An **adjective** modifies or describes a noun or pronoun. An adjective may answer the questions *what kind? how many? which one?* or *whose?*

In this sentence, *beautiful* modifies *woman.* It tells what kind of woman appeared.

A *beautiful* <u>woman</u> suddenly appeared.

In this sentence, *two* modifies *boys.* It tells which boys continued to run together.

The *two* <u>boys</u> continued to run together.

A. DIRECTIONS: *Underline the adjective or adjectives in each sentence.*

1. Mr. Peters drove along a straight, empty stretch of road.
2. He heard strange cries coming from a distant bush.
3. A great white swan suddenly changed into a little man.
4. The grateful stranger granted Mr. Peters several wishes.
5. Mr. Peters soon had a gorgeous wife with pretty blue-green eyes.
6. Antonio was fair, lean, and lanky, while Felix was dark, short, and husky.
7. Antonio's lean form and long reach made him the better boxer.
8. Felix's short and muscular frame made him the better slugger.
9. Large posters were plastered on the walls of local shops.
10. The fighters changed from their street clothes into fighting gear.

B. Writing Application: *Write a sentence in response to each set of instructions.*

1. Write a sentence about Leita, using the adjective *attractive.*

   _____

   _____

2. Write a sentence about the forest, using the adjectives *dark* and *remote.*

   _____

   _____

3. Write a sentence about Antonio Cruz, using the adjectives *lean* and *talented.*

   _____

   _____

4. Write a sentence about Felix Vargas, using the adjectives *short* and *powerful.*

   _____

   _____

"Amigo Brothers" by Piri Thomas
Selection Test A

Critical Reading *Identify the letter of the choice that best answers the question.*

_____ 1. In "Amigo Brothers," what do both Antonio and Felix dream of becoming someday?
  A. a boxing trainer
  B. a lightweight champion
  C. the owner of a gym
  D. the director of the Boys Club

_____ 2. Antonio and Felix have a collection of *Fight* magazines and scrapbooks filled with newspaper clippings and tickets from boxing matches. What do these details show about the boys?
  A. They spend too much money on magazines.
  B. They should invest in new scrapbooks.
  C. They are extremely interested in boxing.
  D. They are the very best of friends.

_____ 3. Felix says that he and Antonio have to act like strangers when they box each other. What inference can you draw from that statement?
  A. They do not want to let their friendship get in the way of winning.
  B. They do not want the spectators to know that they are friends.
  C. Boxers who know their opponents do not usually win championships.
  D. Boxers who know each other are not permitted to fight each other.

_____ 4. What is the main external conflict in "Amigo Brothers"?
  A. the friendship between Antonio and Felix
  B. the boxing match between Antonio and Felix
  C. the race that Antonio and Felix run along the East River
  D. the contest between the lower east side of Manhattan and the South Bronx

_____ 5. In "Amigo Brothers," why does Felix go to the movies?
  A. so that he does not have to talk to his aunt
  B. so that he can enjoy a good boxing movie
  C. so that he can relax on the night before the big fight
  D. so that he can keep from thinking about Antonio

_____ 6. Which passage reveals Antonio's internal conflict over the fight with Felix?

A. "Antonio was passing some heavy time on his rooftop. How would the fight tomorrow affect his relationship with Felix?"

B. "Antonio wore white trunks, black socks, and black shoes. Felix wore sky blue trunks, red socks, and white boxing shoes."

C. "Antonio countered with his own flurry, forcing Felix to the ground."

D. "It was Antonio who came out fast, charging across the ring. Felix braced himself but couldn't ward off the barrage of punches."

_____ 7. In "Amigo Brothers," why does the boxing match take place in a park?

A. The gym is not air conditioned and would be too hot.

B. The promoters are unable to get permission to use the gym.

C. The gym is not large enough to accommodate the crowd.

D. The nearest gym is a long walk from a subway station.

_____ 8. What does this passage from "Amigo Brothers" tell you about the fight?

Rights to the body. Lefts to the head. Neither fighter was giving an inch.

A. Both fighters are saving their strength.

B. Both fighters are the same height.

C. Both fighters are in pain.

D. Both fighters are doing their best.

_____ 9. In "Amigo Brothers," what does the description of the fight suggest about Antonio and Felix?

A. Neither one can win a championship.

B. They are both good boxers.

C. Neither one is doing his best.

D. They have tried hard not to hurt each other.

_____ 10. What inference about Antonio and Felix can you draw from this passage?

The announcer turned to point to the winner and found himself alone. Arm in arm the champions had already left the ring.

A. They care more about their friendship than about who has won the fight.

B. They are too beaten up to wait to hear the announcement of the winner.

C. They will both represent the Boys Club in the championship tournament.

D. They are grateful that the fight is over and have gone to their dressing rooms.

Vocabulary and Grammar

___ 11. When Antonio is *evading* his opponent's fists, what is he doing?

    A. He is avoiding being punched.

    B. He is fighting back with equal force.

    C. He is tricking his opponent.

    D. He is giving in to his opponent.

___ 12. Antonio's blows are *devastating*. What else might be *devastating*?

    A. a car

    B. a movie

    C. a hurricane

    D. a vacation

___ 13. Which word in this sentence from "Amigo Brothers" is an adjective?

    They fooled around with a few jabs at the air, slapped skin, and then took off.

    A. around

    B. few

    C. air

    D. slapped

___ 14. Which word in this sentence from "Amigo Brothers" does *great* modify?

    The fight had created great interest in the neighborhood.

    A. fight

    B. created

    C. interest

    D. neighborhood

Essay

15. In "Amigo Brothers," Antonio and Felix are best friends who fight each other in a boxing match. In an essay, describe Felix and Antonio's friendship. What do they have in common? What dreams are important to them? At the end of the match, how do they show that their friendship is important?

16. In an essay, describe the conflict in "Amigo Brothers." What is the main external conflict between Antonio and Felix? What internal conflicts might there be? How is the main conflict resolved? Support your points with references to the story.

"Amigo Brothers" by Piri Thomas
Selection Test B

Critical Reading *Identify the letter of the choice that best completes the statement or answers the question.*

____ 1. In this passage from "Amigo Brothers," which detail shows that Felix is experiencing an internal conflict about the upcoming boxing match?

"Since we found out it was going to be me and you, I've been awake at night, pulling punches on you, trying not to hurt you."

A. He admits that he is staying awake at night thinking about the fight.
B. He states openly that the fight will be between him and Antonio.
C. He admits that he has been thinking about fighting Antonio.
D. He states that he does not want to hurt Antonio.

____ 2. What does this passage from "Amigo Brothers" say about the conflict in the story?

"We both are *cheverote* fighters and we both want to win. But only one of us can win. There ain't no draws in the eliminations."

A. Each boy is confident that he will be the winner.
B. Each boy thinks that the other will be eliminated.
C. Both boys want to win, and they know that only one of them can win.
D. Both boys want to win, and neither wants the match to end in a draw.

____ 3. What inference can you draw from this speech that Felix makes to Antonio in "Amigo Brothers"?

"When we get into the ring it's gotta be like we never met. We gotta be like two heavy strangers that want the same thing and only one can have it. You understand, don'tcha?"

A. Felix believes that they would be happier if they had never become friends.
B. Felix believes that after the match they will be strangers to each other.
C. Felix believes that after the match they will no longer be friends.
D. Felix believes that they must not think about their friendship during the match.

____ 4. In "Amigo Brothers," why do Felix and Antonio agree not to see each other until after the match?
A. They are ready to fight each other.
B. They are angry with each other.
C. Each wants to focus on the match rather than their friendship.
D. Each is afraid the other will discover something about his fighting style.

____ 5. How are the external and internal conflicts of "Amigo Brothers" related to each other?
A. The external conflict in *The Champion* represents each character's internal conflict.
B. The external conflict of the fight brings about an internal conflict in each character.
C. Their internal conflicts lead them to face each other, bringing about an external conflict.
D. The internal conflict is within Felix, while the external conflict is between the two friends.

___ 6. In "Amigo Brothers," how does Felix attempt to psyche himself for the big fight?
   A. Watching a fight movie, he sees himself as the champ and Antonio as the challenger.
   B. On a run by the East River, he practices his moves while envisioning Antonio's face.
   C. In the South Bronx, he fights a gang of boys who are hanging out on the street.
   D. At the gym with his trainer, he works out harder than he ever has before.

___ 7. What inference can you draw from this passage from "Amigo Brothers"?
   Antonio danced in carefully. He knew Felix had the habit of playing possum when hurt, to sucker an opponent within reach of the powerful bombs he carried in each fist.
   A. Felix can be very violent.
   B. Felix does not fight fairly.
   C. Antonio is more graceful than Felix.
   D. Antonio knows Felix's fighting style.

___ 8. What does this passage from "Amigo Brothers" suggest about Antonio's abilities as a fighter?
   Antonio danced, a joy to behold. His left hand was like a piston pumping jabs one right after another with seeming ease.
   A. He moves gracefully and punches fast.
   B. The spectators love watching him fight.
   C. He must dance better than he boxes.
   D. He punches fast but moves slowly.

___ 9. What can you infer from this passage from "Amigo Brothers"?
   They looked around and then rushed toward each other. A cry of alarm surged through Tompkins Square Park.
   A. The fighters are extremely angry with each other.
   B. The fighters have incited a riot among the spectators.
   C. The crowd is impressed with the fighters' strength and ability.
   D. The crowd thinks that the boxers are going to fight brutally.

___ 10. At the end of the boxing match, the narrator of "Amigo Brothers" says that Felix and Antonio "would always be champions to each other." What is the meaning of that statement?
   A. The boys will always think highly of each other.
   B. Both contestants have won the match.
   C. Both boys will become championship boxers.
   D. The boys are relieved that the fight is over.

___ 11. What do Antonio and Felix have in common throughout the story?
   A. Both are tall and lean.
   B. Both have a long reach.
   C. Both want to fight fairly and win.
   D. Each thinks the other is the better fighter.

Vocabulary and Grammar

_____ 12. When a boxer is *evading* punches thrown by an opponent, he or she may be
A. bobbing and weaving.
B. punching and jabbing.
C. giving in.
D. playing tricks.

_____ 13. What is the meaning of the word *dispelled* in this sentence from "Amigo Brothers"?
If Felix had any small doubt about their friendship affecting their fight, it was being neatly <u>dispelled</u>.

A. increased
B. confirmed
C. driven away
D. thought over

_____ 14. Something that could be described as *perpetual* is
A. a boxing match.
B. the ocean's tide.
C. a big storm.
D. a vacation.

_____ 15. Which two words in this sentence from "Amigo Brothers" are used as adjectives?
In the quiet early dark, he peered over the ledge.

A. quiet, early
B. quiet, dark
C. early, dark
D. dark, ledge

_____ 16. Which word in this sentence from "Amigo Brothers" does *awesome* modify?
Antonio's face, superimposed on the screen, was hit by the awesome blow.

A. face
B. superimposed
C. hit
D. blow

Essay

17. At the end of "Amigo Brothers," the reader never learns which boy has earned the right to represent the Boys Club in the Golden Gloves Championship Tournament. In an essay, explain which contestant deserved to win. Support your choice with examples from the story.

18. In an essay, describe the overall external conflict and the overlapping internal conflicts in "Amigo Brothers." How does Piri Thomas weave the external and internal conflicts together to create an interesting story? Finally, describe the resolution, and tell what it teaches the characters.

Vocabulary Warm-up Word Lists

Study these words from "Zoo." Then, apply your knowledge to the activities that follow.

Word List A

breed [BREED] *n.* a particular kind or type of animal or plant
Alexander's favorite <u>breed</u> of dog is the golden retriever.

clutching [CLUHCH ing] *v.* holding on to something tightly
Kevin was <u>clutching</u> his new baseball mitt to his chest.

constantly [KAHN stuhnt lee] *adv.* happening over and over; endlessly; continually
The annoying child was <u>constantly</u> whining about something.

horrors [HAHR uhrz] *n.* things that cause a strong feeling of fear or disgust
The novel *The Red Badge of Courage* tells of the <u>horrors</u> of war.

limit [LIM it] *n.* the greatest number or amount allowed
The speed <u>limit</u> on this highway is fifty-five miles per hour.

odd [AHD] *adj.* not usual or ordinary; peculiar; strange
The animal's <u>odd</u> behavior worried the zookeeper.

scurried [SKER eed] *v.* ran quickly or hastily; scampered
The mouse <u>scurried</u> across the floor, fleeing from the cat.

seeking [SEEK ing] *v.* searching for; looking for
<u>Seeking</u> answers to her questions, Justine did research online.

Word List B

adults [uh DULTS] *n.* mature persons
<u>Adults</u> pay twice as much as children for the movie.

annual [AN yoo uhl] *adj.* happening or appearing once a year
The bake sale is an <u>annual</u> fund-raising event at our school.

awe [AW] *n.* a mixed feeling of reverence, fear, and wonder, caused by something powerful
The eruption of the volcano inspired <u>awe</u> in the scientists.

clustered [KLUS terd] *v.* gathered together as a bunch
The baby chicks <u>clustered</u> around their mother.

daybreak [DAY brayk] *n.* dawn; the time of morning when daylight first appears
The farmer was up at <u>daybreak</u> to milk the cows.

expense [ek SPENS] *n.* financial cost; fee
The fancy dinner was not worth the <u>expense</u>.

jagged [JAG id] *adj.* having sharp points or notches
Dominic used the <u>jagged</u> rock to cut the branch into firewood.

reveal [ri VEEL] *v.* to expose to view; show; exhibit; display
Charlotte opened the curtains to <u>reveal</u> the spectacular view.

"Zoo" by Edward D. Hoch
Vocabulary Warm-up Exercises

Exercise A *Fill in each blank in the paragraph below with an appropriate word from Word List A. Use each word only once.*

Although she had been dealing with the [1] _____ of training a puppy that [2] _____ misbehaved, Carla decided she wanted another pet. She did some research on cats and found out about a [3] _____ she liked. She spent many weeks [4] _____ a Manx cat. The Manx is an [5] _____ cat—it does not have a tail. Finally, she heard there was one at the pet shop. Carla [6] _____ over there as quickly as she could. The price of the cat was a little over the [7] _____ she had set for herself. Carla was [8] _____ her money in her hand when she decided that the expense was worth it. She was sure her puppy would love the tail-less cat.

Exercise B *Answer the questions with complete explanations.*

Example: If Mr. Greene <u>detests</u> spinach, would he enjoy having it with dinner?
No; <u>detests</u> means "dislikes intensely," so Mr. Greene would not enjoy eating spinach.

1. If something is an <u>expense</u>, are you likely to get it for free?
   _____

2. If you <u>reveal</u> a secret, are others likely to hear about it?
   _____

3. If you attend an <u>annual</u> family gathering, do you go to it every month?
   _____

4. If you walk barefoot on <u>jagged</u> rocks, are you likely to cut your feet?
   _____

5. If only <u>adults</u> are invited to a party, could your grandparents go to it?
   _____

6. If you were in <u>awe</u> of something, would you be bored by it?
   _____

7. If plants are <u>clustered</u> in a garden, are they scattered around the garden?
   _____

8. If you want to be awake at <u>daybreak</u>, would you get up at 9 A.M.?
   _____

"Zoo" by Edward D. Hoch
Reading Warm-up A

Read the following passage. Pay special attention to the underlined words. Then, read it again, and complete the activities. Use a separate sheet of paper for your written answers.

More than 50 million years ago, a horselike creature <u>scurried</u> through the North American forests. This four-legged animal was about the size of a fox, but it was related to the modern horse. It fed on fruit and leaves. Its feet had pads like those of a dog. However, each toe ended in a hoof rather than a claw. Fossil hunters found the bones of this <u>odd</u> animal about a hundred years ago. They named it eohippus, which means "dawn horse." They thought it was a direct ancestor of the horse.

Modern researchers have been <u>seeking</u> a better understanding of the link between the eohippus and the horse. They agree that the modern horse probably descends from a <u>breed</u> of smaller animals. However, they do not believe that the path from eohippus to horse was direct.

Many of the early horselike creatures died out long ago. One branch survived, however. About a million years ago, it produced animals very similar to today's wild horses. Then, less than 10,000 years ago, many of those early horses died out. No one knows why. Climate changes might have had something to do with it. Another cause might have been the humans who <u>constantly</u> hunted the animals. Only the horses of Asia and several zebras survived. All the horses of North America died out.

How, then, did we get all the horses that the American cowboys rode? Imagine those cowboys. They are <u>clutching</u> at the reins of their mighty steeds. Where did those horses come from? Historians believe that the ancestors of those horses were brought to the New World in the 1500s. They were brought on ships by the Spanish explorers.

Today, tens of thousands of wild horses gallop across the American West. There is a danger that the land cannot support all of them. To put a <u>limit</u> on their numbers, the U.S. government captures hundreds of horses each year and puts them up for adoption. By doing that, government workers protect the herds from the <u>horrors</u> of self-destruction.

1. Circle the words that tell what <u>scurried</u> through the North American forests. What does **scurried** mean?

2. Circle the word that tells what is described as <u>odd</u>. What does **odd** mean?

3. Circle the words that tell who have been <u>seeking</u> a better understanding. Use **seeking** in a sentence.

4. Circle the word that further describes the <u>breed</u> of animals from which the modern horse descends. What **breed** of animal would you like to have as a pet?

5. Why is it a bad idea to hunt one kind of animal <u>constantly</u>? Use **constantly** in a sentence.

6. Circle the words that tell what the cowboys are <u>clutching</u>. In your own words, tell what **clutching** means.

7. Circle the words that tell what government workers put a <u>limit</u> on. Use **limit** in a sentence.

8. Circle the words that tell what <u>horrors</u> the government is trying to prevent. What does **horrors** mean?

"**Zoo**" by Edward D. Hoch
Reading Warm-up B

Read the following passage. Pay special attention to the underlined words. Then, read it again, and complete the activities. Use a separate sheet of paper for your written answers.

Since the time of the earliest humans on Earth, <u>adults</u> and children alike have gazed in <u>awe</u> at the night sky. They have marveled until <u>daybreak</u> at its beauty and mystery. We can imagine our ancestors pointing to groups of stars. They would compare them to familiar objects, such as dippers, bears, and crabs. Then they would name the groups of stars, the constellations. Of course we know now that the stars in constellations are not <u>clustered</u> together, even though they appear to be. In fact, they are at greatly varying distances from Earth. Because all the stars in a constellation lie within the same line of sight, they seem to be connected.

Modern tools of astronomy <u>reveal</u> many details about the universe that earlier humans never knew. For example, telescopes and space probes have told us a great deal about Mars. We know more about Mars than we know about any planet other than Earth. Its cold, thin, transparent atmosphere allows us to observe the features of its surface. The spacecraft *Mariner 9* orbited the planet in 1971. It photographed the entire surface. Pictures of a Martian "Grand Canyon" show <u>jagged</u> formations more than two and a half miles deep in some places. *Mariner 9* also showed what appear to be dried riverbeds. These suggest a long-ago presence of water on Mars. We know that a day on Mars lasts 24 hours, 37 minutes, a little longer than a day on Earth. A year on Mars, however, is much longer than a year on Earth. It takes Mars 687 days to orbit the sun, compared with the 365 days it takes the Earth to orbit the sun.

Science-fiction writers delight in writing about Mars as a good place for human beings to live. Is it worth the <u>expense</u> of finding out whether they are right? Many people think so. Who knows? Maybe in the future we will be spending our <u>annual</u> vacations on Mars.

1. Circle the word that tells who gazed at the sky with the <u>adults</u>. Name one responsibility *adults* have that children do not have.

2. Circle the words that tell what the earliest humans gazed at in <u>awe</u>. Use *awe* in a sentence.

3. Underline the words that tell what the people marveled at until <u>daybreak</u>. What is another word for *daybreak*?

4. Underline the words that explain what early humans thought were <u>clustered</u> together. Define *clustered*.

5. Underline the words that tell what modern tools of astronomy <u>reveal</u>. Use *reveal* in a sentence.

6. Underline the words that tell what is <u>jagged</u>. Define *jagged*.

7. What <u>expense</u> is being questioned? Describe an unnecessary *expense*—one that people can do without.

8. Circle the word that tells what kind of <u>annual</u> event is being described. Use *annual* in a sentence.

"Zoo" by Edward D. Hoch

Reading: Make Inferences by Reading Between the Lines and Asking Questions

An **inference** is an intelligent guess, based on what the text tells you, about things *not* stated directly in the text. Suppose a story opens with crowds forming to wait for the arrival of an interplanetary zoo. You can infer from those details that the zoo will soon arrive.

One way to make inferences is to **read between the lines by asking questions,** such as, "Why does the writer include these details?" and "Why does the writer leave out certain information?" In the opening sentence of "Zoo," for example, we learn that "the children were always good during the month of August." The next thing we learn is that the Interplanetary Zoo comes to Chicago every year around August 23. Why does the writer open his story with these details? What conclusion can be drawn about why the children are always good in August? From these details you can infer that the children are good in August because they want their parents to take them to the interplanetary zoo.

DIRECTIONS: *Read the following passages from "Zoo," and answer the questions that follow.*

1. In the following passage, what inference can you draw from the detail that the people are clutching dollars?

   Before daybreak the crowds would form, long lines of children and adults both, each one clutching his or her dollar and waiting with wonderment to see what race of strange creatures the Professor had brought this year.

   _____

   _____

2. In the following passage, what inference can you draw about the Professor from the description of his clothing?

   Soon the good Professor himself made an appearance, wearing his many-colored rainbow cape and top hat.

   _____

3. In the following passage, what inference can you draw about the horse spiders from the way they file out of their cages, listen to Hugo's parting words, and then scurry away?

   The odd horse-spider creatures filed quickly out of their cages. Professor Hugo was there to say a few parting words, and then they scurried away in a hundred different directions, seeking their homes among the rocks.

   _____

4. In the following passage, what inference can you draw from the she-creature's reaction to her mate and offspring's arrival?

   In one house, the she-creature was happy to see the return of her mate and offspring. She babbled a greeting in the strange tongue and hurried to embrace them.

   _____

Name _____ Date _____

"Zoo" by Edward D. Hoch
Literary Analysis: Theme

A story's **theme** is its central idea, message, or insight into life. Occasionally, the author states the theme directly. More often, however, the theme is implied.

A theme is *not* the same as the subject of a work. For example, if the subject, or topic, of a story is similarities and differences, the theme will be a message about that subject, such as "differences between groups of people can keep people from seeing the ways in which they are similar."

As you read, look at what characters say and do, where the story takes place, and objects that seem important in order to determine the theme—what the author wants to teach you about life.

DIRECTIONS: *Answer the following questions about "Zoo."*

1. What is the setting? If there is more than one setting, name and briefly describe each one.

   _____

   _____

2. What do the main characters say? Summarize the words spoken by Hugo, one of the people from Earth, the female horse spider, the male horse spider, and the little one.

   Hugo: _____

   Person from Earth: _____

   She-creature: _____

   He-creature: _____

   Little creature: _____

3. How do the characters act? Describe the actions of the people in Chicago and the actions of the horse-spider people.

   People in Chicago: _____

   _____

   Horse spiders: _____

   _____

4. What object or objects seem important?

   _____

5. What is the subject, or topic, of "Zoo"?

   _____

6. Based on these details, what would you say is the theme of "Zoo"?

   _____

"Zoo" by Edward D. Hoch
Vocabulary Builder

Word List

```
interplanetary    awe    expense
```

A. DIRECTIONS: *Complete each sentence with a word from the Word List.*

1. The _____ of interplanetary travel was high, but Professor Hugo earned the money back by charging admission to his zoo.
2. The crowd gazed in _____ at the terrifying yet unusual creatures.
3. Professor Hugo's _____ zoo visited Earth, Mars, Kaan, and many other planets.

B. DIRECTIONS: *Revise each sentence so that the Word List word is used logically.*

1. The *interplanetary* mission involved travel from Rome to Tokyo.

_____

_____

2. The spectators at the zoo were *awed* by the cute rabbits.

_____

3. The *expense* of the zoo allowed the promoter to make a great profit.

_____

_____

C. DIRECTIONS: *Write the letter of the word or phrase that is most* similar *in meaning to the Word List word.*

____ 1. awe
    A. arrogance and hatred
    B. terror and fear
    C. amazement and fear
    D. compassion and love

____ 2. expense
    A. cost
    B. amount
    C. total
    D. budget

____ 3. interplanetary
    A. between galaxies
    B. between planets
    C. universal
    D. worldwide

"Zoo" by Edward D. Hoch

Support for Writing a Letter to the Editor

Before you write your **letter to the editor,** think about whether zoo animals should live in natural habitats or cages. Then, on this graphic organizer, write down advantages and disadvantages of each environment.

Zoo Animals

Natural Habitats	**Cages**
Advantages: _____	Advantages: _____
Disadvantages: _____	Disadvantages: _____

Decide which position you want to take and draft a letter to the editor of a local newspaper in support of your position. Use your notes to back up your opinion with reasons and details that will persuade readers to take your side.

"Zoo" by Edward D. Hoch
Support for Extend Your Learning

Research and Technology

Answer these questions as you gather information for a **poster** advertising a zoo in your city, town, or state.

Where is the zoo located? _____

What are the zoo's hours? _____

What are the admission fees? _____

What special exhibits are there? _____

_____

What animals or sights would you recommend?

_____

Listening and Speaking

On the chart below, record information about a faraway place you might like to visit.

Name of place:		
Details of Trip	**Challenges**	**Benefits**
Location:		
Transportation:		
Language spoken:		
Approximate expense:		
Sights to see:		

Use your notes to prepare a **short speech** describing the challenges and benefits of travel to the place you have chosen.

"Zoo" by Edward D. Hoch
Enrichment: Characteristics of Imaginary Animals

"Zoo" describes the physical characteristics of the imaginary horse spider. We learn that the horse-spider creatures "looked like horses but ran up the walls of their cages like spiders." Like the horse spider, every animal—real or imagined—is special in its own way.

DIRECTIONS: *Invent an imaginary animal of your own. To prepare to write a description of your imaginary animal, complete this chart. The more detail you include, the better.*

Name of animal:
Size: _____   _____   _____
Color or colors: _____   _____
Number and appearance of legs: _____   _____
Shape and appearance of head: _____   _____
Other details: _____   _____   _____

Now, use your notes to write a description of your imaginary animal.

_____

_____

_____

_____

_____

_____

_____

Name _____   Date _____

"Zoo" by Edward D. Hoch
Selection Test A

Critical Reading *Identify the letter of the choice that best answers the question.*

_____ 1. In "Zoo," how often does Professor Hugo bring his zoo to Chicago?
   A. once every six hours
   B. once every month
   C. once every six months
   D. once every year

_____ 2. In "Zoo," Professor Hugo has brought three-legged creatures from Venus; tall, thin men from Mars; and horse spiders from a distant planet. How might you describe Professor Hugo's zoo?
   A. It displays the kinds of creatures found in any zoo.
   B. It displays a wide selection of interesting creatures.
   C. It displays strange creatures from outer space.
   D. It displays snakes, crocodiles, and other reptiles.

_____ 3. In "Zoo," how much do the people of Earth pay to see the interplanetary zoo?
   A. fifty cents
   B. one dollar
   C. two dollars
   D. five dollars

_____ 4. Why do ten thousand people go to see Professor Hugo's zoo while it is in Chicago?
   A. They have nothing better to do at that time of year.
   B. They are fascinated by the creatures on display.
   C. They want to win a chance to touch the zoo animals.
   D. They have been told by their friends how good the zoo is.

_____ 5. In "Zoo," Professor Hugo urges visitors to call their friends in other cities and tell them how much they enjoyed his zoo. What inference can you draw from this detail?
   A. He wants to make as many people happy as he can.
   B. He wants people in different cities to know each other better.
   C. He wants to promote the use of long-distance telephone service.
   D. He wants people to encourage their friends to see his show.

____ 6. In "Zoo," how does the she-creature from Kaan react when her mate and off-spring come home?

A. She scolds them for having stayed away so long.

B. She expresses concern because they had gone so far.

C. She babbles happily and rushes to hug them.

D. She feeds them dinner and prepares their beds.

____ 7. In "Zoo," what does the little horse spider especially enjoy on its visit around the universe?

A. the place called Earth

B. the men from Mars

C. the creatures from Venus

D. the creatures from Kaan

____ 8. In "Zoo," what do the horse spiders find strange about the people on Earth?

A. Some of them eat cooked meat.

B. Some of them live in apartments.

C. They speak many different languages.

D. They wear clothes and walk on two legs.

____ 9. In "Zoo," the he-creature says that the zoo is "well worth the nineteen commocs it costs." What inference can you draw from this statement?

A. The he-creature does not want to travel with Professor Hugo's zoo again.

B. The he-creature wants his wife to travel with the zoo the next time he goes.

C. The creatures in the zoo are paying Professor Hugo to travel with the zoo.

D. Professor Hugo is extremely popular on all the planets he visits.

____ 10. In "Zoo," Edward Hoch writes that the people of Earth are fascinated by the creatures from Kaan and the creatures from Kaan are fascinated by the people from Earth. What does this tell about the theme of the story?

A. It has to do with people's differences and similarities.

B. It has to do with the strangeness of space creatures.

C. It has to do with everyone's love of creatures in zoos.

D. It has to do with the interplanetary zoos of the future.

____ 11. In "Zoo," Hoch describes different creatures reacting to each other. What is he trying to show about people?

A. They are eager to learn from those who are different from them.

B. They want to get to know those who are different from them.

C. They automatically fear those who are different from them.

D. They are shy when they meet those who are different from them.

Vocabulary and Grammar

_____ 12. Which of the following sentences uses *interplanetary* correctly?

A. The *interplanetary* aircraft traveled from place to place on Earth.

B. The *interplanetary* flight from New York to London was cancelled.

C. The voyage from Earth to the moon was an *interplanetary* mission.

D. The *interplanetary* spaceship traveled from Earth to Mars.

_____ 13. What does a visitor to the zoo feel if he or she is in *awe* of the horse spiders?

A. fear and wonder

B. hostility and tenderness

C. surprise and anger

D. admiration and hatred

_____ 14. In the following sentence from "Zoo," which word is an adverb?

The children were always good during the month of August.

A. always

B. good

C. during

D. of

_____ 15. Which word in the following sentence does the adverb *quickly* modify?

The citizens of Earth clustered around as Professor Hugo's crew quickly collected the waiting dollars.

A. around

B. crew

C. collected

D. waiting

Essay

16. In an essay, answer these questions about the horse spiders of Kaan as they are described by Edward Hoch in "Zoo": How do the horse spiders act in their own home? How does the female act? What does the male say? What does the littlest off-spring say and do? How are the horse-spider creatures similar to human beings? How are they different from them?

17. In "Zoo," Edward Hoch is making a point about the way in which people think about those who are different from them. In an essay, explain Hoch's point more precisely. What two settings does he describe? What kinds of characters does he describe? What are some of the important things that the characters do? What does Hoch want us to learn about how people see those who are different from them?

"Zoo" by Edward D. Hoch
Selection Test B

Critical Reading *Identify the letter of the choice that best completes the statement or answers the question.*

____ 1. In "Zoo," for how long and when does Professor Hugo bring his zoo to the Chicago area?
   A. for twenty-three days every year
   B. for one day every twenty-third year
   C. for a day around the twenty-third of every month
   D. for six hours around the twenty-third of every August

____ 2. Professor Hugo is described as wearing a "many-colored rainbow cape and top hat." What can you infer from these details of his appearance?
   A. He likes colorful clothing.
   B. He is a typically flashy showman.
   C. He dresses up for each show.
   D. He is hiding his true identity.

____ 3. Professor Hugo tells his audience in Chicago, "If you enjoyed our zoo this year, telephone your friends in other cities about it." What can you infer from that remark?
   A. He plans to encourage interplanetary friendships.
   B. He is encouraging people to contact old friends.
   C. He wants to increase his business by word of mouth.
   D. He is being paid to advertise long-distance phone service.

____ 4. When the horse spiders reach Kaan, they listen to Professor Hugo's "parting words" and then "scurr[y] away in a hundred different directions, seeking their homes among the rocks." What can you infer about them based on those details?
   A. They respect Professor Hugo, and they live in cities among the rocks.
   B. They dislike Professor Hugo, and they will never again travel with him.
   C. They are tired from their long journey, and they are eager to get home.
   D. They are eager to get home, and they do not all live in the same region.

____ 5. From the point of view of the creatures from Kaan as they are described in "Zoo," what is strange about the people on Earth?
   A. They visit zoos and speak a strange language.
   B. They are horrified and fascinated by the zoo creatures.
   C. They walk on two legs and wear clothing.
   D. They use telephones and gather in large crowds.

____ 6. In "Zoo," how do the horse spiders view the cages that separate them from visitors?
   A. They believe they protect them.
   B. They believe they imprison them.
   C. They believe they are stage props.
   D. They believe they are unnecessary.

___ 7. In "Zoo," the he-creature remarks that the trip on the spaceship "is well worth the nineteen commocs it costs." Based on that statement, how would you define *commocs*?
   A. the children of the horse-spider creatures
   B. the money that is used on the planet of Kaan
   C. the caves in which the horse-spider creatures dwell
   D. the zoos that are constructed on the planet of Kaan

___ 8. The behavior of the humans and the horse spiders in "Zoo" suggests the story is
   A. about people's differences and similarities.
   B. about people's differences in intelligence.
   C. about people's curiosity about nature.
   D. about people's curiosity about space travel.

___ 9. At the end of "Zoo," we learn that horse spiders pay Professor Hugo to take them on voyages. From that information, the reader may infer that Professor Hugo
   A. is making a mistake.
   B. is a clever showman.
   C. is interested in scientific research.
   D. is an extremely wealthy man.

___ 10. In "Zoo," Edward Hoch takes a look at people's views of those who are different from them. What is his theme?
   A. People want to meet those who are different from them so they can learn from them.
   B. People want to meet those who are different from them because they are curious.
   C. People fear those who are different from them and so fail to see how they are similar.
   D. People shy away from people who are different from them and so fail to learn from them.

___ 11. Which of the following details best supports the theme of "Zoo"?
   A. The people of Chicago crowd around as Professor Hugo's crew collects their money.
   B. The people of Chicago are both horrified and fascinated by the horse-spider creatures.
   C. The creatures of Kaan listen to the professor's parting words and then scurry away.
   D. The young horse spider runs up the wall of its cave before speaking of its adventure.

Vocabulary and Grammar

___ 12. Which of the following scenes from "Zoo" shows characters in *awe*?
   A. Crowds come to the zoo and willingly pay to see the horse-spider creatures.
   B. Professor Hugo greets the crowd wearing a colorful cape and a top hat.
   C. The crowds are both horrified and fascinated by the horse spiders.
   D. The horse spiders leave their cages and scurry away to their homes.

____ **13.** The fact that Hugo's zoo is *interplanetary* means that it travels
   A. from one planet to another.
   B. from place to place on one planet.
   C. with creatures from another planet.
   D. from city to city on one continent.

____ **14.** In the following sentence from "Zoo," which word does the adverb *slowly* modify?
   And the crowds slowly filed by.
   A. And
   B. crowds
   C. filed
   D. by

____ **15.** Which word in the following sentence from "Zoo" is an adverb?
   "We must go now, but we will return next year on this date."
   A. must
   B. now
   C. next
   D. date

Essay

16. In an essay, discuss the theme of "Zoo." Consider these questions: What are the settings, and how do they help you determine the theme? What do characters say and do that helps you discover the theme? Mention at least three details in the story to support your points.

17. In an essay, describe Professor Hugo and the way in which he makes money. What does he look like? What does he say to his audience? Why do people pay him? Does he take advantage of people to make money? Cite at least two examples from "Zoo" to support your points.

Vocabulary Warm-up Word Lists

Study these words from "Ribbons." Then, apply your knowledge to the activities that follow.

Word List A

ankles [ANG kuhlz] *n.* joints that connect the leg to the foot
  Marilyn twisted her <u>ankles</u> when she fell.

ballet [ba LAY] *n.* a performance of dance and music, used to tell a story
  The Nutcracker is a <u>ballet</u> about a girl and her dreams of being carried to a fanciful land.

beginners [bee GIN erz] *n.* inexperienced individuals or those just starting out with something
  Before their first swimming lesson, the <u>beginners</u> were nervous.

clumsily [KLUHM zi lee] *adv.* carried out without grace or skill
  The quarterback <u>clumsily</u> dropped the football.

downward [DOWN wuhrd] *adv.* toward a lower place
  Jake looked <u>downward</u> at his soaking wet shoes.

exercises [EK ser sy zuhz] *n.* activities for the purpose of training or developing
  Lina's yoga <u>exercises</u> made her more flexible.

strapped [STRAPT] *v.* fastened with a strap
  The baby was <u>strapped</u> into the car seat.

wobbly [WAHB lee] *adj.* unsteady or shaky
  The <u>wobbly</u> table legs shook, causing the water to spill.

Word List B

attractive [uh TRAK tiv] *adj.* pleasant or pretty to look at
  The <u>attractive</u> teenager was offered a job as a model.

circulating [ser kyoo LAY ting] *v.* moving or coursing from place to place
  The model shows how blood is <u>circulating</u> throughout the body.

deliberately [di LIB er uht lee] *adv.* purposely
  She <u>deliberately</u> left an extra cookie on the plate for her brother.

illustrating [IL uh stray ting] *v.* explaining or making something clear with pictures
  This diagram is <u>illustrating</u> how to put the toy together.

legal [LEE guhl] *adj.* lawful or having to do with the law
  The defendant has certain <u>legal</u> rights.

mechanical [muh KAN uh kuhl] *adj.* operated by machinery; done in a machinelike way
  She sorted the mail in a <u>mechanical</u> way.

regained [ree GAYND] *v.* got back to, recovered
  The team <u>regained</u> its first-place ranking.

undid [uhn DID] *v.* reversed the doing of something
  Maria <u>undid</u> the buttons on the child's jacket and took it off.

Name _____ Date _____

Excercise A *Fill in each blank in the paragraph below with an appropriate word from Word List A. Use each word only once.*

At the circus last night we saw many sights. A sad clown wore giant shoes that
were [1] _____ to his [2] _____. He walked
[3] _____; he was not graceful at all. Another clown was so
[4] _____ we thought he would fall down—he was walking on stilts.
Baby elephants paraded by in pink ballerina outfits. First, they did warm-up
[5] _____. Then they danced a [6] _____, moving in time
to the classical music. From their high perches, the trapeze artists looked
[7] _____ on the audience before flying through the air. Finally, the
clowns drove toy cars as if they were [8] _____ just learning to drive. We
laughed as they bumped their cars into one another.

Excercise B *Answer the questions with complete explanations.*

Example: If Ms. Grey were feeling <u>blue,</u> would she be happy?
No; to feel blue is to feel sad, so Ms. Grey would not be happy.

1. If you <u>undid</u> the setting on an alarm clock, would you wake up on time?
   _____

2. If a singer performs in a <u>mechanical</u> way, does he sing with feeling?
   _____

3. Would an <u>attractive</u> painting be nice to look at?
   _____

4. Should a driver park her car in a <u>legal</u> parking place?
   _____

5. If someone did something <u>deliberately</u>, did he think about it ahead of time?
   _____

6. If the water in a fountain is not moving, is it <u>circulating</u>?
   _____

7. If a runner <u>regained</u> her lead in a race, would she be in first place again?
   _____

8. If your teacher is <u>illustrating</u> an idea, is she explaining it in words?
   _____

Name _____   Date _____

Read the following passage. Pay special attention to the underlined words. Then, read it again and complete the activities. Write your answers on a separate sheet of paper.

Have you ever been to a theater to see a <u>ballet</u>? This form of dance can be delicately beautiful, for it combines great physical skill with music and a story or special mood. The dancers make the movements look effortless, but in fact the movements take years of practice to perfect.

Many ballet dancers begin taking lessons when they are between eight and ten years old. <u>Beginners</u> learn the five basic positions of ballet. These positions involve turning the feet outward. In each position, the arms are held in a different way. Generally, the elbows are gently bent.

At lessons and practice, dancers do <u>exercises</u> at a *barre*. The *barre* is a wooden pole that runs horizontally along a wall. Dancers hold on to the *barre* when they practice their positions. They also raise their legs and place their feet on it.

The posture of a ballet dancer is important. Dancers must remain upright much of the time, and they must look graceful. Therefore, they must work on their balance. They must always look up and out and never <u>downward</u>, toward their feet.

Female ballet dancers, ballerinas, frequently dance on their toes. Therefore, their shoes have a wooden block built into the toe. The blocks support the dancer's weight. Toe slippers are covered in satin and <u>strapped</u> to the dancer's <u>ankles</u> with ribbon. Dancing on one's toes is very difficult. At first, the feet are <u>wobbly</u> because the position feels so awkward. Beginners may move <u>clumsily</u>. Only with constant practice can a dancer make a performance look easy and graceful.

A successful ballet performance beautifully matches the skillful steps of the dance to the mood of the music and the story. This combination makes ballet a wonderful art form.

1. Circle the words that tell what a <u>ballet</u> is. Define *ballet*.

2. Underline the words that tell when <u>beginners</u> start to learn ballet. What are *beginners*?

3. Circle the words that tell where the dancers do <u>exercises</u>. What kind of *exercises* might you do?

4. What is the opposite of <u>downward</u>? Use *downward* in a sentence.

5. Toe shoes are <u>strapped</u> to the dancer's <u>ankles</u>. Explain what that means. Use *strapped* and *ankles* in a sentence of your own.

6. Rewrite the sentence that contains the word <u>wobbly</u>, using a synonym for *wobbly*. What else might be *wobbly*?

7. Underline the words that tell how dancers stop moving <u>clumsily</u>. Define *clumsily*.

"Ribbons" by Laurence Yep
Reading Warm-up B

Read the following passage. Pay special attention to the underlined words. Then, read it again and complete the activities. Write your answers on a separate sheet of paper.

Hong Kong lies on the southeastern coast of China. The region is part of the mainland but also includes about 235 islands. Today, Hong Kong belongs to China. Before 1997, however, it was a British dependency for a long time. It had been part of Britain since the 1840s. At that time, Britain <u>deliberately</u> established itself in Hong Kong because Hong Kong was an <u>attractive</u> place for a port.

England made a treaty, a <u>legal</u> agreement, with China. According to the treaty, Hong Kong would belong to Britain for 99 years. The treaty <u>undid</u> Britain's rule of Hong Kong on July 1, 1997. That is when China <u>regained</u> control of Hong Kong.

Most people who live in Hong Kong are from other parts of China. In the ten years before Hong Kong was returned to China, many residents of Hong Kong left. They left because they were not sure how the change from British rule to Chinese rule would affect them. They went to the United States, Canada, and Australia.

So far, the change in power has been smooth. China has agreed to let Hong Kong make its own economic decisions for a period of 50 years. Therefore, many residents of Hong Kong who left have since returned. They believe that the Chinese government has shown that the agreement is not just <u>mechanical</u>. It is not just an agreement in name only.

Like the blood that is <u>circulating</u> through the human body, the lifeblood of Hong Kong's economy is trade and shipping. Hong Kong's location makes it an important economic center. Merchants are <u>illustrating</u> this every day by sending their goods from Hong Kong by air and water. For now, Hong Kong remains a strong center of commerce.

1. Underline the words that tell what Britain did <u>deliberately</u>. Define *deliberately*.

2. Circle the words that tell what place made an <u>attractive</u> port. Use *attractive* in a sentence.

3. Circle the word that tells what was <u>legal</u>. What does *legal* mean?

4. Underline the words that tell what the treaty <u>undid</u>. Use *undid* in a sentence.

5. Circle the words that tell what China <u>regained</u>. What does *regained* mean?

6. Circle the words that tell what is meant by a "<u>mechanical</u> agreement." Define *mechanical*.

7. What is similar to the blood that is <u>circulating</u> through the human body? Use *circulating* in a sentence.

8. What are the merchants of Hong Kong <u>illustrating</u>? What might a of Hong Kong map be *illustrating*?

"Ribbons" by Laurence Yep

Reading: Make Inferences by Reading Between the Lines and Asking Questions

An **inference** is an intelligent guess, based on what the text tells you, about things *not* stated directly in the text. One way to make inferences is to **read between the lines by asking questions,** such as, "Why does the writer include these details?" and "Why does the writer leave out certain information?" For example, "Ribbons" opens as Stacy and Ian's grandmother arrives from Hong Kong. The narrator, Stacy, says,

> Because Grandmother's . . . expenses had been so high, there wasn't room in the family budget for Madame Oblomov's ballet school. I'd had to stop my daily lessons.

Why does the writer begin with those details? What conclusion can be drawn? From these details you can infer that Stacy feels some resentment because she has had to give up her ballet lessons so that her grandmother can come from Hong Kong.

DIRECTIONS: *Read the following passages from "Ribbons," and answer the questions.*

1. What inference can you draw from Grandmother's reaction to Stacy's hug?
   When I tried to put my arms around her and kiss her, she stiffened in surprise. "Nice children don't drool on people," she snapped at me.

   _____

2. What can you infer about Grandmother's feelings about her daughter's home?
   Grandmother was sitting in the big recliner in the living room. She stared uneasily out the window as if she were gazing not upon the broad, green lawn of the square but upon a Martian desert.

   _____

3. In the following passage, what inference can you draw from those words, spoken by Stacy's mother, about Grandmother?
   [The girls' feet] were usually bound up in silk ribbons. . . . Because they were a symbol of the old days, Paw-paw undid the ribbons as soon as we were free in Hong Kong—even though they kept back the pain.

   _____

4. In the following passage, what inference about Grandmother can you draw from this attempt to show her affection for Stacy?
   She took my hand and patted it clumsily. I think it was the first time she had showed me any sign of affection.

   _____

5. What inference can you draw from Stacy's description of the invisible ribbon?
   Suddenly I felt as if there were an invisible ribbon binding us tougher than silk and satin, stronger than steel; and it joined her to Mom and me.

   _____

"Ribbons" by Laurence Yep
Literary Analysis: Theme

A story's **theme** is its central idea, message, or insight into life. Occasionally, the author states the theme directly. More often, however, the theme is implied.

A theme is *not* the same as the subject of a work. For example, if the subject or topic of a story is cultural differences, the theme will be a message about that, such as "cultural differences can be overcome by communication."

As you read, look at what characters say and do, where the story takes place, and objects that seem important in order to determine the theme—what the author wants to teach you about life.

DIRECTIONS: *Answer the following questions about "Ribbons."*

1. What is the setting? Briefly describe it.

   _____

2. What do the main characters say? Summarize the important statements made by Grandmother, Mom, and Stacy.

   Grandmother: _____

   _____

   Mom: _____

   _____

   Stacy: _____

   _____

3. How do the characters act? Describe the important actions of Grandmother and Stacy.

   Grandmother: _____

   _____

   _____

   Stacy: _____

   _____

   _____

4. What objects seem important?

   _____

5. What is the subject, or topic, of "Ribbons"?

   _____

6. Based on your answers above, what would you say is the theme of "Ribbons"?

   _____

"Ribbons" by Laurence Yep
Vocabulary Builder

Word List

sensitive	meek	coax	laborious	exertion

A. DIRECTIONS: *Complete each sentence with a word from the Word List.*

1. Because Grandmother's feet had been bound when she was young, she found walking and climbing stairs _____ activities.

2. Stacy loved ballet so much that she hardly realized that it was _____—until she collapsed from exhaustion after each lesson.

3. Because the binding of her feet was painful physically and emotionally, Grandmother was _____ about her feet.

4. Stacy hoped that she could _____ Grandmother into paying attention to her by explaining her love of ballet.

5. In many cultures it is expected that a daughter will be _____ and never challenge her parents' requests.

B. DIRECTIONS: *Write the letter of the word or phrase that is most similar in meaning to the Word List word.*

____ 1. coax
    A. intimidate
    B. sweet-talk
    C. relax into
    D. mock

____ 2. exertion
    A. relaxation
    B. mental strain
    C. idleness
    D. hard work

____ 3. laborious
    A. difficult
    B. easy
    C. effortless
    D. intrusive

____ 4. meek
    A. arrogant
    B. bullying
    C. shy
    D. spirited

____ 5. sensitive
    A. emotional
    B. sharp
    C. unstable
    D. unfeeling

"Ribbons" by Laurence Yep
Support for Writing a Letter to the Editor

Before you write your **letter to the editor,** think about whether young people should participate in extra schooling by taking art classes, for example, or by participating in sports. Then, on this graphic organizer, write down advantages and disadvantages of each position.

**Young People's
Extra Schooling**

Art Classes	**Sports**
Advantages: _____ _____ _____ _____ _____ _____ _____ _____ _____	Advantages: _____ _____ _____ _____ _____ _____ _____ _____ _____
Disadvantages: _____ _____ _____ _____ _____ _____ _____ _____ _____	Disadvantages: _____ _____ _____ _____ _____ _____ _____ _____ _____

Decide which position you want to take and draft a letter to the editor of a local newspaper in support of your position. Use your notes to back up your opinion with reasons and details that will persuade readers to take your side.

"Ribbons" by Laurence Yep
Support for Extend Your Learning

Research and Technology

Answer these questions as you gather information for a **poster** about the benefits of studying ballet.

What is ballet? Define it briefly. _____

What are the basic arm positions? _____

What are the basic foot positions? _____

What are the benefits of studying ballet? _____

_____

Listening and Speaking

Answer these questions as you prepare a **short speech** about the challenges and benefits of Stacy's experiences with her grandmother. Answer the questions from Stacy's point of view—you will be speaking as if you were Stacy.

Where is Grandmother from? What experiences were important to her? _____

_____

_____

What challenges did I face when Grandmother came to live with us? _____

_____

_____

How did Grandmother react to me at first? _____

_____

How did I respond to Grandmother's behaviors? _____

_____

How did my mother help? _____

_____

_____

How did we solve the conflict between us? _____

_____

What are the benefits of solving the conflict? _____

_____

Name _____ Date _____

"Ribbons" by Laurence Yep
Enrichment: Documentary

In "Ribbons," Stacy's ballet shoes mean a great deal to her: They symbolize her passion for ballet. In every person's life there are items that represent his or her interests or accomplishments. They might include an award the person has won, an article of clothing he or she prizes, a souvenir, or a book or movie. Imagine that you were going to make a documentary about someone's life. The subject might be someone you know or someone in history or the news whom you admire. In your film, you plan to include segments on those important items in order to explain your subject most fully.

DIRECTIONS: *Think of at least three items that help to represent the subject of your documentary. On this chart, name those items and make notes describing how each helps to explain the subject of your film—what he or she is interested in, what he or she loves, where he or she lives or has traveled, what he or she thinks.*

Name of person who is the subject of the documentary:	
Item	**Meaning of Item**

Now write some commentary, or narration, for the documentary. Weave into your commentary a discussion of the three items that are important to your subject, and explain their meaning.

_____

_____

_____

_____

_____

_____

"Zoo" by Edward Hoch
"Ribbons" by Laurence Yep
Build Language Skills: Vocabulary

The Prefixes *con-* and *sub-*

The prefix *con-* means "together" or "the same." The word *conclude*, which contains the prefix *con-*, means "to pull together details to reach an opinion or come up with an idea."

The prefix *sub-* means "under" or "below." It is the prefix in the word *subject*. One meaning of *subject* is "a topic under study or discussion."

A. DIRECTIONS: *Write a definition of the italicized word in each sentence. Base your definition on your knowledge of the prefix and the context clues in the sentence. Then, check your definition in a dictionary and revise it, if necessary.*

1. Two major stores announced that they would *consolidate* to form a single company.

   _____

2. He signed a *contract* agreeing to work as a consultant for one year for a fee of $6,000.

   _____

3. After the hurricane, water had to be pumped out of the partially *submerged* boats.

   _____

Academic Vocabulary Practice

B. DIRECTIONS: *Indicate whether the statement is* true *or* false, *and explain your answer.*

1. From the details in "Zoo," one can *conclude* that the events are imagined.

   True/False: _____ Explanation: _____

   _____

2. From the horse spiders' *perspective*, they were the creatures on display in the zoo.

   True/False: _____ Explanation: _____

   _____

3. The horse spiders are *credible*—one can easily believe that such creatures exist.

   True/False: _____ Explanation: _____

   _____

4. The *subject* of "Ribbons" is understanding and communication.

   True/False: _____ Explanation: _____

   _____

5. A significant *object* in "Ribbons" is the message that differences can be resolved by communication.

   True/False: _____ Explanation: _____

   _____

"**Zoo**" by Edward Hoch
"**Ribbons**" by Laurence Yep
Build Language Skills: Grammar

Adverbs

An **adverb** is a word that modifies or describes a verb, an adjective, or another adverb. Adverbs provide information by answering the question *how? when? where? how often?* or *to what extent?* Many adverbs end in the suffix *-ly.*

In the first sentence, the adverb, *always*, tells how often the children are good. In the second sentence, the adverb, *outside*, tells where the car stops:

The children were *always* <u>good</u> during the month of August.

A car <u>stopped</u> *outside.*

A. DIRECTIONS: *Underline the adverb in each sentence once, and underline the word it modifies twice.*

1. The sides slowly slid up to reveal the familiar barred cages.
2. The citizens of Earth clustered around as Professor Hugo's crew quickly collected the waiting dollars.
3. The odd horse-spider creatures filed quickly out of their cages.
4. The little one enjoyed it especially.
5. Mom bowed formally as Grandmother reached the porch.
6. I'd been practicing my ballet privately in the room I now shared with Ian.
7. I clutched the ribbons tightly against my stomach.
8. Suddenly I felt as if there were an invisible ribbon binding us.

B. Writing Application: *Write a sentence in response to each set of instructions. Underline the word or phrase that the adverb you use modifies.*

1. Use *quickly* in a sentence about catching a school bus.

   _____

2. Use *never* in a sentence about a food you dislike.

   _____

3. Use *gently* in a sentence about something you do.

   _____

4. Use *always* in a sentence about something else you do.

   _____

5. Use *finally* in a sentence about a process that involves several steps.

   _____

Name _____ Date _____

Selection Test A

Critical Reading *Identify the letter of the choice that best answers the question.*

___ 1. In "Ribbons," from where has Grandmother just arrived?
   A. China
   B. San Francisco
   C. Hong Kong
   D. Los Angeles

___ 2. Why does Grandmother get out of the car before Stacy's father can help her?
   A. She does not like Stacy's father.
   B. She wants to get out by herself.
   C. She is too shy to accept his help.
   D. She is eager to greet her daughter.

___ 3. In "Ribbons," Ian is relieved when he realizes that Grandmother speaks English. What inference can the reader draw from this detail?
   A. He does not speak Chinese.
   B. He does not want to talk to her.
   C. He wants her to teach him Chinese.
   D. He does not want Stacy to talk to her.

___ 4. In "Ribbons," Grandmother reacts to Stacy's hug by stiffening and snapping at her. What inference can the reader draw from this detail?
   A. She is not used to people showing affection.
   B. She is afraid Stacy will cause her to fall over.
   C. She does not want Stacy to get her dirty.
   D. She thinks that hugs can spread disease.

___ 5. In "Ribbons," what does Stacy ask her father once her grandmother has arrived?
   A. She asks to have her own room back again.
   B. She asks to attend ballet class again.
   C. She asks to share her room with Grandmother.
   D. She asks to read fairy tales to Ian.

___ 6. In "Ribbons," why does Grandmother spoil Ian?
   A. He is young.
   B. He is cute.
   C. He is smart.
   D. He is a boy.

_____ 7. What does Stacy discover when she puts on her satin toe shoe?

    A. The shoe is too small.

    B. The ribbons are too long.

    C. The ribbons have come off.

    D. The shoe has fallen apart.

_____ 8. In "Ribbons," why does Grandmother get angry when she sees the ribbons of Stacy's toe shoe?

    A. She thinks they are too grown-up for Stacy.

    B. She thinks Stacy will hurt her with them.

    C. She thinks they are hurting Stacy's feet.

    D. She thinks Stacy likes ballet too much.

_____ 9. In "Ribbons," why is Grandmother ashamed of her feet?

    A. They were bound when she was a child and are now misshapen.

    B. They were hurt in a childhood accident and are badly scarred.

    C. They were misshapen at birth and made fun of by her parents.

    D. They are not as beautiful as the feet of other Chinese women.

_____ 10. How does Stacy treat her grandmother once she learns about her grandmother's feet?

    A. She flatters her.

    B. She helps her get around.

    C. She makes fun of her.

    D. She stops ignoring her.

_____ 11. Why is "The Little Mermaid" important to the theme of "Ribbons"?

    A. It is a story that Grandmother is familiar with from her childhood in China.

    B. It allows Stacy and Grandmother to talk about Grandmother's bound feet.

    C. It causes Grandmother and Ian to argue about the meaning of the story.

    D. It helps Grandmother feel comfortable about letting Stacy see her feet.

_____ 12. What does the title of "Ribbons" refer to?

    A. both the ribbons that bound Grandmother's feet and the ribbons on Stacy's toe shoes

    B. both the ribbons that bound Grandmother's feet and the ribbons worn by the mermaid

    C. only the ribbons on Stacy's toe shoes

    D. only the ribbons worn by the mermaid

Vocabulary and Grammar

_____ 13. In "Ribbons," what does it mean when Stacy's father's face becomes red from the *exertion* of carrying Grandmother's belongings?

A. He is hot.

B. He is working hard.

C. He is too busy to wash his face.

D. He is angry because no one is helping him.

_____ 14. In "Ribbons," what does the writer mean when he says that Grandmother tries "to *coax* a smile from Ian"?

A. She is forcing him to smile.

B. She really wants him to smile.

C. She is funny, and he wants to smile.

D. She is gently trying to make him smile.

_____ 15. Which word in the following sentence from "Ribbons" is an adverb?

Though she was stiff at first, she gradually softened in my arms.

A. she

B. stiff

C. gradually

D. softened

Essay

16. In "Ribbons," Stacy and her grandmother have trouble getting along. In an essay, describe their conflict, and explain how Stacy and Grandmother are able to grow closer at the end of the story. Consider these questions: How does Grandmother treat Stacy in the beginning of the story? What angers her about Stacy's toe shoes? What does Stacy learn about her grandmother's feet? How does the story of the little mermaid help them to resolve their conflict?

17. The theme of a story is its central message or insight. In "Ribbons," the theme is that cultural differences can be bridged through communication. In an essay, discuss how Laurence Yep reveals this theme. Answer these questions: What objects in the story are important to the theme? How does the title "Ribbons" relate to the theme? How do the main characters' actions support the theme?

"**Ribbons**" by Laurence Yep
Selection Test B

Critical Reading *Identify the letter of the choice that best completes the statement or answers the question.*

_____ 1. In "Ribbons," who has come to stay with Stacy's family, and where has she come from?
   A. Stacy's mother's mother has come from to San Francisco.
   B. Stacy's father's mother has come from Los Angeles.
   C. Stacy's mother's mother has come from Hong Kong.
   D. Stacy's father's mother has come from China.

_____ 2. In "Ribbons," Ian shouts excitedly when he first sees his grandmother, but Stacy thinks about the ballet lessons she has had to give up. What inference can you draw from their behavior?
   A. Ian knows their grandmother better than Stacy does.
   B. Stacy is afraid of their grandmother, but Ian is not.
   C. Ian knows that their grandmother will favor him because he is a boy.
   D. Stacy has had to make sacrifices for their grandmother, but Ian has not.

_____ 3. In "Ribbons," Grandmother reacts to Stacy's hug by stiffening and scolding her. What does her behavior show about cultural differences?
   A. They are caused by a show of affection.
   B. They can never be overcome.
   C. They can lead to misunderstandings.
   D. They are usually preventable.

_____ 4. In "Ribbons," why does Grandmother at first pay more attention to Ian than to Stacy?
   A. Ian is a boy.
   B. Ian is smarter than Stacy.
   C. Stacy has been disrespectful.
   D. Ian is nicer than Stacy.

_____ 5. What can you infer from this passage from "Ribbons"?
   Grandmother was sitting in the big recliner in the living room. She stared uneasily out the window as if she were gazing not upon the broad, green lawn of the square but upon a Martian desert.

   A. Grandmother does not feel at home in this country.
   B. Grandmother is not used to seeing broad, open spaces.
   C. Grandmother is sorry that she has been ignoring Stacy.
   D. Grandmother has studied photographs of Mars.

_____ 6. In "Ribbons," why does Grandmother become angry when Stacy asks for help attaching the ribbons to her toe shoes?
   A. She is jealous of Stacy's talent as a ballet dancer.
   B. She is offended because Stacy has asked her impolitely.
   C. She thinks that ballet is not a proper activity for a girl.
   D. She believes the ribbons will be used to bind Stacy's feet.

_____ 7. In "Ribbons," what does the condition of Grandmother's feet show about the traditional status of women in China?
A. They received inadequate medical care.
B. They were treated differently from men.
C. They were valued for the beauty of their feet.
D. They were forced to do most of the manual labor.

_____ 8. Stacy reads "The Little Mermaid" aloud to Ian and her grandmother. How does the story provide a way for Grandmother and Stacy to connect?
A. It is a starting point for a conversation about their misunderstanding.
B. It has a happy ending and allows them to feel good about each other.
C. It teaches Grandmother to divide her attention between Stacy and Ian.
D. It teaches Stacy to respect her grandmother because she is older.

_____ 9. After Stacy reads "The Little Mermaid" aloud, Grandmother says,

"When I saw those ribbons, I didn't want you feeling pain like I do."

What inference about Grandmother can you draw from this remark?
A. She believes that dancing is as harmful as the binding of one's feet.
B. She does not want Stacy to have pretty ribbons because she favors Ian.
C. She cares about Stacy even if she does not know how to show it.
D. She thinks that the calluses on Stacy's feet are ugly and shameful.

_____ 10. In the final scene of "Ribbons," Grandmother listens as Stacy reads "The Little Mermaid" aloud to Ian. This scene serves mainly to bring out the story's
A. theme.
B. ending.
C. humor.
D. setting.

_____ 11. Which of the following statements best summarizes the theme of "Ribbons"?
A. Families will always be in conflict.
B. Understanding and communication are important.
C. Ethnic pride is important to everyone.
D. Young and old people can never get along.

Vocabulary and Grammar

_____ 12. Why is Grandmother's climb up the stairs described as *laborious*?
A. Climbing stairs is difficult for her.
B. She earns her living climbing stairs.
C. She can climb stairs with her canes.
D. She does not like to climb stairs.

_____ 13. In "Ribbons," why is Stacy's mother described as sounding "*meek* as a child"?
A. She thinks that her mother is a child.
B. She dislikes being an only child.
C. She is timid when her mother is annoyed.
D. She feels angry when her mother complains.

_____ **14.** In the following sentence from "Ribbons," which word is an adverb?

We couldn't run around or make noise because Grandmother had to rest.

A. run

B. around

C. because

D. rest

_____ **15.** In the following sentence from "Ribbons," which word does the adverb *gradually* modify?

Though she was stiff at first, she gradually softened in my arms.

A. stiff

B. she

C. softened

D. arms

Essay

16. In an essay, explain how "Ribbons" illustrates the idea that differences between cultures can lead to misunderstandings and hostility. Consider these questions: What are the main cultural differences? How does Stacy react to her grandmother? How do Stacy and her grandmother resolve their differences? What lessons about cultural differences does the story hold for readers of the story? Use examples from the story to support your points.

17. The theme of a story is its central message or insight. In an essay, explain the theme of "Ribbons." In your explanation, address these questions: What is the setting? What do the main characters say and do? What objects are important? How does the title of the story relate to the theme? Be sure that you state the theme and use examples from the story to support your points.

Vocabulary Warm-up Word Lists

Study these words from the stories. Then, complete the activities.

Word List A

authorities [uh THAWR uh teez] *n.* those in power who enforce laws or orders
The local <u>authorities</u> reviewed plans to build a town park.

consented [kuhn SENT id] *v.* agreed to or gave permission for something
The teacher <u>consented</u> to extend the deadline for the report.

established [uh STAB lisht] *v.* set up something
Laura <u>established</u> an art show for the school.

gusts [GUHSTS] *n.* sudden strong rushes of air or wind
In November, strong <u>gusts</u> blow the leaves from the trees.

outline [OWT lyn] *v.* to summarize by telling the main points of something
The study group began to <u>outline</u> notes for the history course.

profits [PRAHF itz] *n.* gains
The <u>profits</u> from the book sale went to buy new desks.

slight [SLYT] *adj.* small in amount
She had gotten over her cold, but Anna still had a <u>slight</u> cough.

wits [WITS] *n.* people who are very bright or clever
The greatest <u>wits</u> competed on the game show.

Word List B

dwellers [DWEL erz] *n.* those who live in a place
Some early humans were cave <u>dwellers</u>.

expanded [ek SPAN did] *v.* made bigger
We <u>expanded</u> our garden by ten square feet this year.

fate [FAYT] *n.* a force that some people believe determines what happens
It was <u>fate</u> that the two would meet again.

midway [MID way] *adj.* at about the middle of something
When we were <u>midway</u> between the two towns, we turned around.

objection [uhb JEK shun] *n.* the act of objecting to or disapproving of something
Marc had a major <u>objection</u> to the town's plan to expand the road.

proposition [prahp uh ZI shun] *n.* a big proposal or undertaking to be dealt with
It is a <u>proposition</u> to take a new job and move to a new town.

throng [THRAHNG] *n.* a large crowd
A <u>throng</u> gathered to watch the parade.

vicinity [vuh SIN uh tee] *n.* a place near or in something; a neighborhood
This <u>vicinity</u> of the city has many good restaurants.

Name _____ Date _____

Vocabulary Warm-up Exercises

Exercise A *Fill in each blank in the paragraph below with an appropriate word from Word List A. Use each word only once.*

The children of Emerson wanted to form a kite-flying club, but they needed a good place to fly their kites. They were determined and clever, so these young [1] _____ came up with an idea. They presented it to the town council. "We will [2] _____ our plan for you," said one boy. He explained that the club would clean up an old field and hold a kite-flying contest each March, when [3] _____ of wind are plentiful. "There will be a [4] _____ fee to enter the contest," he said, "and [5] _____ will be used to maintain the field." The town [6] _____ [7] _____ to the plan, and that is how Emerson's annual kite-flying contest was [8] _____.

Exercise B *Revise each sentence so that the underlined vocabulary word is used in a logical way. Be sure to keep the vocabulary word in your revision.*

Example: The <u>terrible</u> scene was pleasant to look at.
The <u>terrible</u> scene was awful to look at.

1. When we <u>expanded</u> our storeroom, we reduced its size.
   _____

2. People who believe in <u>fate</u> believe that it does not determine what happens.
   _____

3. When we reached the <u>midway</u> point on the journey, we were more than halfway there.
   _____

4. City <u>dwellers</u> are people who live below the surface of a city.
   _____

5. When a <u>throng</u> gathers in this neighborhood, the place is isolated.
   _____

6. Joan's main <u>objection</u> to the project was that she thought it would work well.
   _____

7. If our <u>proposition</u> wins approval, we will have little to do.
   _____

8. People who live in this <u>vicinity</u> live far from here.
   _____

Name _____ Date _____

"After Twenty Years" by O. Henry
"He—y, Come On Ou—t!" by Shinichi Hoshi
Reading Warm-up A

Read the following passage. Pay special attention to the underlined words. Then, read it again, and complete the activities. Use a separate sheet of paper for your written answers.

The residents of many small islands in the South Pacific are concerned about the effects of global warming. For them, global warming is not just a theory. Seas are rising quickly in the South Pacific. Islands are sinking.

One such island is Tuvalu. Tuvalu is only about 15 feet above sea level. As global warming expands the water in the ocean, more storms blow huge <u>gusts</u> of wind and rough seas on shore. The storms cause higher tides, and the tides are swallowing up the island. On higher land, the tides would be only a <u>slight</u> threat. Low-lying Tuvalu, however, faces extinction.

The population of Tuvalu is about 10,500, and they are making plans for their escape. It is believed that if global warming does not slow down, the island will sink beneath the waves within 50 years. <u>Authorities</u> in New Zealand have <u>consented</u> to help the people of Tuvalu. They have <u>established</u> a plan: They will accept 75 Tuvaluans per year as refugees.

Global warming is caused in large part by the emissions of greenhouse gases by industrialized nations. The heat from those gases gets trapped within the earth's atmosphere, causing temperatures to rise. As ice caps and glaciers melt, the sea level rises. The warmer temperatures also warm the sea water. As the water heats up, it expands.

Tuvaluans believe they must act to reduce the effects of global warming. They have decided to <u>outline</u> a plan. Part of the plan involves suing countries that add to global warming. They also wish to sue oil and fuel companies. They say that those companies make <u>profits</u> from global warming.

What will happen to Tuvalu and other small islands of the South Pacific? With effort, the <u>wits</u> of science, business, and politics can work together to solve the problems of global warming. Then, perhaps, the islands can be saved. Without those efforts, the islands may become part of our planet's past.

1. Circle the words that give a clue to the meaning of <u>gusts</u>. Define *gusts*.

2. Circle the words that tell what would be a <u>slight</u> threat on higher land. What is an antonym of *slight*?

3. Underline the words that tell what <u>authorities</u> in New Zealand have agreed to do. What are *authorities*?

4. Rewrite the sentence that contains the word <u>consented</u>, using a synonym for *consented*. Then, use *consented* in a sentence of your own.

5. Underline the sentence that explains the plan that has been <u>established</u> by the authorities. Define *established*.

6. Underline the words that tell what Tuvaluans have said they will <u>outline</u>. What is something you might *outline*?

7. Circle the words that tell who may be making <u>profits</u> from global warming. What are *profits*?

8. Underline the words that tell what <u>wits</u> might work on the issues of global warming. Use *wits* in a sentence.

"After Twenty Years" by O. Henry
"He—y, Come On Ou—t!" by Shinichi Hoshi
Reading Warm-up B

Read the following passage. Pay special attention to the underlined words. Then, read it again, and complete the activities. Use a separate sheet of paper for your written answers.

Emily and Mia were the best of friends. Whether it was riding bikes, listening to music, or doing homework, they found every activity was more fun when they shared it. They believed that <u>fate</u> had brought them together. How else could either one have been so fortunate as to discover such a friend?

Then one day, everything changed. Emily's father and mother announced that their family would soon be moving far away. Their business had <u>expanded</u>, and they had decided to relocate to a new <u>vicinity</u>.

"Oh, no," Emily protested, "I don't want to go without Mia."

Emily's mother countered her daughter's <u>objection</u> with a <u>proposition</u>. "In six months," she told Emily, "it will be summer vacation, and you and Mia can spend it together at the beach."

The two friends did not want to part, but they realized they had no choice. They decided to concentrate on planning their vacation. After Emily left, Mia was sad. To keep busy, she took up in-line skating. Soon she was a skilled skater and having a lot of fun, too.

As for Emily, her family lived near the ocean. Now that they were almost beach <u>dwellers</u>, Emily took up surfing. She was also adjusting to her new school. Despite her activities, she often thought of Mia and looked forward to seeing her again.

At last the day of their reunion arrived. The girls planned to meet at the beach. They spotted each other amid the <u>throng</u> of beachgoers. Waving excitedly, each girl walked <u>midway</u> down the beach. When they met, they hugged and laughed. Mia showed Emily her in-line skates and promised to teach her how to use them. Emily showed Mia her surfboard. With new things to do, as well as all their old favorites, that summer vacation was the best of all.

1. Underline the words that tell what the girls believed <u>fate</u> had done. What is *fate*?

2. Circle the words that tell what had <u>expanded</u>. Use *expanded* in a sentence.

3. Emily's parents wanted to move their business to a new <u>vicinity</u>. Explain what that means.

4. Underline the words that tell what Emily's <u>objection</u> was. Tell what an *objection* is.

5. What was Emily's mother's <u>proposition</u>? What is a *proposition*?

6. Circle the words that describe what kind of <u>dwellers</u> Emily's family had become. What other sorts of *dwellers* might there be?

7. Circle the word that tells who made up the <u>throng</u> of people. Use *throng* in a sentence.

8. Each girl walks <u>midway</u> down the beach. What does that mean?

"**After Twenty Years**" by O. Henry
"**He—y, Come On Ou—t!**" by Shinichi Hoshi
Literary Analysis: Irony

Irony involves a contradiction or contrast of some kind. In **situational irony** (or **irony of situation**), something takes place that a character or reader does not expect to happen. For example, a student voted Most Likely to Succeed ends up going to prison.

In **verbal irony,** a writer, speaker, or character says something that deliberately contradicts or blurs what he or she actually means. Think of a man who has been dreading a reunion with his best friend from twenty years before. When they meet, he says, "I've been *so* looking forwarding to seeing you." That is verbal irony.

In **dramatic irony,** the reader or audience knows or understands something that a character or speaker does not. For example, readers know that the apple Snow White is about to bite into is poisoned, but Snow White does not know it. That is dramatic irony.

As you read "After Twenty Years" and "He—y, Come On Ou—t!" look for situational irony in particular.

DIRECTIONS: *Answer the following questions.*

1. What is the general situation, or the plot? Describe it briefly.

   "After Twenty Years": _____

   _____

   "He—y, Come On Ou—t!": _____

   _____

2. What outcome do you expect?

   "After Twenty Years": _____

   "He—y, Come On Ou—t!": _____

3. What happens? How does the story end?

   "After Twenty Years": _____

   "He—y, Come On Ou—t!": _____

4. What details in the story lead you to expect a certain outcome? Describe one or two details, and state what they lead you to expect.

   "After Twenty Years": _____

   _____

   "He—y, Come On Ou—t!": _____

   _____

5. What is ironic about the ending of the story?

   "After Twenty Years": _____

   "He—y, Come On Ou—t!": _____

Name _____ Date _____

"After Twenty Years" by O. Henry
"He—y, Come On Ou—t!" by Shinichi Hoshi
Vocabulary Builder

Word List

spectators   intricate   destiny   simultaneously   apparent   plausible   proposal

A. DIRECTIONS: *Revise each sentence so that the italicized vocabulary word is used logically. Be sure to use the vocabulary word in your new sentence.*

1. The plot of the short story was so *intricate* that we followed it easily.

   _____

2. The *destiny* of a criminal is likely to include time spent as a police officer.

   _____

3. The two men arrived *simultaneously,* one reaching the doorway an hour after the other.

   _____

4. Because there were many *spectators* when the crime was committed, no eyewitnesses could testify at the trial.

   _____

   _____

5. The *apparent* smile on the face of the scientist was not visible to anyone.

   _____

6. The *plausible* explanation made sense to no one.

   _____

7. Because he offered no solution, everyone accepted the concessionaire's *proposal.*

   _____

B. DIRECTIONS: *Write the letter of the word whose meaning is most similar to that of the Word Bank word.*

____ 1. intricate
   A. complicated   B. tiny   C. simple   D. intelligent

____ 2. simultaneously
   A. genuinely   B. apart   C. together   D. separately

____ 3. apparent
   A. obvious   B. hidden   C. deceptive   D. similar

"After Twenty Years" by O. Henry
"He—y, Come On Ou—t!" by Shinichi Hoshi
Support for Writing to Compare Literary Works

Before you write an essay that compares your reaction to "After Twenty Years" with your reaction to "He—y, Come On Ou—t!" use this graphic organizer to consider how irony is used in the two stories.

What details make the story believable or realistic?

"After Twenty Years":	"Hey—y, Come On Ou—t!":

How does the believability or the realism of the story affect your response? Do you prefer a believable story to a fantasy one? Why or why not?

"After Twenty Years":	"Hey—y, Come On Ou—t!":

What is the story's message? Is the message easy to understand? Why or why not?

"After Twenty Years":	"Hey—y, Come On Ou—t!":

When you respond to a story, are you influenced by the difficulty of understanding its message? Why or why not?

"After Twenty Years":	"Hey—y, Come On Ou—t!":

Now, use your notes to write an essay in which you compare your reactions to the use of irony in "After Twenty Years" and "He—y, Come On Ou—t!"

"After Twenty Years" by O. Henry
"He—y, Come On Ou—t!" by Shinichi Hoshi
Selection Test A

Critical Reading *Identify the letter of the choice that best answers the question.*

____ 1. In "After Twenty Years," what has happened to the restaurant where the two friends had agreed to meet?
   A. It has closed for the evening.
   B. It has changed management.
   C. It has forbidden the man to enter.
   D. It has been closed for five years.

____ 2. In "After Twenty Years," why does the policeman make a point of asking the man in the doorway whether he plans to wait for Jimmy Wells to show up?
   A. He is testing him to find out whether he is a trusted friend.
   B. He wants to see whether he has time to call another officer to arrest him.
   C. He needs time to change out of his uniform and come back to surprise his friend.
   D. He needs time to find out whether there is an outstanding warrant for his arrest.

____ 3. Which of the following statements best summarizes the meaning of this quotation from "After Twenty Years"?

   "It [twenty years] sometimes changes a good man into a bad one."

   A. A life of crime can change a good man into a bad man.
   B. The West is likely to change a good man into a bad man.
   C. Over the course of twenty years, a good man may turn to crime.
   D. You are lucky that life in the West did not change you into a bad man.

____ 4. What is ironic about Jimmy and "Silky" Bob in "After Twenty Years"?
   A. One has become a police officer, and one has become a criminal.
   B. One has grown taller, while the other has grown shorter with age.
   C. Both of them have become criminals.
   D. Neither of them ever liked the other.

____ 5. In "He—y, Come On Ou—t!" how do the villagers come to discover the hole?
   A. A landslide has swept away a shrine that had covered it.
   B. A typhoon has destroyed a building that had covered it.
   C. A child from the village falls into it.
   D. A construction worker notices it.

____ 6. In "He—y, Come On Ou—t!" how does the scientist who comes to examine the hole behave?

    A. He acts as if the hole will go away on its own.

    B. He acts as if the hole is an unnatural event.

    C. He acts as if the hole is not at all unusual.

    D. He acts as if he has seen many such holes.

____ 7. In "He—y, Come On Ou—t!" who offers to fill the hole?

    A. a newspaper reporter

    B. one of the scientists

    C. a government worker

    D. one of the concessionaires

____ 8. What is ironic about the ending of "He—y, Come On Ou—t!"?

    A. The hole is filled and eventually pollutes the entire village.

    B. The city keeps expanding until the village is swallowed up.

    C. A voice shouts from the sky and a pebble falls toward the city.

    D. The hole never fills up, and the city becomes cleaner and better.

____ 9. Which of the following choices is an example of dramatic irony?

    A. An audience can predict that the hero of a story will die.

    B. A character says, "That dress looks so good on you," while thinking that it looks awful.

    C. Readers know who the villain is, but the other characters do not realize it.

    D. A politician who criticizes his opponent's moral character is convicted of lying under oath.

____ 10. Which of the following choices is an example of situational irony?

    A. A girl who was always in trouble grows up to become a police officer.

    B. Unexpected guests arrive, the house is a mess, and the host says, "I'm glad you came."

    C. Readers know that one character in a story will die, but none of the characters know it.

    D. Readers realize that a plot is based on the plot of a much older story that ends tragically.

____ 11. Which word best describes the endings of "After Twenty Years" and "He—y, Come On Ou—t!"?

    A. sad

    B. surprising

    C. tragic

    D. funny

___ 12. Which part of "He—y, Come On Ou—t!" makes it less realistic than "After Twenty Years"?
  A. a deep hole that never fills up
  B. people burying nuclear waste
  C. constructions workers taking breaks
  D. villagers moving a sacred shrine

Vocabulary

___ 13. When "Silky" Bob says that "each of us ought to have our *destiny* worked out," what does he mean?
  A. Their futures will have been decided.
  B. They will have solved their puzzles.
  C. They will have paid off their debts.
  D. Their unhappiness will have eased.

___ 14. Which of the following choices describes a *plausible* explanation?
  A. one that everyone has rejected
  B. one that makes everyone happy
  C. one that is scientific
  D. one that makes sense

___ 15. Who would be most likely to make a *proposal*?
  A. an architect who hopes to design a building
  B. a nurse who is caring for a sick patient
  C. a student who has finished her homework
  D. a construction worker who is on a break

Essay

16. Both "After Twenty Years" and "He—y, Come On Ou—t!" contain irony. In an essay, discuss use of the irony in these stories. For each story, identify the irony as situational, verbal, or dramatic. Then, explain why you have identified it that way. Cite details in each story that support your choice.

17. Stories that make use of irony often have surprise endings. In an essay, compare the endings of "After Twenty Years" and "He—y, Come On Ou—t!" Consider these questions: What is surprising about each ending? Which ending is more surprising? What makes it more surprising? Why is the other story less surprising—does something tip you off to the ending? If so, what is it?

"After Twenty Years" by O. Henry
"He—y, Come On Ou—t!" by Shinichi Hoshi
Selection Test B

Critical Reading *Identify the letter of the choice that best completes the statement or answers the question.*

_____ 1. Why does the policeman in "After Twenty Years" slow down when he sees the man in the doorway?
A. He is lonely and welcomes the chance to talk to someone.
B. He immediately recognizes the man in the doorway.
C. He is generally suspicious of people standing in doorways.
D. He is keeping the appointment to meet his friend.

_____ 2. In "After Twenty Years," the fact that the man in the doorway provides the police officer with a long explanation shows that
A. he is unfamiliar with the neighborhood.
B. he does not recognize his old friend.
C. he has something to hide.
D. he is guilty of a crime.

_____ 3. In "After Twenty Years," why does "Silky" Bob fail to recognize his old friend?
A. Jimmy had always said that he had no respect for policemen.
B. Jimmy was unattractive as a young man.
C. Bob cannot imagine that Jimmy would become a policeman.
D. Bob does not expect Jimmy to show up.

_____ 4. In "After Twenty Years," when the man claiming to be Jimmy first approaches "Silky" Bob, what *first* arouses Bob's suspicions about him?
A. his height
B. his nose
C. his walk
D. his voice

_____ 5. At what point in "After Twenty Years" does Jimmy first realize that his friend is a wanted criminal?
A. when he sees Bob's large diamond scarfpin
B. when Bob strikes a match that lights up his face
C. as soon as Jimmy walks up to the doorway
D. minutes after Jimmy walks away from Bob

_____ 6. What is ironic about the ending of "After Twenty Years"?
A. Jimmy is the policeman who talks to Bob and then has Bob arrested.
B. The man who shows up claiming to be Jimmy is really a criminal.
C. Bob is sure that Jimmy is alive and that he will keep the appointment.
D. Jimmy arrests Bob when he realizes that he is a wanted criminal.

____ 7. In "He—y, Come On Ou—t!" what is remarkable about the hole found under the shrine?
  A. It is in a holy place.
  B. It is very wide.
  C. It seems to be bottomless.
  D. It is filled with different things.

____ 8. In "He—y, Come On Ou—t!" why does a concessionaire volunteer to fill the hole for the village?
  A. He wants to make a profit by charging for the right to dump material into the hole.
  B. He cares about the people of the village and does not want anyone falling into the hole.
  C. He works for the government and his job is to find a place to dump nuclear waste.
  D. He is an environmentalist and believes that pollution can be dumped into the hole.

____ 9. In "He—y, Come On Ou—t!" what is significant about the fact that "the hole gave peace of mind to the dwellers of the city"?
  A. The city dwellers were glad to have such a wonderfully deep hole to dump waste into.
  B. The city dwellers could produce more without worrying about the consequences.
  C. The city dwellers were relieved that the hole was in the village, miles from the city.
  D. The city dwellers were relieved to know that the nuclear waste was safely underground.

____ 10. What is ironic about the ending of "He—y, Come On Ou—t!"?
  A. As the hole fills up with waste, people in the village and then those in the city become ill.
  B. The echo of the voice of the man who called into the hole at first is heard in the sky.
  C. The city grows so big and produces so much that it swallows up the little village.
  D. As the pollution in the city is eliminated, people realize that the hole is a good thing.

____ 11. Which of the following choices is an example of situational irony?
  A. The clumsiest little girl in the neighborhood grows up to be a respected brain surgeon.
  B. A character says, "You never looked younger," while noticing his friend's gray hair.
  C. Readers know that the Wolf is in the bed, but Little Red Riding Hood thinks it is Grandma.
  D. Goldilocks realizes that the Three Bears have eaten her porridge and slept in her bed.

____ 12. Which word best describes the endings of "After Twenty Years" and "He—y, Come On Ou—t!"?
  A. predictable
  B. humorous
  C. obvious
  D. surprising

____ 13. In which way do "After Twenty Years" and "He—y, Come On Ou—t!" differ?
  A. "After Twenty Years" is persuasive; "Come On Ou—t!" is imaginative.
  B. "After Twenty Years" deals with a social issue; "Come On Ou—t!" is entertaining.
  C. "After Twenty Years" is imaginative; "Come On Ou—t!" is persuasive.
  D. "After Twenty Years" is entertaining; "Come On Ou—t!" deals with a social issue.

Unit 2 Resources: Short Stories
190

____ 14. Which element of "He—y, Come On Ou—t!" makes it less realistic than "After Twenty Years"?
   A. A contractor is granted the right to fill a hole.
   B. A construction worker on a high beam takes a break.
   C. A hole is so deep that it can never be filled up.
   D. A sacred shrine is moved from one place to another.

Vocabulary

____ 15. When two events occur *simultaneously,*
   A. both happen at the same time.
   B. one happens before the other.
   C. one cannot be separated from the other.
   D. both take place for only a short time.

____ 16. A story with an *intricate* plot
   A. involves two characters who are close friends.
   B. probably has many characters and story lines.
   C. is usually straightforward and easy to follow.
   D. always describes events in the same sequence.

____ 17. An *apparent* mistake is one that
   A. is unlikely to happen.
   B. is made during the day.
   C. can definitely be identifed as a mistake.
   D. appears likely to have been a mistake.

____ 18. A *plausible* excuse is one that
   A. is generally liked.
   B. is generally accepted.
   C. can be proved scientifically.
   D. can be upheld in court.

Essay

19. Ironic stories often have surprise endings. Did the endings of "After Twenty Years" and "He—y, Come On Ou—t!" surprise you, or did you guess them in advance? In an essay, compare and contrast the surprise endings of the two stories. Use these questions to guide your writing: In what way are the endings similar? In what way are they different? Which story's ending is more surprising? What makes it more surprising?

20. Although the authors of both "After Twenty Years" and "He—y, Come On Ou—t!" use irony, they deliver different messages. In an essay, compare and contrast the messages behind the irony in these two stories. Use the following questions to guide your writing: What is the message of "After Twenty Years"? What is the message of "He—y, Come On Ou—t!"? How did you react to these messages? Cite details from the stories to support your points.

Writing Workshop—Unit 2, Part 2
Narration: Short Story

Prewriting: Narrowing Your Topic

Use the graphic organizer below to help you identify the conflict you will use in your story.

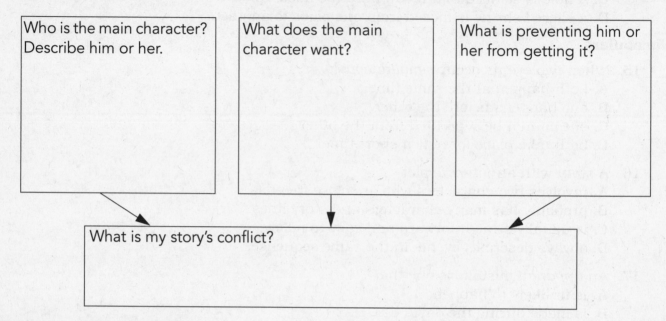

| Who is the main character? Describe him or her. | What does the main character want? | What is preventing him or her from getting it? |

What is my story's conflict?

Drafting: Creating a Plot

Use the graphic organizer below to map out the plot of your story.

Exposition
Introduce the main characters, their situations, and the central conflict.

Conflict
Develop and intensify the conflict during the rising action.

Climax
Create a high point of interest and suspense.

Resolution
Resolve the conflict, and conclude the story.

Writing Workshop—Unit 2, Part 2
Review of a Short Story: Integrating Grammar Skills

Revising for Correct Degrees of Adjectives and Adverbs

Most adjectives and adverbs have three **degrees of comparison:** the positive, the comparative, and the superlative.

Degree	What It Shows	What It Usually Looks Like	Examples
Positive	no comparison	basic adjective or adverb	My dog is *big*.
Comparative	compares two things	ends in *-er* or uses *more*	My dog is *bigger* than yours.
Superlative	compares three or more things	ends in *-est* or uses *most*	My dog is the *biggest* in town.

Generally, one- or two-syllable adjectives and adverbs use *-er* and *-est*, and those of three or more syllables use *more* and *most*. However, if a word sounds awkward one way, use the other. Be careful not to use both at the same time

Incorrect:	My cat is *more playfuller* than my dog.
Awkward:	My cat is *playfuller* than my dog.
Correct:	My cat is *more playful* than my dog.

Identifying Degrees of Adjectives and Adverbs

A. DIRECTIONS: *Circle the adjective or adverb that correctly completes each sentence.*

1. Our new computer works much (more fast, faster) than our old one.
2. On the old computer, the word-processing program worked (more slowly, slowlier).
3. My friend Nate said it was the (more sluggish, most sluggish) machine he ever saw.
4. Of the two computers, this one is (more complex, most complex).

Fixing Incorrect Degrees of Adjectives and Adverbs

B. DIRECTIONS: *On the lines provided, rewrite these sentences so that they use the correct degree of the adjective or adverb.*

1. Mrs. T's garden is the most fine in the city.

_____

2. Her roses smell nice, but her lilies are even more fragranter.

_____

3. Of the two kinds of irises, the bearded irises are the prettiest.

_____

4. The tulips bloom in early May, but the daffodils bloom even more early.

_____

Spelling Workshop—Unit 2
Tricky or Difficult Syllables

To spell words correctly, you must remember to **include all the letters.** Some words are difficult because they have silent letters or letters that are barely pronounced. If any word of this type gives you trouble, try exaggerating its pronunciation to yourself to help you remember the hard-to-hear letters.

Word List

aspirin	biscuit	business	candidate	nuisance
awfully	boundary	cabinet	interesting	pumpkin

A. DIRECTIONS: *Write the word from the Word List that matches each clue.*

1. something you eat   _____
2. place for storing dishes   _____
3. something that irritates you   _____
4. cure for a headache   _____
5. fascinating   _____
6. a store or a company   _____
7. person running for election   _____
8. edge or border   _____
9. terribly   _____
10. large and orange   _____

B. DIRECTIONS: *Write two or three sentences using each group of words below.*

1. *candidate, pumpkin,* and *interesting*

_____

_____

_____

2. *biscuit, cabinet, aspirin,* and *awfully*

_____

_____

_____

3. *boundary, business,* and *nuisance*

_____

_____

_____

Communications Workshop—Unit 2
Organizing and Delivering an Oral Summary

After choosing your news article, fill out the following chart. Use your notes to plan and organize your oral summary so that it summarizes all the important points in the article.

Title of news article: _____

What is the main idea?
What are the important details?
What quotation are you using?
Make a statement of "What it all means."
Describe the visual aids you are using (if any).

For Further Reading—Unit 2

DIRECTIONS: *Think about the books you have read. Then, on a separate sheet of paper, answer the discussion questions and take notes for your literary circle.*

The Jungle Book by Rudyard Kipling

Discussion In Chapter 2, Baloo the bear teaches Mowgli the Law of the Jungle. Why must Mowgli learn more of this law than the wolves? How might some features of this law apply to human nature and society?

Connections: Literary Circle Bagheera tells Mowgli, "You must make your own trail, Little Brother." How might Bagheera's words relate to Kipling's theme, or central idea, about human life and behavior? In your opinion, is Kipling's ending a good one? Explain your response.

Devil's Arithmetic by Jane Yolen

Discussion If you were Hannah and you stepped out of your front door into another world, where would it be? Would you be in the past or in the future? Describe what it would be like.

Connections: Literary Circle What do you think is the meaning of the book's title *Devil's Arithmetic*? How does *Devil's Arithmetic* not only remember the victims, but honor its survivors?

Child of the Owl by Laurence Yep

Discussion Why does the story about the owl charm make Casey feel better? What does the charm symbolize for her? What does the charm symbolize for Paw-Paw?

Connections: Literary Circle When Casey says she wants to grow up to be like Paw-Paw, Paw-Paw says, "I'm afraid you are already like me. And that's a pity." Why do you think she says that?

Miracle's Boys by Jacqueline Woodson

Discussion People in the neighborhood refer to Ty'ree as "St. Ty'ree." Why has he earned that nickname?

Connections: Literary Circle Lafayette has strong memories of his mother as a reader, particularly while reading Toni Morrison. How does the quote, "The function of freedom is to free someone else," relate to Ty'ree, Charlie, and Lafayette?

Unit 2: Short Stories
Part 2 Benchmark Test 4

MULTIPLE CHOICE

Reading Skill: Make Inferences

1. What can you infer about the weather from the details in the following passage?

   Jake's mother tells him to take an umbrella with him when he is leaving for school. However, Jake doesn't think it is necessary.

   A. It is raining.
   B. It is going to rain.
   C. It is snowing.
   D. It is cold.

Read the selection. Then, answer the questions that follow.

   Richard must have looked at the clock twenty times before he finally heard the last bell ring. As soon as he heard it, Richard grabbed his coat and books. As usual, he was the first one out the front door.

2. What can you infer about the setting of the selection?
   A. Richard is at home.
   B. Richard is at school.
   C. Richard is at the gym.
   D. Richard is in the library.

3. Which of the following details does not help you to make an inference about the setting?
   A. the bell rings
   B. Richard grabs his books
   C. Richard is the first one out the door
   D. Richard looks at the clock

4. What can you infer about Richard from the selection?
   A. He is tired.
   B. He is excited.
   C. He is impatient.
   D. He is lazy.

Reading Skill: Make Generalizations

5. Which of the following is an example of a generalization?
   A. Baseball is a sport that is played throughout the summer.
   B. At the last baseball game, the home team won by sheer luck.
   C. All baseball fans are rowdy.
   D. There were a record number of fans at last night's game.

6. Which of the following statements is a fact?
   A. I think students call in sick just to miss a day of school.
   B. Taking vitamin C might help cure a cold.
   C. In one year, about 61 million Americans will suffer from colds.
   D. These tissues are the best to use when you have a cold.

7. What generalization might a person make upon seeing a man playing with three dogs?
   A. Dogs make good pets.
   C. Dogs take a lot of energy.
   B. Dogs are easy to take care of.
   D. Dogs are man's best friend.

Literary Analysis: Conflict

8. Which story situation is an example of a human in conflict with nature?
   A. A character cannot decide whether to learn to ski or to learn to scuba dive.
   C. A teenager wants to try skydiving, but is not yet eighteen years of age.
   B. Two characters disagree about what to do with $1,000 in reward money.
   D. An explorer is in danger as water rapidly rises in the cave she is exploring.

9. In literature, what kind of conflict occurs when there is a struggle between a character and nature?
   A. internal conflict
   C. intense conflict
   B. natural conflict
   D. external conflict

10. Which one of the following is a conflict you might find in a short story?
    A. Don works at the bank on Elm Street.
    C. Don and Fred are related to each other.
    B. Both Don and Fred want to marry Sue Ellen.
    D. Both Don and Fred like to eat hamburgers.

Literary Analysis: Theme

11. What is meant by the term *theme* in a narrative?
    A. Theme is the central message of a story.
    C. Theme is the setting and action of the story.
    B. Theme is the music that goes with the story.
    D. Theme is the conclusion of the story.

12. Which of the following would make the best theme for a short story?
    A. Some types of snakes can be poisonous.
    C. Kindness, in the long run, will be rewarded.
    B. It is easy to prepare a quick, healthful meal.
    D. Many tall buildings sway a little in the wind.

13. How is *theme* most often expressed in a short story?
    A. It is expressed in the first sentence a reader sees.
    C. It is expressed by the first character who speaks.
    B. It is expressed through the characters and events.
    D. It is expressed in an introduction by the author.

14. Which of the following would not be considered a recurring theme in writings about nature?
   A. The beauty of nature is timeless.
   B. Nature is to be preserved for all time.
   C. Time is not to be wasted.
   D. Inspiration can come from nature.

15. Which of the following sentences might be the theme of a story?
   A. Pesticides are used less often today than they once were.
   B. Dublin, Ireland makes an interesting setting for a story.
   C. Honesty is the essential foundation of a relationship.
   D. Spring 1998 was the beginning of Winnie's education.

16. Which of the following would make a good theme for a short story?
   A. a family's history
   B. the history of the Civil war
   C. the definition of kindness
   D. the value of honesty

Literary Analysis: Irony

17. Which of the following best defines the concept of *irony*?
   A. Irony is a comparison between two or more things that are similar.
   B. Irony is a figure of speech in which *like* or *as* is used to compare two ideas.
   C. Irony is figurative language in which a nonhuman subject is given human characteristics.
   D. Irony is the contrast between an outcome and what the reader expects to happen.

18. What makes the following situation *ironic*?

   Feeling cheated after losing the contest, Samuel told the winner that she deserved to win.

   A. Samuel believes he was cheated but tells the winner that she deserved to win.
   B. Samuel feels cheated, because he knows he did the best job on his project.
   C. Samuel lost the contest because he did not spend enough time in preparation.
   D. The winner of the contest deserved to win, and Sam is wrong for feeling upset.

Grammar: Adjectives

19. Which word is modified by the adjective *unusual* in the following sentence?

   The day was most <u>unusual</u>, with its cloudless blue sky and moderate temperature.

   A. cloudless
   B. sky
   C. day
   D. temperature

20. What question does the adjective *shimmering* answer?

   Randy and I are observing the shimmering night sky with our new telescope.

   A. whose?
   B. how many?
   C. which one?
   D. what kind?

21. Which adjective modifies *neck* in the following sentence?

She wrapped the red scarf neatly around her slender neck.

    A. red

    B. slender

    C. wrapped

    D. neatly

22. Which of the following sentences contain an adjective that modifies a noun?

    A. Deb decided she would work on a puzzle.

    B. The puzzle in the box was a jigsaw puzzle.

    C. Quickly, she arranged the pieces in places.

    D. She felt good about completing the puzzle.

23. Which of the following sentences uses the comparative form of *bad* correctly?

    A. The weather was worse today than yesterday.

    B. The weather was the worst today.

    C. The weather was badder today than yesterday.

    D. The weather was worser today than yesterday.

24. Which of the following sentences uses the superlative form of *good* correctly?

    A. The better moment of the trip was when we swam with dolphins.

    B. The good moment of the trip was when we swam with dolphins.

    C. The goodest moment of the trip was when we swam with dolphins.

    D. The best moment of the trip was when we swam with dolphins.

Grammar: Adverbs

25. Which of the following sentences contains three adverbs?

    A. Ty warmly greeted the new visitors with much enthusiasm.

    B. Ty greeted the visitors warmly and enthusiastically.

    C. The very happy visitors warmly and enthusiastically greeted Ty.

    D. The new visitors accepted Ty's warm and enthusiastic greeting.

26. Where should the adverb *only* be placed in a sentence?

    A. Place the adverb *only* directly before the word or phrase it modifies.

    B. Place the adverb *only* directly after the word or phrase it modifies.

    C. Place the adverb *only* at the beginning of sentences.

    D. Place the adverb *only* at the conclusion of sentences.

27. In which of the following sentences does the adverb *only* refer to *retrieves*?

    A. The yellow dog retrieves the blue ball only.

    B. The yellow dog retrieves only the blue ball.

    C. Only the yellow dog retrieves the blue ball.

    D. The yellow dog only retrieves the blue ball.

Vocabulary: Prefixes

28. What is the meaning of the word *obstructed* in the following sentence?

The new building obstructed her view of the ocean.

   A. blocked   C. enhanced

   B. cleared   D. threatened

29. Which word contains a Latin prefix meaning *with* or *together*?

   A. defeated   C. count

   B. connect   D. separate

30. Using your knowledge of the prefix *sub-*, what is the meaning of the word *subservient*?

   A. working in a pool or lake   C. working below someone

   B. working above someone   D. working below ground

Spelling: Homophones

31. Which of the following sentences uses a homophone correctly?

   A. John did not here the telephone ring.   C. Hear is the car!

   B. The teacher asked Philip to come here.   D. Did you here the news?

32. Which of the following pairs of words are homophones?

   A. there, they're   C. stuff, tough

   B. we're, were   D. record, record

ESSAY

Writing

33. On a separate piece of paper, support the following statement with a specific example of your own.

A library is important to a community.

34. Using the statement about libraries and your sentence of support, write a brief letter to a local newspaper editor about why libraries need community support.

35. On a separate piece of paper, support the following idea with an anecdote from your own experience.

Handing homework in on time is a good study habit.

36. On a separate piece of paper, write a sentence or two describing a house in a forest. Include sensory details and use precise language to give a vivid impression.

ANSWERS

"The Treasure of Lemon Brown"
by Walter Dean Myers

Vocabulary Warm-up Exercises, p. 2

A.
1. theaters
2. treasure
3. commence
4. throb
5. swirling
6. brilliance
7. lifetime
8. memories

B. Sample Answers
1. A telegram lying on a kitchen table is an ominous thing that might have awaited someone. The person it was addressed to would not know whether it contained bad news or good news.
2. Yes, my mother has beckoned me with a look.
3. Yes, I read a mystery that kept me in suspense until the identity of the villain was revealed.
4. Yes, the brittle noise of chalk scratching on the blackboard always makes me squirm.
5. Someone might be lecturing a child after he or she has misbehaved.
6. A youngster spends his or her time sleeping, eating, and playing.

Reading Warm-up A, p. 3

Sample Answers
1. a collection of great literature, music, and art; A treasure to me is my coin collection, my family, my best friend, my CD collection.
2. for the first time; *Commence* means "to start."
3. Audiences were thrilled; *Throb* means "to beat strongly" or "pulsate."
4. musical and dramatic works that were written and produced by African Americans; I have seen some great plays in the theaters on Broadway.
5. the African American experience; A memory from my lifetime is the time my sisters and I spent in the country with our grandparents.
6. Swirling colors would be blurred, with one color running into another, as if they were in motion. *Swirling* means "going in circles with a whirling motion."
7. Because of the Depression, and for a variety of other reasons; *Brilliance* means "a great brightness."

Reading Warm-up B, p. 4

Words that students are to circle appear in parentheses.

Sample Answers
1. Christina's mother might have waved to Christina or motioned her with her hand. *Beckoned* means "called or summoned with a silent gesture."

2. the brittle tones of her mother's voice, her mother would be lecturing her all evening; Chores that I have put off have awaited me.
3. tones of her mother's voice; *Brittle* means "having a hard, sharp quality."
4. Christina imagined her mother would be lecturing her because she wanted to refuse to baby-sit for her brother. *Lecturing* means "giving a lengthy scolding."
5. child; A youngster has a lot to look forward to.
6. (feeling); *Ominous* means "threatening" or "sinister, as if something bad is about to happen."
7. Christina found the *suspense* overwhelming because she was anxious to find out whether Jeffrey was behind the shrub. I felt suspense when I was opening my birthday present.
8. her brother. On his lap was a kitten; *Revealed* means "made known" or "disclosed."

Walter Dean Myers

Listening and Viewing, p. 5

Sample answers and guidelines for evaluation:

Segment 1. It was important for Walter Dean Myers to write about his community because he loved Harlem and urban life and those topics had not been written about before. In saying what they would write about their community, students may refer to different aspects of rural, suburban, or urban life.

Segment 2. A scrapbook would be a good basis for a story because it contains remembrances of the most important events of one's life, and those remembrances, taken together, tell a story. Myers puts his experiences into his writing, so his stories, taken together, are in a way a collection of his memories.

Segment 3. Myers uses old photographs as an inspiration for his characters. Students may say that that method would work for them because it would help them describe the appearance of a character and give them clues to the character's personality. Students who say that it would not work for them may say that they would prefer to create a character completely out of their imagination.

Segment 4. Books open new worlds to Myers and make him a better person; they have helped him achieve more than he thought he could. Students may say that books have shown them a larger view of the world and taught them things they did not know.

Unit 2: Learning About Short Stories, p. 6

A. 1. B; 2. A; 3. A; 4. B; 5. B
B. Guidelines for evaluation: Students should clearly identify the setting; use the main character's words, appearance, or actions or the words of another character to show what the main character is like; and describe a basic situation.

"The Treasure of Lemon Brown"
by Walter Dean Myers

Model Selection: Short Story, p. 7

Sample Answers

A. 1. Because Greg is failing math, his father will not let him play basketball with the Scorpions, the Community Center team.

2. Lemon Brown is courageous. Many tragic things have happened in his life (his wife has died; his only child has been killed in a war; he is penniless), yet he does not ask for or seem to need the help of others. He seems very wise.

3. These words are Lemon Brown's explanation for how he ended up penniless and homeless. They are an example of indirect characterization. From that sentence, the reader can conclude that Lemon Brown is very poor but unwilling to pity himself.

4. Some boys or young men who believe that Lemon Brown's treasure is money come to rob the old man.

5. Greg and Lemon Brown confront the thugs who have come to rob Lemon Brown: Greg howls, and Lemon Brown hurls himself down the stairs. They scare the robbers away.

B. 1. The theme of "The Treasure of Lemon Brown" is that a person's treasure is of great personal and emotional value, but it does not necessarily have financial value.

2. Yes, this is a universal theme because many people understand that the things with the greatest value (for example, friendship, love, and trust) often do not have monetary value.

Selection Test A, p. 8

Learning About Short Stories

1. ANS: B	DIF: Easy	OBJ: Literary Analysis
2. ANS: A	DIF: Easy	OBJ: Literary Analysis
3. ANS: C	DIF: Easy	OBJ: Literary Analysis
4. ANS: D	DIF: Easy	OBJ: Literary Analysis
5. ANS: B	DIF: Easy	OBJ: Literary Analysis

Critical Reading

6. ANS: A	DIF: Easy	OBJ: Literary Analysis
7. ANS: D	DIF: Easy	OBJ: Literary Analysis
8. ANS: D	DIF: Easy	OBJ: Literary Analysis
9. ANS: C	DIF: Easy	OBJ: Literary Analysis
10. ANS: C	DIF: Easy	OBJ: Comprehension
11. ANS: D	DIF: Easy	OBJ: Interpretation
12. ANS: A	DIF: Easy	OBJ: Comprehension
13. ANS: B	DIF: Easy	OBJ: Interpretation
14. ANS: C	DIF: Easy	OBJ: Literary Analysis
15. ANS: D	DIF: Easy	OBJ: Interpretation

Essay

16. Guidelines for evaluation: Students should clearly state a theme and support it with two details from the story. They may recognize that the theme is that a person's treasure is what is important or meaningful to him or her. They may say that a treasure has more to do with pride and personal accomplishments than with money. Lemon Brown's harmonica and newspaper clippings became his treasure when he understood that his son respected their worth because he was proud of his father's life.

Difficulty: *Easy*

Objective: *Essay*

17. Guidelines for evaluation: Students should recognize that through his encounter with Lemon Brown, Greg has acquired a new appreciation of his father. He probably is seeing for the first time that his father's life has been difficult, and he may recognize that his father is concerned about his schoolwork because he is concerned about how he will do in life.

Difficulty: *Easy*

Objective: *Essay*

Selection Test B, p. 11

Learning About Short Stories

1. ANS: B	DIF: Average	OBJ: Literary Analysis
2. ANS: D	DIF: Average	OBJ: Literary Analysis
3. ANS: A	DIF: Challenging	OBJ: Literary Analysis
4. ANS: D	DIF: Challenging	OBJ: Literary Analysis
5. ANS: A	DIF: Average	OBJ: Literary Analysis
6. ANS: C	DIF: Average	OBJ: Literary Analysis

Critical Reading

7. ANS: A	DIF: Average	OBJ: Literary Analysis
8. ANS: B	DIF: Average	OBJ: Interpretation
9. ANS: C	DIF: Challenging	OBJ: Literary Analysis
10. ANS: C	DIF: Average	OBJ: Literary Analysis
11. ANS: D	DIF: Challenging	OBJ: Literary Analysis
12. ANS: A	DIF: Average	OBJ: Literary Analysis
13. ANS: D	DIF: Average	OBJ: Interpretation
14. ANS: A	DIF: Average	OBJ: Comprehension
15. ANS: C	DIF: Average	OBJ: Comprehension
16. ANS: C	DIF: Average	OBJ: Literary Analysis
17. ANS: A	DIF: Challenging	OBJ: Interpretation
18. ANS: B	DIF: Average	OBJ: Literary Analysis
19. ANS: D	DIF: Challenging	OBJ: Interpretation
20. ANS: C	DIF: Challenging	OBJ: Literary Analysis

Essay

21. Guidelines for evaluation: Students should demonstrate some understanding that Greg learns from Lemon Brown something about a son's love for his father and a father's love for his son. When Greg sees how poor Lemon Brown is, he may at last understand why his father has been lecturing him to do well in school and why his father takes such pride in his job as a postal worker. He may understand that his father's lecturing is not meant to be a punishment but is the way his father demonstrates his love for his son.

   Difficulty: *Average*

   Objective: *Essay*

22. Guidelines for evaluation: Students should clearly state a theme and support it with two details from the story. They will likely say that the theme is that a person's treasure is what is important to him or her and that a treasure cannot be measured by its monetary value. In supporting their claim that the theme is or is not universal, students should demonstrate an understanding of the meaning of a universal theme. For example, they may say that the theme is universal because all cultures and people in all ages have stressed that certain values or beliefs are more important than money.

   Difficulty: *Average*

   Objective: *Essay*

23. Guidelines for evaluation: Students should note that Brown's ragged appearance and lack of a home are evidence of the difficult times he has experienced. The value he places on his "treasure" suggests that financial achievement has been less important to him than pride in his accomplishments as a blues singer—and his pride in his son's recognition of those accomplishments. Students may note that he appears to be motivated by a desire to remain true to himself and to cherish the memory of his wife and son.

   Difficulty: *Challenging*

   Objective: *Essay*

Unit 2, Part 1 Answers

Diagnostic Test 3, p. 15

MULTIPLE CHOICE

1. ANS: C
2. ANS: B
3. ANS: D
4. ANS: C
5. ANS: B
6. ANS: C
7. ANS: A
8. ANS: D
9. ANS: A
10. ANS: C
11. ANS: C
12. ANS: C
13. ANS: D
14. ANS: B
15. ANS: C

"The Bear Boy" by Joseph Bruchac

Vocabulary Warm-up Exercises, p. 19

A.
1. lodge
2. result
3. neglected
4. preparations
5. weapons
6. lance
7. timid
8. wrestling

B. Sample Answers

1. Yes, you are being helpful because to encourage someone is to give him or her confidence to try to do something.
2. No; violence is physical force that could hurt someone, so a scene of violence would not be a pleasant sight.
3. Yes; an initiation is an introduction into a group or club, so when you go through an initiation into a club, you become a member.
4. No; your relatives are the members of your family, and usually the people in your neighborhood are not all members of your family.
5. Yes; a responsibility is a duty or a job, and most people feel good when they fulfill a duty or complete a job.
6. Yes; *powerful* means "having great strength or authority," so a person with a powerful personality would likely stand out in a group.
7. No; boys enter manhood when they become adults.
8. Yes; guidance is helpful advice, and people are usually happy to receive helpful advice.

Reading Warm-up A, p. 20

Words that students are to circle appear in parentheses.

Sample Answers

1. They had survived cold and hunger to get to Gluskonba's island. People had seen them wrestling with strong animals; A timid person would run away from danger.
2. (strong animals); The brothers wrestling outside the lodge were skilled athletes.
3. (home); Once he was in his lodge, each man was supposed to open the pouch that Gluskonba had given him.
4. (lance); He might have wanted a bow and arrow or a hunting knife.

5. (the hunt); A lance is a long spear.

6. (duties); My neighbor neglected to mow her lawn, and now there are weeds growing everywhere.

7. A hunter might make preparations respectfully by sharpening his weapons and practicing his aim so that he can kill his prey with as little pain to the animal as possible. Preparations are the work involved in making something ready.

8. he got his wish: He became the best hunter among his people; His understand had that result because he learned to have respect for the animals he hunted.

Reading Warm-up B, p. 21

Words that students are to circle appear in parentheses.

Sample Answers

1. During a child's earliest years the mother provided for his or her wellbeing, giving the child much love and attention; Mothers can provide guidance by teaching their children to tell the difference between right and wrong.

2. (Children), (parents), (mother); Other relatives include sisters, brothers, aunts, uncles, cousins, and grandparents.

3. If a boy had a pony of his own, he would care for it and get to know it and therefore develop the confidence and the skills that are necessary for horsemanship.

4. *formal*; An initiation is an introduction into a group or club.

5. A boy enters manhood when he earns enough money to support himself.

6. Only after he had killed a buffalo and survived the violence of a raiding party was a boy considered a man; The powerful machine did the work of six people.

7. (a raiding party); peace

8. A married couple accepted the responsibility of taking care of themselves. That responsibility might have involved finding their own food, providing for their own shelter, and raising children.

"The Bear Boy" by Joseph Bruchac

Reading: Use Prior Knowledge to Make Predictions, p. 22

Story Details and Prior Knowledge / What I Predict Will Happen / What Actually Happens

Sample Answers

A shadow comes over the bear cubs. I know that something large casts a shadow. / The mother bear will appear. / The mother bear does appear.

The medicine man criticizes Kuo-Haya's father. I know that people often feel bad when they have been criticized. / Kuo-Haya's father will feel bad because he has neglected his son. / Kuo-Haya's father does feel bad because he has neglected his son.

Kuo-Haya's father gets honey from a beehive. I know that bears like honey. / Kuo-Haya's father will take the honey to the bears. / Kuo-Haya's father uses the honey to distract the bears.

Kuo-Haya's father tells his son that he will treat him as a son should be treated. I know that people are often forgiven after they accept responsibility for their mistakes. / Kuo-Haya will forgive his father. / Kuo-Haya does forgive his father.

Literary Analysis: Plot, p. 23

1. The characters are Kuo-Haya and his father. The setting is a Pueblo village; the time is long ago.

2. The event introduces a conflict in the story.

3. Kuo-Haya's father sees a bee and gets the idea of distracting the bears with honey in order to get to his son.

4. Sample answer: Kuo-Haya's father tells his son that he has come to take him home and that he has learned a lesson from the bears.

5. Students' answers should include at least some of the following information: Kuo-Haya returns to the village with his father. The father keeps his promise to be friends with the bears, demonstrates his love for his son, and teaches his son. The villagers see that the Kuo-Haya is no longer timid. Kuo-Haya, having learned to wrestle from the bears, becomes the best wrestler. With his father's coaching, he also becomes a great runner. His story continues to be told to remind parents to show love for their children.

Vocabulary Builder, p. 24

A. Sample Sentences

1. The timid rabbit hid from the fox in the low bushes.

2. For her initiation into adulthood, Amanda read a passage from an ancient book and gave a speech about the importance of charity.

3. The family neglected the garden all summer, and by August it was overgrown with weeds.

B. 1. C; 2. D; 3. A

Enrichment: Initiation Into Adulthood, p. 27

Sample Answers

A. 1. Young people should know how to get along well with others.

2. Young people should know the rules of common courtesy.

3. Young people should know how to read.

4. Young people should know how to drive a car or use public transportation.

5. Young people should know how to apply for a job.

6. Young people should know how to use a checkbook and a credit card.

7. Young people should know how to cook.

8. Young people should know how to wash clothes.

B. 1. Adults are responsible for getting and holding a job.

2. Adults are responsible for feeding, clothing, and sheltering themselves and their families.

3. Adults are responsible for taking part in their community and being good citizens.

Selection Test A, p. 28

Critical Reading

1. ANS: C   DIF: Easy   OBJ: Comprehension
2. ANS: A   DIF: Easy   OBJ: Comprehension
3. ANS: A   DIF: Easy   OBJ: Reading
4. ANS: D   DIF: Easy   OBJ: Reading
5. ANS: B   DIF: Easy   OBJ: Comprehension
6. ANS: B   DIF: Easy   OBJ: Reading
7. ANS: A   DIF: Easy   OBJ: Interpretation
8. ANS: D   DIF: Easy   OBJ: Literary Analysis
9. ANS: D   DIF: Easy   OBJ: Literary Analysis
10. ANS: C   DIF: Easy   OBJ: Comprehension
11. ANS: A   DIF: Easy   OBJ: Interpretation
12. ANS: C   DIF: Easy   OBJ: Interpretation

Vocabulary and Grammar

13. ANS: C   DIF: Easy   OBJ: Vocabulary
14. ANS: C   DIF: Easy   OBJ: Vocabulary
15. ANS: D   DIF: Easy   OBJ: Grammar

Essay

16. Students may have known that bears like honey. Based on that knowledge and on the suggestion in the story that the father noticed the bee, many students may have predicted that the father would try to get honey for the bears. Students who did not make that prediction might have thought the father would use the bees in another way to try to get his son back.

Difficulty: *Easy*

Objective: *Essay*

17. Students should note one event for each element; they might note that the exposition explains why Kuo-Haya's father has neglected his son; the rising action describes how Kuo-Haya goes with the bears, how the trackers look for him, how the medicine man advises his father, and how his father tries to get him back; the climax reveals how Kuo-Haya's father gets him back; the falling action explains how and why Kuo-Haya returns to the village; the resolution tells what happens when Kuo-Haya returns home. Most students will probably think that the elements create a satisfying story about a timid boy who learns to overcome his timidness and a neglectful father who learns to pay attention to his son.

Difficulty: *Easy*

Objective: *Essay*

Selection Test B, p. 31

Critical Reading

1. ANS: C   DIF: Challenging   OBJ: Comprehension
2. ANS: A   DIF: Average   OBJ: Comprehension
3. ANS: A   DIF: Average   OBJ: Reading
4. ANS: B   DIF: Challenging   OBJ: Literary Analysis
5. ANS: D   DIF: Average   OBJ: Reading
6. ANS: C   DIF: Average   OBJ: Comprehension
7. ANS: A   DIF: Average   OBJ: Interpretation
8. ANS: B   DIF: Average   OBJ: Reading
9. ANS: A   DIF: Challenging   OBJ: Interpretation
10. ANS: D   DIF: Average   OBJ: Literary Analysis
11. ANS: C   DIF: Average   OBJ: Literary Analysis
12. ANS: B   DIF: Challenging   OBJ: Literary Analysis
13. ANS: A   DIF: Average   OBJ: Interpretation
14. ANS: C   DIF: Average   OBJ: Interpretation

Vocabulary and Grammar

15. ANS: C   DIF: Average   OBJ: Vocabulary
16. ANS: C   DIF: Challenging   OBJ: Vocabulary
17. ANS: A   DIF: Average   OBJ: Grammar
18. ANS: A   DIF: Challenging   OBJ: Grammar

Essay

19. If students are familiar with the commonly held knowledge that bears like honey, they may say that the outcome of the story was easy to predict. On the other hand, students may note that the outcome took careful observation. The story says only this: "A bee flew up to him, right by his face. Then it flew away. The father stood up. Now he knew what to do!" To predict the outcome, a reader must not only know that bears like honey; he or she must also see the connection between the bee flying right by the father's face and his then knowing "what to do."

Difficulty: *Average*

Objective: *Essay*

20. Students should explain that the lesson teaches that parents should love their children and show their love. Kuo-Haya's father learns that if he does not show his love for his son, he risks losing his son forever. Students might note that readers are expected to learn the lesson the father learns and may point out that the story of Kuo-Haya is told to teach parents and other listeners this lesson.

Difficulty: *Challenging*

Objective: *Essay*

"Rikki-tikki-tavi" by Rudyard Kipling

Vocabulary Warm-up Exercises, p. 35

A.
1. brood
2. peculiar
3. bred
4. thickets
5. balancing
6. clenched
7. fraction
8. splendid

B. Sample Answers

1. No, I would not be pleased because to speak *scornfully* is to speak with contempt.

2. Yes; to *inherit* something is to receive something that has been passed down by a family member, so if I inherited my father's looks, I would look like him.

3. No, if my jaw were *paralyzed*, it would be unable to move, and I would not be able to open my mouth.

4. No; a *bungalow* is a small house; it does not have room for many guests.

5. Yes; *valiant* means "brave" or "courageous," so I would admire someone who did something valiant.

6. No; *scuttled* means "moved quickly with short steps," so if someone scuttled away, he or she would probably be in a hurry.

7. No; *savagely* means "wildly," so if the wind were blowing savagely, I would stay inside.

8. No; someone who was been revived has been woken up or brought back to life.

Reading Warm-up A, p. 36

Words that students are to circle appear in parentheses.

Sample Answers

1. reputation for bravery; *unimpressive*

2. (newly hatched); The mongoose gained its reputation in ancient Egypt because it found crocodiles and ate their eggs or their newly hatched offspring.

3. (heavy brush), (tangled); Birds build their nests in *thickets*.

4. lightly on its feet; *Balancing* means "keeping steady and not falling over."

5. it leaps in any direction; In a *fraction* of a second, a computer performs a number of processes.

6. (the snake's head); Finally the mongoose is holding the snake's head between its sharp teeth, and it snaps the snake's spine.

7. (as pets); German shepherds are *bred* to be watchdogs.

8. (a mongoose); A mongoose is not a *peculiar* pet because it is intelligent and entertaining.

Reading Warm-up B, p. 37

Words that students are to circle appear in parentheses.

Sample Answers

1. The heat and humidity *paralyzed* Heather; (She could not move)

2. (on the porch); You might see a *bungalow* in the country or by the shore.

3. The heat of the sun beat *savagely* down on the roof. The wild dogs tore savagely into the raw meat.

4. (beetle); *scurried*

5. her grandfather's love of travel; Money or possessions can be *inherited*.

6. (independence); *Valiant* means "brave" or "courageous."

7. India would not be able to rule itself; The rude man, thinking himself better than everyone else, treated his guests *scornfully*.

8. (the thought of rain); A swim has *revived* my energy on a hot day.

"Rikki-tikki-tavi" by Rudyard Kipling

Reading: Use Prior Knowledge to Make Predictions, p. 38

Story Details and Prior Knowledge / What I Predict Will Happen / What Actually Happens

Sample Answers

Rikki-tikki hears a hiss from the thick grass. I know that snakes hiss. / A snake will appear. / Nag, a cobra, appears.

When Rikki-tikki and Chuchundra are in the house, Chuchundra says, "Nag is everywhere." I know that cobras enter houses. / Nag will come into the house. / Nag plans to attack in the bathroom.

Darzee's wife flutters before Nagaina with a broken wing. I know that Darzee's wife is clever. / Darzee's wife will distract Nagaina. / Rikki-tikki goes to the melon patch and begins to destroy Nagaina's eggs.

When Nagaina is about to attack Teddy, Rikki-tikki shows her that he has one of her eggs. I know that Nagaina feels strongly about her eggs. / Nagaina will be distracted and Rikki-tikki will be able to kill her. / Rikki-tikki fights with Nagaina and eventually kills her.

Literary Analysis: Plot, p. 39

1. The characters are the mongoose Rikki-tikki-tavi; an English boy, Teddy; and his parents. The setting is a house in India that the English family has recently moved into.

2. Nag appears when Rikki-tikki is in the garden. Their meeting sets up one of the central conflicts in the story.

3. Rikki-tikki kills Nagaina, the female cobra.

4. Sample answer: All of the garden animals celebrate the death of the cobras.

5. Rikki-tikki feels proud of himself—but not too proud. He keeps the garden safe from then on, making sure a cobra never again would enter it.

Vocabulary Builder, p. 40

A. Sample Sentences

1. Once we fed the bird and mended its broken wing, it revived.

2. Although Christopher lost the race, he found consolation in the knowledge that he had run faster than he ever had before.

3. Grover, my Labrador retriever, likes swimming immensely; he will spend hour after hour in the water.

B. 1. B; 2. C; 3. D

Enrichment: Real-Life Animals, p. 43

Sample Answers

Physical features: Mongoose—about 15 inches long, including a 10-inch tail; yellowish-gray hair that is streaked with brownish black; similar to a ferret / Cobra—about 6 feet long and 6 inches around; yellowish to dark brown; seemingly "hooded" when nervous or excited

Where it lives: Mongoose—Africa, southern Asia / Cobra—Southern Asia, East Indies

What it eats: Mongoose—birds' eggs, young birds / Cobra—frogs, fish, birds, small mammals

Its defense weapons: Mongoose—swiftness, fierceness / Cobra—deadly poison spread by biting or squirting

Other feature reproduction: Mongoose—litters consist of between one and seven offspring; Cobra—clutch consists of between 12 and 15 eggs

"The Bear Boy" by Joseph Bruchac
"Rikki-tikki-tavi" by Rudyard Kipling

Build Language Skills: Vocabulary, p. 44

A. Sample explanations follow each definition:

1. manner of expression; A person's manner of expression is the way the person speaks.

2. a book that lists words alphabetically and tells how they are pronounced and what they mean; A dictionary tells how a word is to be spoken.

B. Sample Answers

1. Yes, I anticipate seeing the movie because I want to find out whether I agree with my friend's opinion of it.

2. I thought the plot of "Rikki-tikki-tavi" was good because at each point I wanted to know what happened next.

3. Yes, I always predict the ending, because I can usually figure it out ahead of time, and I like to see if I'm right.

4. If I want to see something in a display case, I indicate the item by pointing to it.

5. I would verify the date by looking up the movie on my favorite Web site.

Build Language Skills: Grammar, p. 45

A. 1. is linking verb

2. seem linking verb; fight action verb

3. lives action verb; love action verb

4. threatens action verb; is linking verb

5. defeats action verb; is linking verb

B. Students should write cohesive, grammatically correct paragraphs in which they use at least three action verbs and three linking verbs. They should correctly identify each verb as an action verb or a linking verb.

"Rikki-tikki-tavi" by Rudyard Kipling

Selection Test A, p. 46

Critical Reading

1. ANS: D	DIF: Easy	OBJ: Comprehension
2. ANS: D	DIF: Easy	OBJ: Literary Analysis
3. ANS: B	DIF: Easy	OBJ: Reading Skill
4. ANS: C	DIF: Easy	OBJ: Comprehension
5. ANS: A	DIF: Easy	OBJ: Interpretation
6. ANS: B	DIF: Easy	OBJ: Literary Analysis
7. ANS: A	DIF: Easy	OBJ: Comprehension
8. ANS: A	DIF: Easy	OBJ: Interpretation
9. ANS: C	DIF: Easy	OBJ: Reading Skill
10. ANS: B	DIF: Easy	OBJ: Literary Analysis
11. ANS: C	DIF: Easy	OBJ: Interpretation

Vocabulary and Grammar

12. ANS: B	DIF: Easy	OBJ: Vocabulary
13. ANS: D	DIF: Easy	OBJ: Vocabulary
14. ANS: A	DIF: Easy	OBJ: Grammar
15. ANS: C	DIF: Easy	OBJ: Grammar

Essay

16. Students might note that the first paragraph reveals that Rikki-tikki fought a "great war" and that prior knowledge of stories leads readers to expect they will then learn of the war and of Rikki-tikki's triumph. They may also point out that Rikki-tikki is successful in all of his major tests leading up to the climax—his fights with Karait and Nag, leading the reader to expect him to prevail in the climactic battle against Nagaina.

Difficulty: *Easy*

Objective: *Essay*

17. Students should note one event for each element; they might note that the exposition gives the history of Rikki-tikki's arrival at the home of the English family; the rising action outlines his meetings with Nag and Nagaina and his battles with Karait and Nag; the climax occurs when Rikki-tikki fights Nagaina; the falling action describes Rikki-tikki's recovery and the announcement of his victory; in the resolution, Rikki-tikki is reunited with the English family. Most students will probably think that the elements create an exciting tale of courage and loyalty.

Difficulty: *Easy*

Objective: *Essay*

Selection Test B, p. 49

Critical Reading

1. ANS: B	DIF: Average	OBJ: Reading Skill
2. ANS: A	DIF: Average	OBJ: Interpretation
3. ANS: C	DIF: Average	OBJ: Reading Skill
4. ANS: C	DIF: Average	OBJ: Reading Skill
5. ANS: C	DIF: Average	OBJ: Literary Analysis
6. ANS: C	DIF: Average	OBJ: Literary Analysis
7. ANS: B	DIF: Average	OBJ: Comprehension
8. ANS: C	DIF: Average	OBJ: Literary Analysis
9. ANS: C	DIF: Challenging	OBJ: Interpretation
10. ANS: B	DIF: Average	OBJ: Comprehension
11. ANS: D	DIF: Challenging	OBJ: Literary Analysis
12. ANS: D	DIF: Challenging	OBJ: Comprehension
13. ANS: B	DIF: Challenging	OBJ: Interpretation
14. ANS: B	DIF: Average	OBJ: Interpretation

Vocabulary and Grammar

15. ANS: B	DIF: Average	OBJ: Vocabulary
16. ANS: C	DIF: Average	OBJ: Vocabulary
17. ANS: C	DIF: Average	OBJ: Grammar
18. ANS: C	DIF: Average	OBJ: Grammar

Essay

19. Students might note that the first paragraph reveals that Rikki-tikki fought a "great war." Readers need to know that such an opening suggests that the story will tell about the war and Rikki-tikki's triumph. In addition, as the story proceeds, Rikki-tikki is successful in the tests leading up to the climax—the fights with Karait and Nag—so readers may well expect him to prevail as well in the climactic battle against Nagaina. Students will likely say that it was not difficult to predict that outcome and that few, if any, events suggest that the story will end any other way.

Difficulty: *Average*

Objective: *Essay*

20. Students may note that Rikki-tikki's bravery, his loyalty to the English family, and the responsibility he takes in protecting the birds lead him to confront the snakes repeatedly. His intelligence allows him to outwit the snakes and win in the end. Students may say that the snakes' cruelty and selfishness lead them to attack the other animals. They may also note that the snakes' natural fear causes them to try to wipe out the English family so that they can live safely in the garden. They may add that the snakes are also motivated by family loyalty—Nag's loyalty to his wife and Nagaina's to her husband and their unborn offspring.

Difficulty: *Challenging*

Objective: *Essay*

from *Letters from Rifka* by Karen Hesse

Vocabulary Warm-up Exercises, p. 53

A.
1. regiment
2. peasants
3. belongings
4. bales
5. huddled
6. flickering
7. vanished
8. details

B. Sample Answers
1. Everyone admired the child's *dimpled* cheeks.
2. The crowded *boxcar* was full of crates.
3. We placed new candles in the *candlesticks*.
4. As a *precaution*, we brought our umbrellas with us.
5. The hiker explained that a *rucksack* is a kind of knapsack.
6. Because the children were hungry, they devoured their lunch like *vultures*.
7. The *burlap* felt uncomfortable against his skin.
8. The house was very dirty; even the curtains were *filthy*.

Reading Warm-up A, p. 54

Words that students are to circle appear in parentheses.

Sample Answers
1. (in Russia); *Peasants* are poor farm laborers.
2. (soldiers); A *regiment* is a military unit made up of two or more battalions.
3. caring for the animals in the barn; The *details* of her job annoyed her.
4. daydreaming of how different things would be if he were rich; *Huddled* means "hunched" or "drew oneself together." *Bales* are large bundles of something.

5. (candlelight); *Flickering* means "having the look of darts of light."

6. Tevye's family may have packed clothes, some food, and a few small valuables. *Belongings* are the things that belong to someone.

7. the life they knew; I could not find my socks anywhere; they had *vanished*.

Reading Warm-up B, p. 55

Words that students are to circle appear in parentheses.

Sample Answers

1. to celebrate the Sabbath; *Candlesticks* are holders for candles.

2. (ragged clothing); clean

3. The dimpled cheeks of children are probably round with tiny indentations in them. *Dimpled* means "having dimples, the small natural indentations on the cheeks or chin."

4. the few possessions they were allowed to take with them; A *rucksack* is a knapsack.

5. (a sack); *Burlap* might be used to protect the roots of a tree that is for sale, or it might be used to ship potatoes.

6. The Nazis were like vultures because they stole from helpless people; *Vultures* are large birds that eat the flesh of dead animals.

7. Groups of prisoners were loaded into boxcars. A *boxcar* is a car on a freight train.

8. sending members of the family away before they could be captured and sent to the camps; *Precaution* means "something done ahead of time to keep away danger."

from *Letters from Rifka* by Karen Hesse

Reading: Read Ahead to Verify Predictions and Reread to Look for Details, p. 56

For incorrect predictions, **Event and Detail** follow **Verification:**

2. Incorrect / Rifka never reveals just what happens between her and the guards, but readers can tell from the first line of the selection ("We made it!") that she somehow succeeded.

3. Correct

4. Incorrect / They leave without the papers. Papa says, "There is no time for papers."

Literary Analysis: Character, p. 57

A. Sample Answers

1. brave, thoughtful, caring

2. decisive, careful, loving

B. 1. C; 2. A; 3. E; 4. B; 5. D

Vocabulary Builder, p. 58

A. Sample Answers

1. She might have made up a story about what she was doing on the train.

2. Most likely, he would have been arrested by the guards.

3. They were gathered close together to hide from the soldiers who were coming in search of Nathan.

B. 1. C; 2. D; 3. A

Enrichment: Aleksandr Pushkin, p. 61

Sample Answers

1. The speaker might mean lands to which Russians immigrate.

2. The speaker might be referring to the Russian people who are trapped by "age-old rites," old beliefs and customs.

3. Rifka is like the bird set free in that she has fled old Russia and its "age-old rites" to find a new home and a new life where she will be freer.

Selection Test A, p. 62

Critical Reading

1. ANS: B	DIF: Easy	OBJ: Comprehension
2. ANS: D	DIF: Easy	OBJ: Comprehension
3. ANS: C	DIF: Easy	OBJ: Interpretation
4. ANS: D	DIF: Easy	OBJ: Reading Skill
5. ANS: A	DIF: Easy	OBJ: Literary Analysis
6. ANS: D	DIF: Easy	OBJ: Literary Analysis
7. ANS: C	DIF: Easy	OBJ: Interpretation
8. ANS: A	DIF: Easy	OBJ: Comprehension
9. ANS: B	DIF: Easy	OBJ: Reading Skill
10. ANS: B	DIF: Easy	OBJ: Literary Analysis
11. ANS: D	DIF: Easy	OBJ: Comprehension
12. ANS: C	DIF: Easy	OBJ: Interpretation

Vocabulary and Grammar

13. ANS: C	DIF: Easy	OBJ: Vocabulary
14. ANS: B	DIF: Easy	OBJ: Vocabulary
15. ANS: A	DIF: Easy	OBJ: Grammar

Essay

16. Students might note that Rifka's family is likely to encounter dangers and will certainly be uncomfortable on their journey. Assuming they arrive safely in America, Rifka will have to learn a new language and new customs. She will most likely attend school. She will miss her relatives and old friends, and she will have to

make new friends. She will be reunited with brothers whom perhaps she has not seen in a long time, and she will have to get to know them again.

Difficulty: *Easy*

Objective: *Essay*

17. Students will likely note that both Nathan and Rifka demonstrate courage, Nathan when he deserts the army to warn Saul that he will soon be forced to join and Rifka when she declares that she will be able to distract the guards. That courage will help them face other dangers on the journey. Both also care deeply about their family, as Nathan's desertion and Rifka's remarks about her family members show—she is grateful to Avrum, loves her grandmother, treasures a gift given her by Tovah. Students might point out that their bravery and commitment to the family may motivate the less courageous family members.

Difficulty: *Easy*

Objective: *Essay*

Selection Test B, p. 65

Critical Reading

1. ANS: B	DIF: Average	OBJ: Interpretation
2. ANS: A	DIF: Challenging	OBJ: Interpretation
3. ANS: C	DIF: Challenging	OBJ: Interpretation
4. ANS: D	DIF: Average	OBJ: Reading Skill
5. ANS: B	DIF: Average	OBJ: Reading Skill
6. ANS: B	DIF: Challenging	OBJ: Reading Skill
7. ANS: C	DIF: Average	OBJ: Comprehension
8. ANS: D	DIF: Average	OBJ: Literary Analysis
9. ANS: A	DIF: Average	OBJ: Reading Skill
10. ANS: B	DIF: Challenging	OBJ: Literary Analysis
11. ANS: A	DIF: Challenging	OBJ: Interpretation
12. ANS: C	DIF: Challenging	OBJ: Literary Analysis
13. ANS: A	DIF: Average	OBJ: Comprehension
14. ANS: C	DIF: Average	OBJ: Interpretation

Vocabulary and Grammar

15. ANS: C	DIF: Average	OBJ: Vocabulary
16. ANS: A	DIF: Average	OBJ: Vocabulary
17. ANS: D	DIF: Average	OBJ: Grammar
18. ANS: C	DIF: Average	OBJ: Grammar
19. ANS: B	DIF: Challenging	OBJ: Grammar

Essay

20. Students will likely note that both Nathan and Rifka demonstrate courage, Nathan when he deserts to warn his brother and Rifka when she declares that she will be able to distract the guards. Their courage will help them face other dangers on the journey. Both also care deeply about

their family, as Nathan's desertion and Rifka's remarks about her family members show—she is grateful to Avrum, loves her grandmother, treasures a gift given her by Tovah. Students might point out that their bravery and commitment to the family may motivate the less courageous family members. Students may also comment on Rifka's ability to adapt to change, a trait that will probably help her deal with the uncertainties of the future.

Difficulty: *Average*

Objective: *Essay*

21. Students might note that Rifka is clearly extremely fond of Nathan (when she sees him at the door, joy fills her heart), so she probably wants to win his admiration. She may also wish to prove that Saul is wrong about her—she is not too small to be noticed. Finally, she knows the extreme danger her family faces. Their safety depends on her efforts, and because she loves them deeply, she will act to make sure they escape safely. Her courage and imagination are traits that may help her succeed.

Difficulty: *Challenging*

Objective: *Essay*

"Two Kinds" by Amy Tan

Vocabulary Warm-up Exercises, p. 69

A. 1. sulky
2. uneven
3. nervousness
4. regret
5. arched
6. talented
7. exist
8. assured

B. Sample Answers

1. F; *Images* are mental pictures, and most artists do have mental pictures of what they plan to paint.

2. T; *Heaving* means "moving up and down," and when you breathe heavily, your chest rises and falls, or heaves.

3. F; An *assortment* is a collection or a variety, so if there is a large assortment, there are many choices.

4. T; *Fascinated* means "very interested by something," so its opposite would be *bored,* which means "uninterested in anything."

5. F; *Miniature* means "very small," so an adult would not fit comfortably in a miniature chair.

6. F; *Throughout* means "from start to finish," so if you leave early, you will not have stayed for the whole performance.

7. T; *Purely* means "entirely," so something that happens purely by design was planned.

8. F; *Petals* are the colorful parts of flowers that are shaped like leaves; all flowers have petals.

Reading Warm-up A, p. 70

Words that students are to circle appear in parentheses.

Sample Answers

1. the results of their efforts; *Uneven* means "rough" or "irregular."

2. if the other team scored a goal, the Hawks would stop trying; Does a company *exist* that can handle this challenge?

3. (mood); A person with a *sulky* expression would frown or look moody.

4. lots of practice and belief in yourselves; *Talented* means "gifted" or "having natural ability."

5. feel her old feeling; *Nervousness* is a state of being worried or anxious.

6. If you lose without trying; It was with *regret* that Sue decided not to attend the meeting.

7. (net); An *arched* object is curved and has space under it.

8. we like to win games, but that is not the only way to measure victory; *Assured* means "promised confidently."

Reading Warm-up B, p. 71

Words that students are to circle appear in parentheses.

Sample Answers

1. *everywhere;* The colorfully dressed trick-or-treaters marched *throughout* the neighborhood.

2. smells, sounds, and sights; An *assortment* is a variety.

3. Flower markets, red, yellow, pink, and white flowers; My favorite flower is a daisy, and its *petals* are white.

4. the many objects in souvenir shops; *Fascinated* means "bewitched or very interested by."

5. (statues of animals); Other *miniature* objects sold in stores include model cars and dollhouse furniture.

6. *entirely;* The action movie is *purely* entertaining.

7. (of Asian culture); *Images* are mental pictures.

8. Spicy food may bring about a heaving chest. *Heaving* means "rising and falling, as when breathing."

"Two Kinds" by Amy Tan

Reading: Read Ahead to Verify Predictions and Reread to Look for Details, p. 72

For incorrect predictions, **Event and Detail** follow
Verification:

2. Correct

3. Incorrect / The daughter performs very badly. The narrator says, "I dawdled over it, playing a few bars and then cheating. . . . I never really listened to what I was playing. I daydreamed."

4. Incorrect / The daughter leaves the piano at her mother's. She says, "Are you sure? . . . I mean, won't you and Dad miss it?"

Literary Analysis: Character, p. 73

A. Sample Answers

1. stubborn, guilt ridden, angry

2. determined, proud, stubborn

B. 1. B; 2. E; 3. D; 4. C; 5. A

Vocabulary Builder, p. 74

A. Sample Answers

1. No, she would not have been, because no one is ever perfect, and to be beyond reproach, one must be perfect.

2. She would have felt as if she had been destroyed.

3. The idea was both of theirs. I know because to *conspire* means to "plan together."

B. 1. C; 2. B; 3. D

Enrichment: Performing Arts, p. 77

A. In responding to the questions, students should assume the real possibility of pursuing the performing art they have chosen.

B. Students should realistically budget their waking hours, including time spent with family.

from *Letters from Rifka* by Karen Hesse
"Two Kinds" by Amy Tan

Build Language Skills: Vocabulary, p. 78

A. 1. The meteorologists *predict* it will rain heavily.

2. The scientists conducted a study to *verify* their theory.

3. The jurors delivered their *verdict* solemnly.

B. Sample Answers

1. The street signs indicate that we are in the wrong neighborhood.

2. Matthew and Tyler anticipate that the best actors will be trying out for the major parts.

3. The movie's plot was complicated and hard to follow.

4. I have studied hard and predict that I will do well on the math test.

5. The scientists submitted their lab notes so that reviewers could verify the results of the experiment.

Build Language Skills: Grammar, p. 79

A. 1. ran irregular, past

2. fled irregular, past; is starting regular, present participle

3. was irregular, past; saved regular, past

B. Students should write cohesive, grammatically correct paragraphs in which they use, and correctly identify, at least three regular verbs and three irregular verbs.

"Two Kinds" by Amy Tan

Selection Test A, p. 80

Critical Reading

1. ANS: D	DIF: Easy	OBJ: Interpretation
2. ANS: C	DIF: Easy	OBJ: Literary Analysis
3. ANS: C	DIF: Easy	OBJ: Reading
4. ANS: B	DIF: Easy	OBJ: Literary Analysis
5. ANS: D	DIF: Easy	OBJ: Comprehension
6. ANS: C	DIF: Easy	OBJ: Comprehension
7. ANS: D	DIF: Easy	OBJ: Interpretation
8. ANS: B	DIF: Easy	OBJ: Reading
9. ANS: B	DIF: Easy	OBJ: Interpretation
10. ANS: D	DIF: Easy	OBJ: Comprehension
11. ANS: B	DIF: Easy	OBJ: Literary Analysis
12. ANS: C	DIF: Easy	OBJ: Interpretation

Vocabulary and Grammar

13. ANS: C	DIF: Easy	OBJ: Vocabulary
14. ANS: B	DIF: Easy	OBJ: Vocabulary
15. ANS: A	DIF: Easy	OBJ: Grammar

Essay

16. Students should note that the mother has a greater adjustment to make because she grew up in a very different culture. The daughter, in contrast, has experienced only the culture of the United States. Therefore, the mother firmly believes that children owe their parents strict and unquestioning obedience, while the daughter believes that she must be true to herself. In addition, students might note that the daughter faces a conflict within herself. On the one hand, she feels loyalty to her mother and her mother's traditions; on the other hand, she wishes to assert her independence.

Difficulty: *Easy*

Objective: *Essay*

17. Students might note that both the daughter and her mother are strong willed and stubborn. The mother shows these traits by persisting in finding an area in which her daughter can excel even after her daughter clearly indicates that she does not share her mother's enthusiasm. The daughter shows her stubbornness by refusing to share her mother's enthusiasm and by refusing to put effort into practicing the piano. In pointing out the characters' differences, students might note that the mother is demanding, while the daughter is defiant. For example the mother demands that her daughter practice the piano and expects to be obeyed. The daughter defies her mother by studying the piano halfheartedly and eventually refusing to practice anymore. Finally, the characters differ in that the mother

believes that one can become whatever one wants. The daughter holds that one can be only what one is capable of being.

Difficulty: *Easy*

Objective: *Essay*

Selection Test B, p. 83

Critical Reading

1. ANS: C	DIF: Average	OBJ: Literary Analysis
2. ANS: C	DIF: Challenging	OBJ: Interpretation
3. ANS: A	DIF: Average	OBJ: Literary Analysis
4. ANS: B	DIF: Challenging	OBJ: Reading
5. ANS: D	DIF: Average	OBJ: Reading
6. ANS: B	DIF: Challenging	OBJ: Interpretation
7. ANS: B	DIF: Average	OBJ: Reading
8. ANS: C	DIF: Challenging	OBJ: Comprehension
9. ANS: A	DIF: Challenging	OBJ: Literary Analysis
10. ANS: C	DIF: Challenging	OBJ: Literary Analysis
11. ANS: C	DIF: Challenging	OBJ: Literary Analysis
12. ANS: A	DIF: Average	OBJ: Interpretation
13. ANS: C	DIF: Average	OBJ: Interpretation

Vocabulary and Grammar

14. ANS: B	DIF: Average	OBJ: Vocabulary
15. ANS: C	DIF: Average	OBJ: Vocabulary
16. ANS: D	DIF: Average	OBJ: Vocabulary
17. ANS: C	DIF: Challenging	OBJ: Grammar

Essay

18. Students may note that the mother hopes to realize her dreams through her daughter. Her daughter stubbornly fights her mother's wishes, wanting to be herself and to find her own dreams. Each keeps hoping the other will give in. Students should point out that neither one does: The mother continues to believe that her daughter could be anything if only she would try, and the daughter continues to look for acceptance. Students might note that in the end the mother offers her daughter the piano, a sign of forgiveness and acceptance, and the daughter plays the composition that she had played at the recital, which then signifies her reconciliation and the resolution of her childhood conflict.

Difficulty: *Average*

Objective: *Essay*

19. Students should explain that both the title of the story and the titles of Schumann's compositions refer to the conflict the daughter experiences—a struggle between being her mother's daughter and being her own person. Students might note that at first she tries to win acceptance from her mother by going along with her wild

ambitions, but later she realizes that she is beginning to dislike herself for ignoring her own wishes and desires. Students might further recognize that the resolution comes when she recognizes that "Pleading Child" and "Perfectly Contented" are two halves of the same song—they represent the two stages she has to pass through in order to grow up.

Difficulty: *Challenging*

Objective: *Essay*

"Seventh Grade" by Gary Soto
"Stolen Day" by Sherwood Anderson

Vocabulary Warm-up Exercises, p. 87

A. 1. provide
2. bustled
3. confusing
4. formed
5. conviction
6. squirmed
7. affects
8. unison

B. Sample Answers

1. They took the carp home and ate it for dinner.
2. He cast an admiring glance at the capable clerk.
3. They attended the play and afterwards went out to dinner.
4. People who bluff their way to success are dishonest.
5. He remembered the recent trip he made, the one he went on last month.
6. After he saw his train arrive at the station, he lingered on the platform, waiting for it to be time to get onboard.
7. The solemn music made me think serious thoughts.
8. Their failure to win the game depressed the team.

Reading Warm-up A, p. 88

Words that students are to circle appear in parentheses.

Sample Answers

1. (act together); I might march in unison with the other members of the band.
2. always on the move, looking for this, borrowing that; Someone who does not bustle moves around slowly or just sits quietly.
3. (stay put); *wriggled*
4. (opinions); I formed a language club at school.
5. (growing); A conviction is a strong opinion or belief.
6. Trying to be yourself and still be like your friends; *puzzling*
7. It affects the way you act from hour to hour; Self-esteem also affects behavior.

8. Knowing about the behaviors of seventh graders may provide an understanding; *offers*

Reading Warm-up B, p. 89

Words that students are to circle appear in parentheses.

Sample Answers

1. (warm-water fish); My dad caught a carp during his fishing trip.
2. The coach was solemn when he talked about the bad game.
3. (latest); A recent event in my life was planning my dad's birthday party.
4. a carp will pretend to give up; A possum will bluff by pretending to be dead.
5. (succeeded); Sometimes there is a power failure during a storm.
6. (the size of the fish); I have been admiring a pair of boots at the department store.
7. a few minutes; *stayed*
8. smiled when she remembered the fish; *time*

Literary Analysis: Comparing Characters, p. 90

A. Sample answers are provided for each character, as follows:

Words that describe the character directly / What the character says and does / How other characters talk about or act toward the character

Victor: "He already spoke Spanish and English." / To impress Teresa, he claims to know French. / After French class, Teresa is friendly to him.

Teresa: Not applicable / In homeroom, she reads a novel. After class, she asks the teacher about ballet. / Victor thinks she is cute and good in math; Victor blushes when he talks to her.

The narrator of "Stolen Day": Not applicable / He imagines that he has "inflammatory rheumatism" but does not want to tell his family because he thinks they will laugh at him. / The narrator claims that his sister, brothers, and mother laugh at him.

The mother in "Stolen Day": She was "pretty busy." / The narrator says that she laughs at him often. She takes care of her younger children, instructs the narrator to go to bed when he says he does not feel well, and says she's glad when he says he is feeling better. She also discovers a drowned child and carries the body to his or her family's home. / The narrator implies that she has no time for him.

Vocabulary Builder, p. 91

A. Sample Answers

1. An elective is an optional class. Victor does not like math, so if it had been an elective, he would not have had to take it.

2. Michael has a strong belief about the benefits of scowling; he believes that girls are attracted to men who scowl.

3. He is serious and somber.

4. The weather causes a change in the person's mood.

5. He will frown, and his eyebrows will come together.

B. 1. C; 2. A; 3. B; 4. A

Selection Test A, p. 93

Critical Reading

1. ANS: B   DIF: Easy   OBJ: Comprehension
2. ANS: B   DIF: Easy   OBJ: Literary Analysis
3. ANS: D   DIF: Easy   OBJ: Comprehension
4. ANS: A   DIF: Easy   OBJ: Interpretation
5. ANS: C   DIF: Easy   OBJ: Comprehension
6. ANS: B   DIF: Easy   OBJ: Interpretation
7. ANS: D   DIF: Easy   OBJ: Interpretation
8. ANS: A   DIF: Easy   OBJ: Interpretation
9. ANS: D   DIF: Easy   OBJ: Interpretation
10. ANS: B   DIF: Easy   OBJ: Literary Analysis
11. ANS: C   DIF: Easy   OBJ: Literary Analysis
12. ANS: A   DIF: Easy   OBJ: Literary Analysis

Vocabulary

13. ANS: B   DIF: Easy   OBJ: Vocabulary
14. ANS: C   DIF: Easy   OBJ: Vocabulary
15. ANS: A   DIF: Easy   OBJ: Vocabulary

Essay

16. Students should define direct and indirect characterization according to the definitions in their textbooks. They might describe Teresa, Michael, or Mr. Bueller in "Seventh Grade" or the narrator's mother in "Stolen Day." They should show how the character's words or actions, or the words or actions of another character, reveal something about him or her.

    Difficulty: *Easy*

    Objective: *Essay*

17. Students should describe the two main characters and then mention any of the following details, or any others that reveal their characters: Victor likes Teresa and blushes when he talks to her. He feels foolish when he tries to imitate Michael's scowl. He embarrasses himself by pretending to know French. Michael is friendly to him; girls in his English class giggle when he embarrasses himself; Teresa likes him. The narrator of "Stolen Day" comes to believe that he has "inflammatory rheumatism." He implies that he is ignored by his mother and says he is laughed at by members of his family. He daydreams a great deal, about the disease and the boy who actually has it, about how his family treats him,

and about how people would react if he died. Forgetting to be careful about what he says, he tells his family that he has inflammatory rheumatism. They laugh at him, and he regrets his admission.

Difficulty: *Easy*

Objective: *Essay*

Selection Test B, p. 96

Critical Reading

1. ANS: C   DIF: Average   OBJ: Comprehension
2. ANS: B   DIF: Average   OBJ: Literary Analysis
3. ANS: C   DIF: Challenging   OBJ: Literary Analysis
4. ANS: A   DIF: Average   OBJ: Comprehension
5. ANS: A   DIF: Average   OBJ: Interpretation
6. ANS: D   DIF: Average   OBJ: Interpretation
7. ANS: D   DIF: Average   OBJ: Interpretation
8. ANS: C   DIF: Average   OBJ: Interpretation
9. ANS: A   DIF: Average   OBJ: Interpretation
10. ANS: B   DIF: Challenging   OBJ: Interpretation
11. ANS: B   DIF: Average   OBJ: Literary Analysis
12. ANS: C   DIF: Challenging   OBJ: Literary Analysis
13. ANS: A   DIF: Average   OBJ: Literary Analysis
14. ANS: C   DIF: Average   OBJ: Literary Analysis
15. ANS: B   DIF: Average   OBJ: Literary Analysis

Vocabulary

16. ANS: B   DIF: Challenging   OBJ: Vocabulary
17. ANS: B   DIF: Average   OBJ: Vocabulary
18. ANS: C   DIF: Average   OBJ: Vocabulary
19. ANS: B   DIF: Challenging   OBJ: Vocabulary

Essay

20. Students might point out that Gary Soto tells the reader why Victor wants to study French, how he feels when he tries to scowl, how he plans to speak to Teresa after homeroom, and so on. As examples of indirect characterization in "Stolen Day," they might point to the boy's preoccupation with inflammatory rheumatism, the way his pains come and go, and his thoughts about dying. Students may realize that the characterization of Victor in "Seventh Grade" is predominantly direct while the characterization of the narrator of "Stolen Day" is indirect.

    Difficulty: *Average*

    Objective: *Essay*

21. Students should recognize that Victor's problem is that he likes Teresa and makes a fool of himself in an attempt to impress her. He is fully responsible for his problem: He claims that he knows French when he does not and then is called on to speak it—and feels embarrassed by his failure. Students may say that the embarrassment will

teach him not to lie in the future. Alternatively, students may argue that because Teresa believes that the gibberish he speaks is French and the story ends happily, Victor will not be motivated to be honest in the future. In describing the narrator of "Stolen Day," students may recognize that the boy feels neglected by his family, especially his mother. They should recognize that like Victor, he is responsible for his own problem: Although he knows that his family will laugh at him if he tells them he has "inflammatory rheumatism," he tells them anyway—and feels embarrassed by their laughter. Students are likely to say that the narrator's final remarks, about the regret he feels for admitting his thoughts, teach him not to speak out in the future. They may also point out that the boy's basic problem—his feeling of being neglected by his family—is not resolved at the end of the story; the story does not end happily.

Difficulty: *Challenging*

Objective: *Essay*

Writing Workshop—Unit 2, Part 1

Review of a Short Story: Integrating Grammar Skills, p. 100

A. 1. present perfect; 2. present; 3. past; 4. past perfect; 5. future

B. 1. Yesterday I borrowed four books from the library.

2. I have used the library many times in the past.

3. Yesterday, after I had traveled to the library, I walked up to the second floor.

4. I (had) asked the librarian for help but she ignored me.

Unit 2, Part 1 Answers

Benchmark Test 3, p. 101

MULTIPLE CHOICE

1. ANS: C
2. ANS: A
3. ANS: A
4. ANS: D
5. ANS: B
6. ANS: C
7. ANS: A
8. ANS: D
9. ANS: B
10. ANS: C
11. ANS: C
12. ANS: D
13. ANS: A
14. ANS: A
15. ANS: B

16. ANS: D
17. ANS: C
18. ANS: D
19. ANS: B
20. ANS: C
21. ANS: B
22. ANS: C
23. ANS: A
24. ANS: B
25. ANS: D
26. ANS: B
27. ANS: B
28. ANS: B
29. ANS: A
30. ANS: C
31. ANS: C
32. ANS: A
33. ANS: C

ESSAY

34. Students should make the plot of the story clear to readers. There should be transitions between events.

35. Students should demonstrate their understanding of the use of questions to help them narrow their focus.

36. Students should demonstrate their understanding of writing in the first person. Students should also be able to use transition words correctly in order to explain sequence of events.

Unit 2, Part 2 Answers

Diagnostic Test 4, p. 108

MULTIPLE CHOICE

1. ANS: C
2. ANS: A
3. ANS: B
4. ANS: C
5. ANS: B
6. ANS: D
7. ANS: A
8. ANS: D
9. ANS: A
10. ANS: B
11. ANS: B
12. ANS: A
13. ANS: D
14. ANS: A
15. ANS: C

"The Third Wish" by Joan Aiken

Vocabulary Warm-up Exercises, p. 112

A. 1. frantically
2. canal
3. tremendous
4. thrashed
5. occasions
6. reflecting
7. granted
8. utter

B. Sample Answers
1. I wear a waterproof jacket and heavy boots to protect myself in harsh weather.
2. If a friend is distressed, I might try to help by talking with him or her.
3. On a Saturday night, I prefer to watch a movie with my family.
4. A remote place that I would like to visit is Denali National Park.
5. It would be rash for someone to spend all his or her money because there would be nothing left for an emergency.
6. Someone who has been kept waiting is likely to have an angry expression.
7. People are likely to lose their composure in an embarrassing situation.
8. One way of communicating is by talking face to face.

Reading Warm-up A, p. 113

Words that students are to circle appear in parentheses.

Sample Answers
1. (your wish); *given*
2. some of my past wishes; The girl was reflecting on her future.
3. (huge); *tiny*
4. wishes for things I thought would make me happy; The shy girl would not utter a word.
5. The writer's wishes came true when he made them happen. Wishes might also come true by chance.
6. (boaters); Pleasure boats and boats carrying freight might use a canal.
7. like a badly loaded washing machine; The dog thrashed his tail as I prepared his dinner.
8. The boy frantically called the writer; I ran frantically down the hall because I was late for class.

Reading Warm-up B, p. 114

Words that students are to circle appear in parentheses.

Sample Answers
1. (to fly); After school I prefer to play basketball with my friends.
2. (serene); *look*

3. puppylike barking notes or loud high-pitched purring sounds; My sister and I were communicating with sign language.
4. It is as if nothing in the world could upset a mute swan; The swan's silence contributes to its supreme composure.
5. The swan will drive out the offending bird with an angry hiss and a flapping of her wings; a person who is distressed might go someplace to be alone.
6. It invades a swan's nesting territory; Taking an important test without studying for it is a rash thing to do.
7. Arctic Islands, northern Russia, and as far south as Brazil and Australia; *nearby*
8. (clamor); A harsh sound is the pounding of a hammer.

"The Third Wish" by Joan Aiken

Reading: Make Inferences by Recognizing Details, p. 115

Sample Answers
1. The swan has become a man. The swan and the man are different versions of the same magical being.
2. Leita's beauty is extraordinary, and she appears out of nowhere, so she must be magical, too. Perhaps, like the man in green, she has been transformed from a creature in nature.
3. Leita is wandering around because she misses the forest or her life before she was transformed into a woman.
4. The two swans are Leita and her sister. Although she is now a swan, Leita still cares for Mr. Peters.

Literary Analysis: Conflict, p. 116

Sample Answers
1. Internal—Leita is a human, and her sister is a swan. Leita struggles to overcome the loneliness she feels because she is separated from her sister.
2. External—Mr. Peters and Leita struggle to find happiness together.
3. Internal—Leita is torn between her old life as a swan and her current life as a human being.

Vocabulary Builder, p. 117

Sample Answers
A. 1. Most humans put little or no thought into their choices.
2. Yes; it is clear that the old King is overconfident because the sentence states that he is presumptuous, and *presumptuous* means "overconfident."
3. He acts in a spiteful, hateful way.
4. Mr. Peters's home is not close to town. It is *remote*, which means that it is far from everything.

B. 1. D; 2. B; 3. A; 4. B

Enrichment: A Scientific Look at Swans, p. 120

Sample Answers

A. 1. The mute swan is the species most often found in North American parks and ponds. Is has white feathers, may be as long as five feet from bill to tail, and has a wing-span of seven feet. It is used to living among people. Like other swans, it is precocial—it is born with feathers and open eyes and soon after hatching is ready to leave the nest, swim, and find its own food.

2. Young swans are called cygnets.

3. Swans search for food by sticking their necks under-water. They eat the leaves, stems, and roots of plants that grow in the water. They tear the plants with the sharp edges of their bills.

B. Students should supply three facts for the species they have chosen—for example, physical appearance, range, and breeding habits.

Selection Test A, p. 121

Critical Reading

1. ANS: A	DIF: Easy	OBJ: Literary Analysis
2. ANS: C	DIF: Easy	OBJ: Comprehension
3. ANS: B	DIF: Easy	OBJ: Comprehension
4. ANS: A	DIF: Easy	OBJ: Comprehension
5. ANS: D	DIF: Easy	OBJ: Reading
6. ANS: B	DIF: Easy	OBJ: Interpretation
7. ANS: C	DIF: Easy	OBJ: Comprehension
8. ANS: B	DIF: Easy	OBJ: Interpretation
9. ANS: D	DIF: Easy	OBJ: Reading
10. ANS: A	DIF: Easy	OBJ: Interpretation
11. ANS: C	DIF: Easy	OBJ: Interpretation

Vocabulary and Grammar

12. ANS: A	DIF: Easy	OBJ: Vocabulary
13. ANS: D	DIF: Easy	OBJ: Vocabulary
14. ANS: B	DIF: Easy	OBJ: Grammar
15. ANS: C	DIF: Easy	OBJ: Grammar

Essay

16. Among the many examples of her unhappiness are her restlessness, her wandering in the garden, her unex-plained absences from the house, the tenderness she shows a particular swan, and her weeping. Students should realize that Leita is a swan and cannot be happy living as a human. She misses her sister, and although she cares for Mr. Peters, she misses her life in the forest. For her, life as a human is harder than life as a swan.

Difficulty: *Easy*
Objective: *Essay*

17. Students might say that the main conflict is external, between Mr. Peters and Leita. It comes about because Leita, a swan, is unhappy living as a human. She misses her sister and her life in the forest. Alternatively, students might say the main conflict is internal, within Leita, as she struggles between her devotion to Mr. Peters and her desire to live as a swan again. Or, they could cite the internal conflict in Mr. Peters as he strug-gles between his desire for Leita's companionship and his desire to see her happy again as a swan. All of these conflicts are resolved when Mr. Peters makes his second wish, that Leita be turned back into a swan.

Difficulty: *Easy*
Objective: *Essay*

Selection Test B, p. 124

Critical Reading

1. ANS: C	DIF: Challenging	OBJ: Literary Analysis
2. ANS: B	DIF: Challenging	OBJ: Reading
3. ANS: C	DIF: Average	OBJ: Comprehension
4. ANS: B	DIF: Average	OBJ: Comprehension
5. ANS: B	DIF: Average	OBJ: Interpretation
6. ANS: C	DIF: Average	OBJ: Reading
7. ANS: B	DIF: Average	OBJ: Interpretation
8. ANS: A	DIF: Challenging	OBJ: Reading
9. ANS: D	DIF: Challenging	OBJ: Literary Analysis
10. ANS: C	DIF: Average	OBJ: Comprehension
11. ANS: D	DIF: Challenging	OBJ: Interpretation
12. ANS: D	DIF: Challenging	OBJ: Interpretation

Vocabulary and Grammar

13. ANS: D	DIF: Average	OBJ: Vocabulary
14. ANS: C	DIF: Average	OBJ: Vocabulary
15. ANS: C	DIF: Average	OBJ: Grammar
16. ANS: A	DIF: Challenging	OBJ: Grammar
17. ANS: B	DIF: Challenging	OBJ: Grammar

Essay

18. Students should recognize that Mr. Peters does eventu-ally prove the old King wrong. His first wish brings him sadness because Leita does not provide the companion-ship he had longed for. After he changes Leita back into a swan, however, he finds the companionship in the company of the two swans that are "always somewhere close at hand." Furthermore, by using his second wish to turn Leita back into a swan, he puts an end to her terrible unhappiness and therefore uses his wish for a good cause.

Difficulty: *Average*
Objective: *Essay*

19. Students should note the distinction between an external conflict and an internal conflict. They may cite the external conflict between the King and Mr. Peters or the one between Mr. Peters and Leita, both of which are resolved when Mr. Peters makes his second wish. They may cite the internal conflict within Mr. Peters as he struggles between his desire to keep Leita in her human form and his desire to see her happy again, or they may cite the internal conflict within Leita as she struggles between her devotion to Mr. Peters and her desire to live as a swan again. Both of those conflicts are resolved by the granting of the second wish.

Difficulty: *Challenging*
Objective: *Essay*

"Amigo Brothers" by Piri Thomas

Vocabulary Warm-up Exercises, p. 128

A. 1. nimble
2. opponent
3. shuffle
4. style
5. fitful
6. surged
7. barrage
8. achieve

B. Sample Answers

1. Yes; To answer with clarity means to answer clearly, in a way that people will understand.

2. No; *Emerging* means "coming out," so you would not have seen the tail of a snake that is just emerging.

3. Yes; To improvise music is to make it up on the spot, and you have to be a good musician to do that.

4. No; *Numerous* means "many," so someone with numerous things to do does not have a lot of free time.

5. No; A challenger is a person who opposes a champion.

6. Yes; Someone who is muscular is strong and therefore can lift heavy objects.

7. No; Only light blows are used in a sparring match, so the participants are not likely to get seriously injured.

8. No; A person with a mild manner is easygoing and unlikely to get angry often.

Reading Warm-up A, p. 129

Words that students are to circle appear in parentheses.

Sample Answers

1. to become a champion middleweight boxer; I want to *achieve* my high school diploma and go to college.

2. stay steady on the course; My *fitful* attempt to become a guitarist never worked out.

3. (eyes); Always keep your eyes on the *enemy*.

4. He bounced here, now there, never still, never in the same place; A synonym for *nimble* is *quick*.

5. tight, controlled, and quick as a viper; Basketball requires a similar *style* because the players have to be quick on their feet and controlled in their movements.

6. (of soft jabs); Our car had to drive through a *barrage* of hailstones.

7. with a jab to his brother's ribs; Sal *rushed* forward with a forceful jab to his brother's ribs.

8. as if dancing on sand; My tired feet *shuffled* up the stairs.

Reading Warm-up B, p. 130

Words that students are to circle appear in parentheses.

Sample Answers

1. (rules); I quickly *made up* an excuse for being late.

2. by defining what boxers can and cannot do. The *clarity* of the actor's diction allowed the audience to take in every word.

3. in amateur boxing; *Many* rules in amateur boxing are different from professional boxing.

4. women's boxing; Skateboarding is an *emerging* sport among my friends.

5. small cuts; slight bruising; *Minor* injuries such as small cuts and slight bruising happen in all boxing events.

6. (where the boxers use light blows); The kittens were *sparring* with their little paws.

7. defeated the English champion Joe Goss, in 1880 after 87 rounds; In the 2004 World Series, the Boston Red Sox was a *challenger* to the New York Yankees.

8. (female boxers); A racehorse's body is lean and *muscular*.

"Amigo Brothers" by Piri Thomas

Reading: Make Inferences by Recognizing Details, p. 131

Sample Answers

1. Antonio believes in fighting fair. As the lighter of the two boys, he identifies with the tugboat's "courage."

2. The boys are not eager to fight against each other and must prepare themselves mentally.

3. Felix does not want trouble with the boys on the street, so he plays at boxing in order to scare them and avoid violence.

4. Felix also hits hard, and he has the attitude of a professional.

5. Both Felix and Antonio see their friendship as more important than enjoying the glory of winning. The narrator calls both boys champions. That suggests that both of them are winners of a kind.

Literary Analysis: Conflict, p. 132

Sample Answers

1. Internal—Antonio struggles to put Felix out of his mind while knowing that he must fight his friend.
2. External—Felix is aware that the neighborhood boys see him as a stranger and may challenge him.
3. Internal—Antonio wonders how the fight will affect his friendship with Felix while knowing that he must fight him.
4. External—Felix and Antonio fight each other in the boxing match.

Vocabulary Builder, p. 133

Sample Answers

A. 1. The hurricane destroyed the island.
   2. She never stops moving.
   3. It disappeared.
   4. They allowed him to keep from getting punched.

B. 1. B; 2. D; 3. C; 4. A

Enrichment: Describe an Activity, p. 136

Students may write about any activity, from playing chess to snorkeling. They should focus on one aspect of the activity, using vivid details that make the activity come alive for the reader. Their final description should be a vivid, cohesive narrative.

"The Third Wish" by Joan Aiken
"Amigo Brothers" by Piri Thomas

Build Language Skills: Vocabulary, p. 137

A. 1. obstacle
   2. obstruct
   3. obstinate
   4. obstructive

B. Yes / No / Explanation

1. No / A person has to conclude something based on evidence.
2. Yes / An object is something that can be seen or touched, so what the witness swore that he had seen would have been an object.
3. No / A well-written paper has to have a subject.
4. No / *Credible* means "easy to believe," so someone with a reputation for lying is not credible.
5. Yes / An assessment of a situation is likely to be influenced by one's background.

Build Language Skills: Grammar, p. 138

Sample Answers

A. 1. straight, empty
   2. strange, distant
   3. great, white, little

4. grateful, several
5. gorgeous, pretty, blue-green
6. fair, lean, lanky, dark, short, husky
7. lean, long, better
8. short, muscular, better
9. large, local
10. street, fighting

B. 1. Leita was a swan who became an attractive woman.
   2. The dark, remote forest is the setting of the story.
   3. Antonio Cruz is lean, talented boxer.
   4. Felix Vargas is short but powerful boxer.

"Amigo Brothers" by Piri Thomas

Selection Test A, p. 139

Critical Reading

1. ANS: B	DIF: Easy	OBJ: Comprehension
2. ANS: C	DIF: Easy	OBJ: Interpretation
3. ANS: A	DIF: Easy	OBJ: Reading
4. ANS: B	DIF: Easy	OBJ: Literary Analysis
5. ANS: D	DIF: Easy	OBJ: Comprehension
6. ANS: A	DIF: Easy	OBJ: Literary Analysis
7. ANS: C	DIF: Easy	OBJ: Comprehension
8. ANS: D	DIF: Easy	OBJ: Interpretation
9. ANS: B	DIF: Easy	OBJ: Interpretation
10. ANS: A	DIF: Easy	OBJ: Reading

Vocabulary and Grammar

11. ANS: A	DIF: Easy	OBJ: Vocabulary
12. ANS: C	DIF: Easy	OBJ: Vocabulary
13. ANS: B	DIF: Easy	OBJ: Grammar
14. ANS: C	DIF: Easy	OBJ: Grammar

Essay

15. Students might note that Felix and Antonio have grown up in the same apartment building, have shared a love of boxing, and work out together. Both dream of being the lightweight champion. In the match they will fight, both want to fight fairly, and each boy believes he can win. After the match, they show that their friendship is important by hugging each other and leaving the ring with their arms around each other before they hear the announcement of the name of the winner.
    Difficulty: *Easy*
    Objective: *Essay*
16. Students should recognize that the main external conflict is the boxing match between Antonio and Felix. Both boys also deal with the internal conflict of wanting to win but not wanting to hurt his friend. The conflicts are resolved when the boys fight as best they can and

then leave the ring together, arm in arm, without waiting to hear the name of the winner announced.

Difficulty: *Easy*
Objective: *Essay*

Selection Test B, p. 142

Critical Reading

1. ANS: A   DIF: Average   OBJ: Literary Analysis
2. ANS: C   DIF: Challenging   OBJ: Literary Analysis
3. ANS: D   DIF: Average   OBJ: Reading
4. ANS: C   DIF: Average   OBJ: Comprehension
5. ANS: B   DIF: Challenging   OBJ: Literary Analysis
6. ANS: A   DIF: Average   OBJ: Interpretation
7. ANS: D   DIF: Average   OBJ: Reading
8. ANS: A   DIF: Challenging   OBJ: Interpretation
9. ANS: D   DIF: Challenging   OBJ: Reading
10. ANS: A   DIF: Average   OBJ: Interpretation
11. ANS: C   DIF: Average   OBJ: Comprehension

Vocabulary and Grammar

12. ANS: A   DIF: Challenging   OBJ: Vocabulary
13. ANS: C   DIF: Average   OBJ: Vocabulary
14. ANS: B   DIF: Average   OBJ: Vocabulary
15. ANS: A   DIF: Challenging   OBJ: Grammar
16. ANS: D   DIF: Average   OBJ: Grammar

Essay

17. Students who choose Antonio might say that it is noted throughout the selection that he is the better boxer and, with his tall frame and long reach, has the advantage. They could also point to all the times he is able to avoid Felix's punches and make contact with his own punches. Students who choose Felix might point to his powerful fists and the high energy in his short, muscular frame. They might also point to some good punches that almost knocked Antonio out.

Difficulty: *Average*

Objective: *Essay*

18. Students should recognize that the external conflict is the boxing match between two friends. That conflict serves as a frame for each boy's internal conflict: the desire to win versus the desire to maintain a friendship. The resolution occurs when the boys leave the ring before the winner is announced, choosing friendship over what would be one boy's moment of glory before the crowd and the other boy's moment of great disappointment. The resolution teaches Antonio and Felix how important their friendship is to them.

Difficulty: *Challenging*

Objective: *Essay*

"Zoo" by Edward D. Hoch

Vocabulary Warm-up Exercises, p. 146

A.
1. horrors
2. constantly
3. breed
4. seeking
5. odd
6. scurried
7. limit
8. clutching

B. Sample Answers
1. No; an expense is something that costs money, so it would not be free.
2. Yes; *reveal* means "expose to view," so if you reveal a secret, anyone might hear about it.
3. No; an annual event takes place every year, not every month.
4. Yes, because something that is jagged has sharp points.
5. Yes; any grownup is an adult, so someone's grandparents could go to an event that is for adults only.
6. No; awe is a feeling of fear or wonder, so someone would not be bored by something he or she was in awe of.
7. No; *clustered* means "gathered together in a bunch," so plants that are clustered would not be scattered.
8. No; *daybreak* is the time when the sun rises, and that is way before 9 A.M.

Reading Warm-up A, p. 147

Words that students are to circle appear in parentheses.

Sample Answers
1. (a horselike creature); *Scurried* means "ran quickly."
2. (animal); *Odd* means "unusual."
3. (Modern researchers); The collector has been seeking a rare orchid.
4. (smaller); I would love to have a Labrador retriever as a pet.
5. If one kind of animal is hunted constantly, the species may become extinct; My sister plays her favorite CD constantly.
6. (the reins of their mighty steeds); *Clutching* means "holding on to something."
7. (their numbers); There is no limit to the human imagination.
8. (of self-destruction); *Horrors* means "things that cause feelings of fear or disgust."

Reading Warm-up B, p. 148

Words that students are to circle appear in parentheses.

Sample Answers

1. (children); *Adults* have the responsibility of taking care of their families.
2. (the night sky); I felt awe when I visited the planetarium.
3. its beauty and mystery; *dawn*
4. the groups of stars, the constellations; *Clustered* means "bunched together in a group."
5. many details about the universe that earlier humans never knew; Darla will reveal her science-fair project on Monday.
6. formations more than two and a half miles deep in some places; *Jagged* means "having sharp, ragged edges."
7. The expense of finding out whether humans could live on Mars is being questioned; An unnecessary expense is a luxury car.
8. (vacations); Some families hold an annual reunion.

"Zoo" by Edward D. Hoch

Reading: Make Inferences by Reading Between the Lines and Asking Questions, p. 149

Sample Answers

1. Admission to the zoo is a dollar, and people are so eager to go in that they are clutching their money in their hands.
2. The Professor is a flashy showman.
3. The horse-spider creatures are tame, not wild.
4. The creatures' emotions, behaviors, and relationships are similar to those of human beings.

Literary Analysis: Theme, p. 150

Sample Answers

1. "Zoo" is set in "the huge tri-city parking area just outside of Chicago," where the Professor's spaceship lands. It is also set among "the familiar jagged rocks of Kaan" and in the home of a family of horse spiders. (Their home is a cave.)
2. *Hugo:* He urges the crowd to hurry and encourages them to spread the word about the show.

   Person from Earth: One spectator says that the show is worth a dollar and declares that he will bring his wife to see it.

   She-creature: She asks her mate and offspring about their adventure.

   He-creature: He says that they all enjoyed the show, that they were safe, and that the show was worth the money they paid for it.

   Little creature: It says that Earth was "the best" because "the creatures there" wear clothes and walk on two legs.

3. *People in Chicago:* Ten thousand people in Chicago eagerly pay a dollar to view the show. They are horrified and fascinated by the creatures they see.

   Horse spiders: They act like human beings. After leaving the spaceship, they go home, meet their mates, and have conversations.

4. Important objects include the barred cages, the spaceship, Hugo's cape and top hat, and the money—the dollars and commacs.
5. The subject of the story is people and their differences and similarities.
6. People often fear the differences between them rather than seeing the similarities.

Vocabulary Builder, p. 151

A. 1. expense; 2. awe; 3. interplanetary

B. Sample Answers

1. The interplanetary mission involved travel from Earth to Mars.
2. The spectators at the zoo were awed by the ferocious tigers.
3. The expense of the zoo kept the promoter from making a great profit.

C. 1. C; 2. A; 3. B

Enrichment: Characteristics of Imaginary Animals, p. 154

Students should write detailed descriptions of an imaginary animal, including information about its size, color, number and appearance of legs, and shape and appearance of head.

Selection Test A, p. 155

Critical Reading

1. ANS: D	DIF: Easy	OBJ: Comprehension
2. ANS: C	DIF: Easy	OBJ: Interpretation
3. ANS: B	DIF: Easy	OBJ: Comprehension
4. ANS: B	DIF: Easy	OBJ: Interpretation
5. ANS: D	DIF: Easy	OBJ: Reading
6. ANS: C	DIF: Easy	OBJ: Interpretation
7. ANS: A	DIF: Easy	OBJ: Comprehension
8. ANS: D	DIF: Easy	OBJ: Comprehension
9. ANS: C	DIF: Easy	OBJ: Reading
10. ANS: A	DIF: Easy	OBJ: Literary Analysis
11. ANS: C	DIF: Easy	OBJ: Literary Analysis

Vocabulary and Grammar

12. ANS: D	DIF: Easy	OBJ: Vocabulary
13. ANS: A	DIF: Easy	OBJ: Vocabulary
14. ANS: A	DIF: Easy	OBJ: Grammar
15. ANS: C	DIF: Easy	OBJ: Grammar

Essay

16. Students should recognize that in each situation, the horse-spider creatures act like human beings. The female creature embraces her family members and asks about their adventure. The male creature responds to her questions, reassures her that the trip was safe, and suggests that she go along next time. The little one shows its excitement by running up the walls of the cave and describing its favorite things. Students should see that the creatures show affection and interact just as human beings do. They may notice that their appearance, language, and physical capabilities differ from those of human beings.

    Difficulty: *Easy*
    Objective: *Essay*

17. Students should state that the story takes place on Earth and on the planet Kaan and that the characters are human beings from Earth and horse-spider creatures from Kaan. They should recognize that each group of characters is fascinated by the other and that their actions demonstrate that interest. Finally, they should realize that Hoch is making the point that people are afraid of those who are different from them and are failing to see the ways in which they are all basically alike.

    Difficulty: *Easy*
    Objective: *Essay*

Selection Test B, p. 158

Critical Reading

1. ANS: D DIF: Average OBJ: Comprehension
2. ANS: B DIF: Challenging OBJ: Reading
3. ANS: C DIF: Average OBJ: Reading
4. ANS: D DIF: Average OBJ: Reading
5. ANS: C DIF: Average OBJ: Interpretation
6. ANS: A DIF: Average OBJ: Interpretation
7. ANS: B DIF: Average OBJ: Comprehension
8. ANS: A DIF: Average OBJ: Literary Analysis
9. ANS: B DIF: Challenging OBJ: Reading
10. ANS: C DIF: Challenging OBJ: Literary Analysis
11. ANS: B DIF: Challenging OBJ: Literary Analysis

Vocabulary and Grammar

12. ANS: C DIF: Average OBJ: Vocabulary
13. ANS: A DIF: Average OBJ: Vocabulary
14. ANS: C DIF: Average OBJ: Grammar
15. ANS: B DIF: Average OBJ: Grammar

Essay

16. Students should name the two settings as Earth (specifically, the Chicago area) and the planet of Kaan (especially one family's home). They should describe how the people on Earth are fascinated by the horse-spider creatures and how the horse-spider creatures are fascinated by the people on Earth, and they should recognize that the theme of "Zoo" is that when viewing others, people focus on the ways in which they are different rather than on similarities.

    Difficulty: *Average*
    Objective: *Essay*

17. Students should describe Professor Hugo's colorful cape and his top hat; they might suggest that he dresses like a circus ringmaster. They should realize that he tries to stir up excitement in his audience by telling them to hurry, by declaring that they are getting their money's worth, and by claiming that he has gone to "great expense" to bring them his zoo. By urging his audience to spread the word about his zoo, he is attempting to get free advertising. Students should recognize that the Professor makes money from both the creatures in the show and those who come to see it. Both groups pay him because they are curious about other creatures and other places. Some students might think that because Professor Hugo is not honest, he is taking advantage of those who pay him; others might say that because those who pay him get something for their money, they are not taken advantage of.

    Difficulty: *Challenging*
    Objective: *Essay*

"Ribbons" by Laurence Yep

Vocabulary Warm-up Exercises, p. 162

A.
1. strapped
2. ankles
3. clumsily
4. wobbly
5. exercises
6. ballet
7. downward
8. beginners

B. Sample Answers

1. No; to undo the setting on an alarm is to turn it off, so an alarm would not wake you up on time if it had been undone.
2. No; *mechanical* means "done in a machinelike way," so a mechanical performer would not sing with expression.
3. Yes; something that is attractive is pleasing to look at.
4. Yes; a legal parking spot is one that is permitted by the law.
5. Yes; *deliberately* means "purposely," so something done deliberately is planned.
6. No; *circulating* means "moving around," so if water is not moving, it is not circulating.

7. Yes; *regained* means "recovered" or "got back to something," so if a runner regained her lead, she was again in first place.

8. No; *illustrating* means "explaining with pictures," so the teacher is not illustrating an idea if she is only talking about it.

Reading Warm-up A, p. 163

Words that students are to circle appear in parentheses.

Sample Answers

1. (form of dance); Ballet is a performance of dance and music that tells a story.

2. when they are between eight and ten years old; Beginners are people who are just starting out with something.

3. (at a *barre*); I do sit-ups and stretching exercises.

4. *upward*; From the balcony the spectators looked downward at the performers.

5. The shoes are fastened with straps to the part of the leg between the calf and the foot; The model strapped on her sandals and lifted her skirt to reveal her ankles.

6. At first the feet are shaky because the position feels so awkward. Someone who is not used to ice skating might be wobbly.

7. Only with constant practice can a dancer make a performance look easy and graceful; *Clumsily* means "carried out without skill or grace."

Reading Warm-up B, p. 164

Words that students are to circle appear in parentheses.

Sample Answers

1. established itself in Hong Kong; *Deliberately* means "purposely."

2. (Hong Kong); The beautifully kept garden was attractive.

3. (treaty) or (agreement); *Legal* means "lawful" or "having to do with the law."

4. Britain's rule of Hong Kong; With the click of the mouse, I undid my mistakes.

5. (control of Hong Kong); *Regained* means "got back to" or "recovered."

6. (an agreement in name only); *Mechanical* means "done in a machinelike way."

7. In Hong Kong, trade and shipping are like the blood circulating through the human body. If someone's blood is circulating poorly, his or her hands and feet might feel cold.

8. The merchants are illustrating Hong Kong's importance as an economic center. A map of Hong Kong would be illustrating the region's location.

"Ribbons" by Laurence Yep

Reading: Make Inferences by Reading Between the Lines and Asking Questions, p. 165

Sample Answers

1. Grandmother is not used to physical affection.

2. Grandmother does not feel at home.

3. Grandmother would rather feel pain than be reminded of the practices of the past.

4. Grandmother is uncomfortable showing affection, but she wants to show that she cares for Stacy.

5. Stacy believes that she and Grandmother are overcoming their differences and discovering how strongly they are connected.

Literary Analysis: Theme, p. 166

Sample Answers

1. The setting is a two-story, three-bedroom apartment in San Francisco. (Note that students are unlikely to determine the number of bedrooms.)

2. *Grandmother:* She scolds Stacy for many things: for hugging her, for complaining when Grandmother gives Ian her ice cream, for the ribbons on her toe shoes, which Grandmother says will ruin Stacy's feet, for going into the bathroom when Grandmother is bathing her feet. At the end, however, she explains to Ian the importance of the little mermaid's wish to walk despite the pain that walking causes her.

   Mom: She explains her mother's behavior to Stacy. She tells her that in China, boys are considered more important than girls. She explains how and why her mother's feet were bound.

   Stacy: She complains to her mother about her grandmother's behavior. When given the chance, she explains her love of dance to her grandmother and explains that the ribbons are for tying on her dancing shoe, which she loves.

3. *Grandmother:* She ignores or scolds Stacy and pays attention to Ian. Finally, though, she listens as Stacy reads "The Little Mermaid" aloud, and she uses that story to talk about her bound feet. Then she listens and watches as Stacy explains her love of ballet.

   Stacy: She tries to show affection for her grandmother by hugging her. She tries to get her grandmother's attention by asking for help with her toe shoes. She gets angry and ignores her grandmother. Finally, though, after her grandmother talks about her bound feet by talking about the little mermaid, Stacy tries again to explain her toe shoes and her love of ballet to Grandmother, and this time she succeeds.

4. The important objects are the satin toe shoes, the silk ribbons, Grandmother's feet, and the fairy tale "The Little Mermaid."

5. The subject is cultural differences.

6. The theme is that cultural differences can be bridged through communication.

Vocabulary Builder, p. 167

A. 1. laborious; 2. exertion; 3. sensitive; 4. coax; 5. meek

B. 1. B; 2. D; 3. A; 4. C; 5. A

Enrichment: Documentary, p. 170

The items that students choose should relate to and have significance in the life of their subjects. In their commentary, students should write coherently and demonstrate an understanding of the narrative form.

"Zoo" by Edward Hoch
"Ribbons" by Laurence Yep

Build Language Skills: Vocabulary, p. 171

A. 1. to unite

2. a formal agreement that spells out the terms of an arrangement

3. underwater

B. Sample Answers

1. True / One concludes something based on evidence, and the evidence, or details, in "Zoo" indicate that the story is a fantasy.

2. False / In "Zoo," the horse spiders' assessment is that they are the spectators, and the creatures on the other planets are the ones that are on display.

3. False / One cannot easily believe that the horse spiders exist.

4. True / "Ribbons" is about understanding and communication; that is the subject of the story.

5. False / An object is something that can be seen or touched, so a message cannot be called an object.

Build Language Skills: Grammar, p. 172

A. The adverbs to be underlined are followed by the words they modify.

1. slowly—slid; up—slid
2. around—clustered; quickly—collected
3. quickly—filed
4. especially—enjoyed
5. formally—bowed
6. privately—practicing; now—shared
7. tightly—clutched
8. suddenly—felt

B. Sample Answers

1. If I do not <u>move</u> quickly in the morning, I will miss the school bus.

2. I never <u>eat</u> spinach.

3. When I groom my dog, I <u>comb</u> his fur gently.

4. In the summer, I always <u>check</u> the dog for fleas and ticks.

5. Finally, I <u>give</u> the dog a bath.

"Ribbons" by Laurence Yep

Selection Test A, p. 173
Critical Reading

1. ANS: C	DIF: Easy	OBJ: Interpretation
2. ANS: B	DIF: Easy	OBJ: Interpretation
3. ANS: A	DIF: Easy	OBJ: Reading
4. ANS: A	DIF: Easy	OBJ: Reading
5. ANS: B	DIF: Easy	OBJ: Comprehension
6. ANS: D	DIF: Easy	OBJ: Comprehension
7. ANS: C	DIF: Easy	OBJ: Comprehension
8. ANS: C	DIF: Easy	OBJ: Interpretation
9. ANS: A	DIF: Easy	OBJ: Interpretation
10. ANS: D	DIF: Easy	OBJ: Interpretation
11. ANS: B	DIF: Easy	OBJ: Literary Analysis
12. ANS: A	DIF: Easy	OBJ: Literary Analysis

Vocabulary and Grammar

13. ANS: B	DIF: Easy	OBJ: Vocabulary
14. ANS: D	DIF: Easy	OBJ: Vocabulary
15. ANS: C	DIF: Easy	OBJ: Grammar

Essay

16. Students should recognize that the conflict occurs because Grandmother dotes on Ian and scolds Stacy and ignores her. Grandmother misunderstands the purpose of Stacy's toe-shoe ribbons: She thinks that Stacy is binding her feet with them. Stacy then learns how Grandmother's feet had been bound and are deformed as a result. After they read "The Little Mermaid" together, Stacy and Grandmother talk about the mermaid's decision to walk and the challenge that decision presented. Talking about the story's message allows Stacy and Grandmother to talk about Grandmother's feet and Stacy's love of ballet, and that discussion allows them to understand each other better and get along better.

Difficulty: *Easy*

Objective: *Essay*

17. Students should identify the important objects as Grandmother's feet and the ribbons on Stacy's ballet slippers, and they should recognize that both objects relate to the title of the story. They relate to the theme as well because they represent the cultural differences that separate Grandmother and Stacy. To Grandmother, ribbons represent pain; to Stacy, they represent her passion for ballet. Students should recognize that Grandmother and Stacy demonstrate the theme after Grandmother listens to Stacy read the story about the mermaid. The mermaid learns to walk despite the pain it causes. Grandmother then listens as Stacy explains that the ribbons she'd shown her earlier are used to tie her dancing shoes, not to bind her feet. Therefore, through communication, Stacy and her grandmother overcome their differences.

Difficulty: *Easy*
Objective: *Essay*

Selection Test B, p. 176

Critical Reading

1. ANS: C	DIF: Average	OBJ: Interpretation
2. ANS: D	DIF: Challenging	OBJ: Reading
3. ANS: C	DIF: Average	OBJ: Literary Analysis
4. ANS: A	DIF: Average	OBJ: Comprehension
5. ANS: A	DIF: Average	OBJ: Reading
6. ANS: D	DIF: Average	OBJ: Comprehension
7. ANS: B	DIF: Challenging	OBJ: Interpretation
8. ANS: A	DIF: Challenging	OBJ: Interpretation
9. ANS: C	DIF: Average	OBJ: Reading
10. ANS: A	DIF: Average	OBJ: Literary Analysis
11. ANS: B	DIF: Challenging	OBJ: Literary Analysis

Vocabulary and Grammar

12. ANS: A	DIF: Average	OBJ: Vocabulary
13. ANS: C	DIF: Average	OBJ: Vocabulary
14. ANS: B	DIF: Average	OBJ: Grammar
15. ANS: C	DIF: Average	OBJ: Grammar

Essay

16. Students might note these cultural differences: Grandmother stiffens and scolds Stacy when Stacy hugs her. Grandmother favors Ian because he is a boy. Grandmother reacts angrily when she sees the ribbons to Stacy's toe shoes. Students should note that Stacy feels hurt. She tries to win her grandmother's affection by sharing with her her love of ballet. When that attempt fails, Stacy chooses to ignore her grandmother. Students should recognize that Stacy's reading of "The Little Mermaid" aloud provides the opportunity for her and her grandmother to talk about Grandmother's bound feet and Stacy's dancing shoes and so allows them to resolve their differences. Students might note

that "Ribbons" suggests that people must recognize and discuss cultural differences so that they can understand each other and even grow close.

Difficulty: *Average*
Objective: *Essay*

17. Students should describe the setting (Stacy's family's apartment), identify the main characters (Stacy and Grandmother), and briefly describe the conflicts between them. They should identify the important objects as Grandmother's feet and the ribbons on Stacy's ballet slippers, and they should recognize that both the feet and the ballet shoes relate to the title. To Grandmother, the ribbons represent pain and deformity; to Stacy, they represent passion and appreciation of beauty. The theme is the importance of communication and understanding.

Difficulty: *Average*
Objective: *Essay*

"After Twenty Years" by O. Henry
"He—y, Come On Ou—t!" by Shinichi Hoshi

Vocabulary Warm-up Exercises, p. 180

A. 1. wits
2. outline
3. gusts
4. slight
5. profits
6. authorities
7. consented
8. established

B. Sample Answers
1. When we expanded our storeroom, we increased its size.
2. People who believe in fate believe that it determines what happens.
3. When we reached the midway point on the journey, we were halfway between the beginning and the end.
4. City dwellers are people who live in cities.
5. When a throng gathers in this neighborhood, the place is crowded.
6. Joan's main objection to the project was that she thought it would not work.
7. If our proposition wins approval, we will have a lot to do.
8. People who live in this vicinity live here.

Reading Warm-up A, p. 181

Words that students are to circle appear in parentheses.

Sample Answers
1. (storms blow), (huge), (wind); Gusts are sudden, strong rushes of air or wind.
2. (the tides); *great*

3. help the people of Tuvalu, They will accept
   75 Tuvaluans per year as refugees; Authorities are the
   people who are in power or in control.

4. Authorities in New Zealand have agreed to help the people of Tuvalu; Scott consented to rake the leaves for
   Mrs. Wiggins.

5. They will accept 75 Tuvaluans per year as refugees.
   Established means "set up something."

6. a plan; I might outline the major points of a topic that
   will be on a test.

7. (oil and fuel companies); Profits are gains.

8. the wits of science, business, and politics; It took great
   wits, like Steven Jobs and Bill Gates, to make personal
   computers a part of our everyday lives.

Reading Warm-up B, p. 182

Words that students are to circle appear in parentheses.

Sample Answers

1. brought them together; Fate is a force that some people
   believe controls things or causes things to happen.

2. (Their business); We expanded our kitchen, and now it
   is much larger.

3. A new vicinity means a new place, so Emily's parents
   wanted to move their business to a new location.

4. I don't want to go without Mia; An objection is an act of
   objecting to or disapproving of something.

5. Emily's mother's proposition was that the girls could
   spend summer vacation together at the beach. A proposition is a big proposal or undertaking.

6. (almost beach dwellers); Other kinds of dwellers include
   city dwellers, apartment dwellers, and country dwellers.

7. (beachgoers); The throng of shoppers crowded the store
   during the sale.

8. It means that each girl traveled halfway along the
   beach, and the two girls met at the midpoint.

Literary Analysis: Irony, p. 183

Sample Answers

1. A man tells a police officer that he is waiting for a friend
   he hasn't seen for 20 years, and that they had agreed to
   meet in that spot on that night. / After a storm, the people of a village discover a deep hole that appears to be
   bottomless. Everyone agrees it should be filled, and so
   people fill it with waste, including contaminated material.

2. The old friend will arrive, and the two men will discover
   how much each has changed. / The hole will be filled,
   and the ground will be contaminated.

3. The man in the doorway is arrested because he is a
   wanted criminal. / A construction worker hears the
   echo of the voice of the man who shouted into the hole
   at first, and the very first item thrown into the hole, a
   pebble, falls from the sky.

4. The scar near the man's eyebrow and the diamond pin
   led me to expect that the man would reveal that he has
   lived a hard life and earned a lot of money. / The scientist cannot explain why the hole appears to be bottomless. That leads me to expect that the people will be able
   to go on filling the hole forever.

5. The policeman is the man's old friend, and the man is a
   wanted criminal. / Everything that the people put into
   the hole begins to fall out of the sky—everything the
   people thought they had thrown away is going to be
   returned to them.

Vocabulary Builder, p. 184

A. Sample Answers

1. The plot of the short story was so intricate that we
   could not follow it.

2. The destiny of a criminal is likely to include time
   spent in prison.

3. The two men arrived simultaneously, both reaching
   the doorway at the same time.

4. Because there were many spectators when the
   crime was committed, many eyewitnesses testified at
   the trial.

5. The apparent smile on the face of the scientist was
   noticed by everyone.

6. The plausible explanation made sense to everyone.

7. Because he offered a good solution, everyone
   accepted the concessionaire's proposal.

B. 1. A; 2. C; 3. A

Selection Test A, p. 186

Critical Reading

1. ANS: D	DIF: Easy	OBJ: Comprehension
2. ANS: B	DIF: Easy	OBJ: Interpretation
3. ANS: C	DIF: Easy	OBJ: Interpretation
4. ANS: A	DIF: Easy	OBJ: Literary Analysis
5. ANS: A	DIF: Easy	OBJ: Comprehension
6. ANS: C	DIF: Easy	OBJ: Interpretation
7. ANS: D	DIF: Easy	OBJ: Comprehension
8. ANS: C	DIF: Easy	OBJ: Literary Analysis
9. ANS: C	DIF: Easy	OBJ: Literary Analysis
10. ANS: A	DIF: Easy	OBJ: Literary Analysis
11. ANS: B	DIF: Easy	OBJ: Literary Analysis
12. ANS: A	DIF: Easy	OBJ: Literary Analysis

Vocabulary

13. ANS: A	DIF: Easy	OBJ: Vocabulary
14. ANS: D	DIF: Easy	OBJ: Vocabulary
15. ANS: A	DIF: Easy	OBJ: Vocabulary

Essay

16. Students may identify the irony in both stories as situational, or they may identify the irony in "After Twenty Years" as situational and the irony in "He—y, Come On Ou—t" as dramatic. They should demonstrate an understanding of the forms of irony they name. They may point out that in "After Twenty Years" the irony lies in the situation of one man becoming a police officer while his old friend becomes a criminal whom the officer must arrest, or they may suggest that the irony is that Bob goes out of his way to honor a twenty-year-old pledge to a best friend only to be arrested by that friend. Students may say that in "He—y, Come On Ou—t!" it is ironic that although the hole cannot be explained, the people come to accept it and seem not to think that their actions will have negative consequences. In the end, however, it becomes clear that there will be serious negative consequences. Students who identify the irony in "He—y, Come On Ou—t!" as dramatic should point out that readers recognize the negative consequences while the characters in the story do not.

Difficulty: *Easy*

Objective: *Essay*

17. Students should identify the aspect of each ending that makes it surprising, and they should cite details from the stories that logically support their choices of the story with the more surprising ending and the story with the less surprising ending.

Difficulty: *Easy*

Objective: *Essay*

Selection Test B, p. 189

Critical Reading

1. ANS: D	DIF: Challenging	OBJ: Interpretation
2. ANS: B	DIF: Average	OBJ: Interpretation
3. ANS: C	DIF: Challenging	OBJ: Interpretation
4. ANS: A	DIF: Average	OBJ: Comprehension
5. ANS: B	DIF: Average	OBJ: Comprehension
6. ANS: A	DIF: Average	OBJ: Literary Analysis
7. ANS: C	DIF: Average	OBJ: Interpretation
8. ANS: A	DIF: Average	OBJ: Interpretation
9. ANS: B	DIF: Challenging	OBJ: Comprehension
10. ANS: B	DIF: Average	OBJ: Literary Analysis
11. ANS: A	DIF: Average	OBJ: Literary Analysis
12. ANS: D	DIF: Average	OBJ: Literary Analysis
13. ANS: D	DIF: Challenging	OBJ: Literary Analysis
14. ANS: C	DIF: Average	OBJ: Literary Analysis

Vocabulary

15. ANS: A	DIF: Average	OBJ: Vocabulary
16. ANS: B	DIF: Average	OBJ: Vocabulary
17. ANS: D	DIF: Average	OBJ: Vocabulary
18. ANS: B	DIF: Challenging	OBJ: Vocabulary

Essay

19. Students should identify aspects of the endings that are surprising, cite similarities between the endings, and then identify differences between them (for example, "After Twenty Years" is more realistic; the resolution of "After Twenty Years" is more predictable than that of "He—y, Come On Ou—t!"). Students should cite details from the stories to support their choice of the more surprising ending.

Difficulty: *Average*

Objective: *Essay*

20. Students should state a clear message for each story. They are likely to suggest that O. Henry is writing about friendship or justice; they should realize that Hoshi is addressing the need to recognize the consequences of various events (production of goods, creation of pollution, the use of nuclear energy) in contemporary society. Students should support their opinions of the stories with well-reasoned explanations and relevant details from the stories.

Difficulty: *Challenging*

Objective: *Essay*

Writing Workshop—Unit 2, Part 2

Review of a Short Story: Integrating Grammar Skill, p. 193

A. 1. faster; 2. more slowly; 3. most sluggish; 4. more complex

B. 1. Mrs. T's garden is the finest in the city.
2. Her roses smell nice but her lilies are even more fragrant.
3. Of the two kinds of irises, the bearded irises are the prettier.
4. The tulips bloom in early May, but the daffodils bloom even earlier.

Spelling Workshop—Unit 2

Tricky or Difficult Syllables, p. 194

A. 1. biscuit; 2. cabinet; 3. nuisance; 4. aspirin; 5. interesting; 6. business; 7. candidate; 8. boundary; 9. awfully; 10. pumpkin

B. Answers will vary.

Unit 2, Part 2 Answers

Benchmark Test 4, p. 197

MULTIPLE CHOICE

1. ANS: B
2. ANS: B
3. ANS: D

4. ANS: C
5. ANS: C
6. ANS: C
7. ANS: A
8. ANS: D
9. ANS: D
10. ANS: B
11. ANS: A
12. ANS: C
13. ANS: B
14. ANS: C
15. ANS: C
16. ANS: D
17. ANS: D
18. ANS: A
19. ANS: C
20. ANS: D
21. ANS: B
22. ANS: B
23. ANS: A

24. ANS: D
25. ANS: C
26. ANS: A
27. ANS: D
28. ANS: A
29. ANS: B
30. ANS: C
31. ANS: B
32. ANS: A

ESSAY

33. Libraries provide a place for people to study and do homework as well as to enjoy reading.

34. Students' responses should demonstrate an understanding of the letter form. The essays should also show students' ability to support statements with specific examples.

35. Students' responses should demonstrate an understanding of anecdotes.

36. Sample response: The creaky old house stood in the middle of the forest, dwarfed by giant, shapeless trees.